INTERSECTING HEARTBEATS

By
Yvonne Aarden

To: Linda
May you enjoy the many different "heartbeats" in my life's story with my amazing husband. May your "heartbeats" be filled with love and great memories.
♡♡ Yvonne Aarden
'22

Intersecting Heartbeats
© 2018, Yvonne Aarden

ISBN: 9781981715503

All rights reserved.

No reprint rights granted without the written permission of the author.

Reasonable excerpts or quotes used for review, educational, or other fair use purposes are permitted and encouraged.

CONTENTS

Prologue: Living My Vows (1961-68)..1

Ch.1: Questioning My Vows (1969) 13

Ch.2: Summer of Uncertainties (1969)...35

Ch.3: Rethinking My Vows (1969)..49

Ch.4: Learning to Live in the "Real" World (1969)........................57

Ch.5: Discovering Each Other's Past Lives (1970).........................71

Ch.6: Wedding & Building of Home (1970-1972).........................95

Ch.7: Working on our House and Having Babies (1973-74).....115

Ch.8: Rejected by the Church (1976-1977)...................................127

Ch.9: Busy Lives (1976-1980)...137

Ch.10: Tangled Alcohol Roots (1982)...147

Ch.11: Family Fun (1982-1986)...155

Ch.12: Memorable School and Family Events (1987-1988).......167

Ch.13: Changes for the Aarden Family (1989-91).......................181

Ch.14: Life Changes for Everyone (1992-97)................................197

Ch.15: Travels and Tribulations (1998-2002)...............................209

Ch.16: The Year That Totally Changed Us Forever (2003).......223

Epilogue: Life After Piet: (2003-2017)..245

This book is dedicated, with love,

to my parents,
Bo and Phil Rumreich,
who created my heartbeat;

to Piet Aarden,
who stole my heart;

and

to our children, Bret and Pyra,
who captured our hearts
forever.

PROLOGUE
Living My Vows: 1961-68

Staring in disbelief, I read and re-read the slip of paper in my hands. It was the summer of 1961 and I was a twenty-one-year-old, junior nun who had not yet made her final vows. I was living in our Benedictine Motherhouse located in Crookston, Minnesota, near the Canadian border. The Reverend Mother had just presented me with my first teaching assignment.

With only two years of community college under my cincture, I was being sent to teach Mexican migrant children in Asherton, Texas. This was the only remote mission of our Motherhouse. All the other teaching missions were located in Minnesota. Five nuns (out of the three hundred in our community) were chosen for this assignment, and I was one of the chosen! Maybe the Rev. Mother had made a mistake? But even though I knew nothing about teaching, I knew that one was not to question the yearly obedience assignment.

Anxious for my first teaching assignment in Texas.

On the morning of our departure, we squeezed our five suitcases and a variety of boxes into the trunk of an old Ford that had seen better days. During that five-day drive to Texas, the principal outlined my responsibilities for the coming school year: I would be cooking all the noon meals, doing the laundry on Monday mornings, cleaning the convent every Friday afternoon, and teaching whatever classes the other nuns assigned me each day. After our regular school day, I would then help teach catechism classes to the public school children. As I listened, I began to wonder if I should change my name from Sr. Mona to Sr. Cinderella!

Asherton was located near the Mexican border. Nearing our Texas mission, the waves of oppressive desert heat seeped into our car and drenched my layers of traditional nun's clothing. Plumes of dust from the village dirt roads surrounded the car, so we quickly rolled up the windows. In the stifling heat, I caught sight of my future home: a limestone building that stood a few feet from a majestic stone church. This stark structure, the nuns told me, was our convent and school.

As we entered our building, there was a small entryway leading to three barren classrooms. Each room contained rows of desks connected to wooden slats and slate blackboards that had seen better days. The entrance to the school was also the entrance to the convent. Everything was under one roof, complete with unfinished wooden floors, cracks in the walls, and no signs of an air conditioner in the hundred-degree temperatures.

In front of us, as we walked into the convent, was a narrow, dimly-lit hallway. The wall on our left was actually the wall we shared with the upper-grade classroom. The first room on the right was the private office and bedroom of our principal/superior. I thought it looked somewhat spacious. The bedroom dormitory for the rest of us nuns was the next room on the right. It contained four cot-like beds that stood stiffly, like sentinels crowded next to small dressers, with a narrow walking space to the only bathroom. Our tiny bedroom closet had four huge nails protruding from the walls—one nail for each of us to hang the two habits we possessed. The same hallway connected the bedrooms to a small living-dining room situated next to the sparsely-furnished kitchen. On the bright side, we had running water!

We nuns lived in poverty among our migrant families, but nothing like the poverty that they struggled with from day to day. I will never forget the Dias family, with ten children, living in a one-room shack. The mother had just given birth to her tenth baby in the fields. When we visited them, we brought baby clothes, bottles, and some milk.

Mrs. Dias' milk supply was so limited that we found her trying to feed her newborn some tea from a chipped cup. We promised to bring milk and food supplies every day for the family. The next evening, the children appeared at our back door with the gift of warm, flour tortillas. It was their way to say thank you and to show their deep appreciation. In Texas, the Mexican families didn't considered us nuns to be Anglos; we were seen as very special, holy women, next in line to the Virgin Mary.

After teaching two years and being the Flunky Cinderella nun in Asherton, my yearly obedience slip assigned me the task of starting a new school in the neighboring parish of Carrizo Springs. This larger parish was predominantly Mexican, but the town had a real downtown with lots of stores and businesses owned by affluent Anglos. I was given the role of principal and first-grade teacher at the ripe age of twenty-three!

This assignment did not sit well with Sr. Caroline, the superior and principal of our Asherton convent school. She had boldly stated—a year before—that she was SURE the Rev. Mother would choose her to start the new school, certainly not the "baby" nun, Sr. Mona.

Since I would be living in the same Asherton convent with the other nuns, the neighboring parish furnished me with a brand new, bright-red car to drive the ten miles to and from my new school. It became necessary for me to become quite independent, and make quick decisions on my own. I had to learn not only how to teach first-graders, but also how to become an administrator at the same time.

Washing the car on the dusty Asherton street by our convent. (L) Sr. Mary Ellen, Sr. Marian, Sr. Marguerite. (R) Sr. Mona. (Yours Truly!)

When I returned to the convent after my first day of school, Sr. Caroline took me aside. She sternly said, "I want a report every single day, to know what is happening at the new school, as well as whatever the pastor tells you." She then told me that even though I was the principal of the new school, she was still the superior at the convent. "You are much too young and inexperienced. I certainly don't know what the Mother Superior was thinking!"

I was upset, but did not dare say what I was thinking. During the day, I was expected to be a responsible adult, running a school with all of its demands. Returning to the convent each evening, I was treated like a little girl, telling her mommy all the things she had done in school.

After four years of being a principal and teaching little first-graders in Texas from 1963-1967, my next yearly assignment stated that I was going to be teaching eighth grade in Mahtomedi, Minnesota. Once again I stared in disbelief at the paper in my hands. I did not want to leave my precious, poverty-stricken Mexican children and teach in a world of affluence. Mahtomedi was a bedroom community of the Twin Cities, dripping with sophisticated families. As I rebelled inside, I knew that I must not question the Rev. Mother's decision.

On the first day of class in Mahtomedi, I introduced myself to my eighth-graders. I told my new, much bigger students how I had grown up on an Indian reservation in northern Minnesota. They laughed when I told them how I had gone duck hunting with my dad, but had always talked too much and scared the ducks away.

In Texas, I had become used to bending down to be at eye-level with my little ones, wiping noses, and showing eager first-grade hands how to hold pencils. Rick Brewster was a tall, big-boned eighth-grader who needed to bend down to my eye level. He would have had a real problem if I'd offered to hold the Kleenex while he blew his nose, much less shown him how to hold a pencil.

"Sr. Mona," Rick said, addressing me by the name I had been given when I entered the order ten years before. It was a name I had not chosen, and still had trouble recognizing as my own. "My dad and I went duck hunting over the weekend. Mom said I could invite you for supper tomorrow night."

"Of course, Rick," I said. My mouth watered at the thought of wild duck and rice, a dish I hadn't had in years. "It'll be fun to meet your family. What time? If you give me directions, I can drive over."

That night at supper, I told the other nuns that I would be going to Brewster's home the next day for my evening meal.

Dead silence.

The nine nuns around the table turned and stared at me.

"Sr. Mona, we don't go to our students' homes to eat or visit," replied Sr. Agatha, our superior and principal. In a shocked voice, she continued, "I don't know what they allowed you to do in Texas. Here in Minnesota, we teach at the school and stay in the convent for meals."

It was my turn to stare at them. "Well, I already told Rick I'd come." More stunned silence. "How do you get to know your students if you just sit here in the convent?" I retorted.

"Sister Mona, see me in my office after supper," was Sr. Agatha's response. I looked around and all the nuns had their eyes riveted on their plates. The silence was deafening.

In Texas, we had all been young nuns, except for the superior. Now here I was living with old nuns who were set in their ways. Was I hearing these nuns correctly? Did they live quarantined from their students and families? How could I ever live in such a stifling environment?

Trying to break the unbearable, icy silence, I asked how everyone's day had gone. I quickly shared how happy I was to have had a break in my day when the new assistant pastor came to talk with my students. "Wow, he brought his guitar. We had such fun, singing and laughing," I shared excitedly. "We decided it would be great fun to plan a Friday night sing-along with my eighth-graders, out in the woods by the lake."

More deadly silence.

This was definitely not going well. Dessert came none too soon. As I choked down the bread pudding, I caught the Superior's eyes. She explained to the rest of the nuns that she and I would be a bit late for recreation that evening. With that dismissal, I followed her to her office.

"Sr. Mona, you remind me so much of Maria in *The Sound of Music*. She, too, was impetuous and found it difficult to follow the rules."

I nodded in agreement. I shared with Sr. Agatha how *The Sound of Music* had always been more than just a movie to me. Her mouth hung open as I told her the story of how we Texas nuns had seen the movie in San Antonio. (We had driven there for a teacher's conference during my first year in Texas.) There just happened to be a music store around the corner from the movie theatre. After the movie, I spied a shiny, new guitar in the window—a guitar that looked, to my eyes, just like Maria's. I asked the nuns to wait a minute while I ran into the shop.

Pointing to the guitar in the window, I told the shopkeeper that I had just seen the movie, *The Sound of Music*. Now I wanted to buy a guitar, so I could be just like Maria and teach songs to the poor little Mexican kids at our mission school. He asked how much money I had.

Since I was dressed in my nun's habit (just like the Benedictine nuns in the movie), I reached into my flowing black garb. Searching for my pocket under the mysterious wrappings, I found it and pulled out some crumpled bills. My parents had sent me $25.00 that I just never managed to give to our superior.

He shook his head in bewilderment. "That would hardly buy the case," he said. "Sorry."

I couldn't believe my ears and started to cry. "Please, sir, it would mean the world to the kids—and to me."

The shopkeeper stared as I pulled out my white handkerchief to wipe away tears of disappointment. He proceeded to tell me he was Jewish and that he had never seen a crying nun before. As he stared some more, I heard him mutter something under his breath. I waited and watched as he walked to a shelf and came back with a baritone ukulele.

He explained to me that this ukulele cost much more than my $25.00, but, at least, it was cheaper than a guitar. I looked at him, jumped up and down for joy, and thanked him over and over. Tears of joy streamed down my cheeks.

"But, sir, just one more thing. Maria had her guitar in a case!"

He guffawed, stared at me in disbelief, went to the back room, and came back with a case for my new ukulele.

"Now, Sister, go and think of me, a Jewish shopkeeper, whenever you play that ukulele for those kids." He chuckled and said under his breath, "I can't wait to hear what the rabbi will say when I tell him what happened in my store today,"

Trying to be like Maria in The Sound of Music.

I grinned, winked, and told him I would definitely do that. I would pray for him every day. Then, with my new ukulele in its case, I had skipped out of the music store, just like Maria had skipped on her way to the Baron's home.

When I finished telling my *The Sound of Music* story in Sr. Agatha's office, she started to laugh. "Maybe we do need to make some changes around here. You really are a breath of fresh air," she chuckled. "But change is difficult and takes time. Be patient, Sister!"

I couldn't believe my ears. Sr. Agatha might prove to be my saving grace, after all! I jumped up, hugged her, and said I knew we were going to be great friends. She explained that since I had already told Rick I would come for supper, I could go. Next time, though, I should talk with her first.

How different this convent and school setting were from my Texas days! It was like day and night. This stucco-built home sheltered all the modern conveniences and offered a separate bedroom for each nun, as well as several shared bathrooms. The modern school building had custodians and tile floors with spacious classrooms. We even had moveable desks and no lack of school supplies.

In Texas, we nuns had been our own custodians. We made due with outdoor toilet facilities and cramped classrooms spilling over with students. I longed for the rich spirit and overflowing love that I had experienced with my dear Mexican families.

Halfway through the school year, I realized that burning the candle at both ends, while trying to keep a page ahead of the bright eighth-graders, was getting the best of me. At Christmas break, I proposed a plan I had been hatching for several months: "Sr. Agatha, I've been thinking that we should departmentalize the sixth- through eighth-grade classes. You are so talented in math and physical education. Sr. Hyacinth loves teaching social studies and spelling. I enjoy teaching language arts, and I'd even attempt to learn how to teach science, if we could do this."

I also explained that the kids had told me the public high school was getting rid of their old science tables. If I could get those tables, I could create a "hands-on" science lab, and learn with the kids. With departmental teaching, we would all be teaching to our strengths, and not be expected to know everything in every subject.

Sr. Agatha liked the idea. She said if we did this, she would have more time for her principal's duties. Sr. Agatha was in her forties and quiet in nature. With her innate disposition, she possessed the ability to get along with every type of temperament—even outspoken ones like mine. How different she was from Sr. Caroline, my Texas superior!

"Well, let's call the nuns together, present this idea, and see how it goes," she said, with a twinkle in her eye. "We have all Christmas vacation to work on this."

When the students returned after vacation, they learned that they now had three teachers instead of one. My room no longer had desks. The second-hand tables made my room look like a science lab, without equipment. (That was my next project.) I had applied—and would be accepted the following summer—to an eight-week, hands-on science workshop at Macalester College in St. Paul.

Things started to look up with the changes at school, but I still faced disapproval of many of my actions within the convent walls.

One afternoon, walking past the sixth-grade classroom, I overheard two of the nuns talking. "So what do you think she'll come up with next? Have the kids be the teachers?" complained Sr. Hyacinth to Sr. Rosaria, the first-grade teacher.

Both nuns had more than forty years of teaching under their cinctures. "Does she think she can sweet talk our Superior and get everything she dreams up? Next thing you know, she'll try and take over directing my Spelling Bee champions!" lamented Sr. Hyacinth.

Every evening after supper, all nine nuns gathered in the spacious, well-furnished living room for recreation time before prayers. The older nuns picked up their crochet hooks and knitting needles by their rocking chairs. Some nuns corrected student papers, others read the newspaper, but all were expected to be busy with something. It was like living in a bubble without any fresh air or new ideas. Talking was allowed, but each evening became like the one before, with little interaction.

In Texas, we had laughed and talked and shared teaching ideas, as well as funny things that happened in the classrooms that day. We took turns helping each other with the gelatin copier—using newsprint paper that was a premium commodity—to make one set of worksheets each day for each classroom. All of us helped create activity papers for Chewie, our blind first-grader. We punctured holes into coloring book pages with the sharp tip of a drafting compass to create a Braille-like effect. Chewie used these as a guide for coloring. Laughter had never been absent in our Asherton convent, despite the difficulties and long hours.

In Mahtomedi, we never left the convent's recreation room to go on walks or visit families.

"We didn't join the convent to run around the town or ride bicycles, Sr. Mona!" said one of the older nuns. "The Klein boy said you want to ride a horse at their farm. Don't you think that's going a bit too far?"

I shared my frustrations with my mom. I wrote to her, explaining how I had been very happy in Texas, but now living with some of those cranky, old nuns was becoming extremely difficult. I never wanted to become like them. I would leave the convent before that happened to me.

My mom was distraught. She made the five-hour trip from the reservation down to Mahtomedi the following weekend.

"Vonnie, we didn't raise you to give up when things got hard," she said in a determined, yet loving way.

"I know, Mom, but I just don't fit in here," I lamented. "I loved working with poor people in Texas. They appreciated every little thing we did for them. Here, there is not that same need."

Mom listened. Then she reminded me that she and Dad—as well as my childhood parish priest, Fr. Gus—had done everything they could to stop me when I wanted to leave home (at age thirteen!) to join the convent. "But, no. You knew best and refused to listen to us. Now you're telling me you want to give that life up?"

"Mom, I love teaching, but it feels like I'm living in an old people's home. The old nuns are content to just sit every night and vegetate. It isn't the life I want."

Mom reminded me how I would chase boys when I'd come home for the summers during my high school years. "You acted like most teenage girls. Not like one who wanted to become a nun. Is there a man behind your reason for wanting to quit the convent?"

"NO, Mom. I just never realized how different it would be to be a nun here."

She then patiently asked me, "Vonnie, is it just the old nuns' behaviors? Or is it your inability to do all the things that you want to do that is making you want to leave?"

After a weekend of difficult conversations, and lots of tears and hugs, I decided that I was not a quitter. I would try to be more patient and accept the older nuns. Mom always knew best. She possessed that amazing quality of helping people step back, and look at the entire picture before making a decision.

I kept thinking and praying about my vocation. If I had a real vocation, why would I keep questioning it? Was Mom right when she asked if I was a quitter? It was true, I missed my Texas challenges and freedom, but I had taken a vow of obedience. That meant I was to accept my yearly assignments without questioning them.

It was June, and my first year of teaching older kids was over. Our Motherhouse always sent pairs of nuns to the parishes in our Crookston Diocese to teach two-week summer catechism classes for kids not able to attend a Catholic School. The paired sisters prepared the younger children to receive the sacraments of First Communion and First Confession. Older children would learn more doctrine and prayers. Since the Rev. Mother had given me the special privilege of attending an eight-week science workshop, she had to find another nun to fill my place for the catechism classes. I could hardly wait to attend the workshop. I realized how grateful I should be for the opportunity. Maybe next summer...

The hands-on science workshop was mind boggling. I could hardly wait for each day to learn more. As I experienced each new concept, my head whirred with ideas of how I could modify it to fit my classroom.

The following September, I was armed and ready to challenge my eager students in the world of biology. Thanks to generous parishioners, my science lab even included a special microscope to fit on top of the overhead projector. This microscope gave us the ability to study and watch live pond-water specimens projected onto an overhead screen. It was 1968, and even the public school in Mahtomedi did not have such a modern microscope for their science lab! Animal cages, terrariums, insect nets, and fish tanks all provided live specimens for our science lab. Our classroom began to look like a mini-zoo. My dream had come true: We were living and learning our science without textbooks!

Students in my language arts classes informed me that the public school had a drama club, so why couldn't we? I realized that not every student was a biology enthusiast. Why not begin our own drama club? Students created posters to put up in the school hallways inviting anyone interested in starting a drama club to attend an after-school meeting.

"Wanna-be" thespians were chomping at the bit to join. We met weekly after school in my classroom. If only there had been a crash course on how to direct theatrical productions! The students' enthusiasm overlooked my many blatant errors—after all, we weren't preparing for Broadway—but it would have helped if the director had known a few basics of stage directions.

We decided to start with a Grimm's fairytale production. The kids went wild when Danny tried out for the Queen's role. His admirer, Lynn, then switched to trying out for the King. It truly became a fairy tale in more ways than one, and even drew a few laughs from some of the older nuns. St. Jude's Drama club became a haven for non-sport enthusiasts. Now they had an after-school activity to be proud of.

Life on the convent front remained, for me, an uphill battle. The older nuns still shook their heads at Sr. Mona's "escapades." When the assistant priest and I planned a weekend retreat with the eighth graders, they rolled their eyes even more and wondered what the world was coming to.

Fr. Mielke came armed with his guitar, and I with my ukulele. We started a new eighth-grade tradition: Camping out and experiencing the wonders of God's nature in the wild. Sitting around the campfire, singing songs and telling stories, created bonds that the inside of classroom walls could never do.

For me, these after-school activities kept me believing that I had made the right choice to remain in the convent. I had written to my mom to tell her I had given it much thought and prayer, and was going to remain a nun.

One spring day in May, that second year of teaching at St. Jude's, a letter arrived from our Crookston Motherhouse. It was from our Rev. Mother and contained my summer catechism teaching assignment, as well as my summer college assignment. The letter stated that Sr. Judith and I had been assigned, together, to teach catechism in Kelliher. The parish priest was Fr. Aarden. After two weeks in Kelliher, I was to report to St. Catherine's College in St. Paul, MN, for more college credits.

Coincidentally, just the day before, I received a letter from Sr. Judith. Our paths had crossed in so many different ways. She had been a year behind me in high school and had also been assigned to teach in Texas when I was there. Sr. Judith was now teaching at a school about three hours from mine and was happy as a lark with her first-graders. She wondered how it had happened that we two young nuns were assigned to teach together. The Rev. Mother always sent an old nun with a young nun. What did I think? Was it a mistake and what should we do about it?

CHAPTER ONE

Questioning my Vows: 1969

The end of May arrived and I was supposed to be preparing for my summer catechism classes. Since I was the older nun (by one whole year), I would be the nun in charge of the summer assignment. I liked the idea of being in charge, but I really had no clue how to proceed.

The problem was, I wasn't sure how to prepare. I had never taught the two-week sessions before, and it had been more than fifteen years since I had been a catechism student myself. Surely the teaching of catechism had evolved in the years since the Benedictine nuns had come to our Indian village in northern Minnesota. During their two-week visits, I had spent many hours memorizing prayers and learning rote answers to the rigorous *Baltimore Catechism* questions so I could earn holy cards and framed pictures of Jesus, Mary, and the saints. The biggest prize of all was earning my very own set of rosary beads. Did nuns still make catechism prizes? Did the nuns still teach that way?

Sr. Agatha was someone I could confide in. I knew she wouldn't tell the other sisters what I was asking her. I showed her my summer obedience letter and explained I had not taught summer catechism before. Now I was to be the senior nun in charge. Did she think that this was some mistake by the Rev. Mother?

"What should I do?" I asked her. "Do you think I should ask the Rev. Mother if she made a mistake? If not, what is the protocol for teaching catechism, and what are the duties of the older nun?"

Sr. Agatha told me that she had been the older nun numerous times. She would help me, and assured me that the Rev. Mother must have had her reasons for this assignment. "It's proper to write to the pastor to introduce yourself," she explained. "Then ask what curriculum he wants you to teach during the two weeks. You will also have to ask him the best way to travel to his parish."

I told her, "I don't know much about Kelliher, but my family and I used to go near there every summer to pick blueberries. And, besides that, some of my high school classmates at boarding school were from there." At least I would have a few things to talk about when we got there.

Sr. Agatha told me that the pastor was a well-loved Dutch priest from Holland. He had been an assistant pastor at East Grand Forks when she taught there. He had a great rapport with the parishioners and students. She was sure he would be very welcoming to us nuns. With that information, I decided to compose my letter to this friendly, well-liked priest.

"Dear Father Aarden..." Wait a minute, was it proper to start with the word "Dear" to a priest? Should I just write, "Father Aarden"? In all my letter-writing lessons, it always started with "Dear" for a friendly letter. If he were so friendly with his parishioners, then it would seem proper to use the word "Dear." This was too trivial to ask Sister Agatha. I decided to go with the "Dear."

> Dear Father Aarden,
>
> Sister Judith and I are so pleased to be coming to your parish to teach Catechism for two weeks. We will be arriving in Bemidji on the Greyhound bus on Sunday, June 13 at 5:00 pm. You will recognize us as the two veiled women in black, and I will be carrying my ukulele case. How will we recognize you?
>
> This is so exciting. We went to school at the Mount with the Moen girls (Sr. Gregory and Sr. Jacqueline) from Shooks, MN. My parents used to take me blueberry picking near your area, so I am acquainted with the northern woods. It will be great to have fun up there and meet you and your parishioners.
>
> We look forward to our two weeks.
>
> Sincerely,
>
> Sister Mona, O.S.B.
>
> P.S. What did you want us to teach?

A week after I sent my letter to the pastor, I received this curt reply.

> Sister Mona,
>
> Up here it is all work and no play. You will be teaching from the Baltimore Catechism. Since I am speaking at the First Mass of one of the new priests, I will be unable to pick you and Sister Judith up at the Greyhound bus station in Bemidji. Mrs. Moen will be there, and she assures me that she will recognize you.
>
> Sincerely,
>
> Father Aarden

I immediately wrote Sr. Judith to tell her the disastrous news of the *Baltimore Catechism*, and the terse letter from this Fr. Aarden. I suggested that she teach the First Communion class, since she was currently working with Primary students. I would teach the older kids because I had the sixth-graders through eighth-graders at St. Jude's.

In my letter, I also mentioned that I would be brushing up on chords for my ukulele. We could have group sing-alongs. Singing songs like *Kumbaya* and *Michael, Row the Boat Ashore* would be a good break each day from learning catechism and doctrine. As a quick post-script, I shared how the nuns at my convent had offered to help make framed holy cards to take along. I suggested she have a supply also, if she didn't already.

It was the first week of June, and school had finished for the year. I had one week to get my classroom materials put away as I had no idea what my next year's assignment would be.

Sr. Judith and I met in the Twin Cities and boarded the Greyhound bus for our five-hour trip to Bemidji, Minnesota. We talked nonstop, like two magpie birds catching up on the past year of activities, as well as regaling ourselves with Texas memories.

Heads turned in the bus as we shrieked with laughter when we re-lived the story of Sr. Judith's Yul Bruner hairstyle. Years earlier, I had counseled Sr. Judith to shave her head before she joined us in Texas. The heat there was intense, and I had reasoned that we wore very conservative habits and no one would ever see her baldness.

Unfortunately for Sr. Judith, we received permission to modify our dress, not long after she arrived with her shaved head. As the Greyhound rolled on, we recalled that infamous night when we had invited the pastor for a sneak preview of our "transformed" nun's attire.

(It really wasn't all that transformed. Instructions from the Motherhouse said that we needed to keep the long veil, as well as our black cotton stockings and matronly black shoes. BUT we could modify and shorten our black habit to *thirteen inches from the floor* AND let *some* of our hair show.)

Our parish priest stuttered all the time, but never as badly as when he saw the five of us on display that day. The color drained from his face. He was as white with shock as the few snowy hairs left his head. Our faces looked like bandits with the lined demarcations of previously sun-protected areas, versus the rest of the face that had been exposed to the Texas heat. There the five of us sat, with a few wisps of our hair peeking out of our small, Clorox–fashioned headpieces. Each of our hairstyles spoke to the era when we had entered the convent. One nun had her hair in waves, one in pin curls, and one with natural curls.

Then there was Sr. Judith with her stubble.

The pastor pointed and stuttered, "Oh, m-m-my G-g-g-g-od, y-y-y-ou l-l-l-ook j-j-j-ust l-l-ike J-j-j-ulius C-c-c-easer!"

We giggled uncontrollably. Sr. Judith rushed out of the room sobbing. After that horrible experience, she wore the more-traditional garb until her hair grew back.

As Sr. Judith and I talked, the hours flew by. The bus driver called out to say that Bemidji was our next stop. Reality quickly set in, and we wondered what on earth lay ahead of us for the next two weeks. Here we were, two young nuns who really didn't know why and how we had been chosen to teach together.

Where it all began: The rectory and church in Kelliher, MN.

When we arrived at the Bemidji Greyhound bus station, Mrs. Moen was there waiting. "Welcome, Sisters. I so wished the Reverend Mother would have sent my two girls," she wistfully said. "I have a meeting tonight, so when we get to the rectory, I'll get you settled before I leave. Fr. Aarden will return later this evening."

An hour later, we were in Kelliher. The town had one main street and no stoplights. Mrs. Moen pointed out a few stores, a cafe, a school, and said there were about two hundred people in town. She went on to say that children from Shooks, an even smaller village nearby, would also participate in our two weeks of catechism.

The newly-built rectory was nestled in the woods near a white-steeple church. When we entered the rectory, Mrs. Moen took us into the kitchen where she had prepared a meal for us. She explained that she would be cooking our meals while we were there. Since she lived only about a mile away from the church, it would be no problem to help us.

"Fr. Aarden built housekeeper's quarters but does not need them," she explained. "He likes to cook his own meals. I just come in once a week to clean."

Just before Mrs. Moen left for her meeting, she showed us our separate bedrooms and told us to make ourselves at home until the pastor arrived.

"Let's eat first," I said, "I think we'll have enough time before he returns to check out this big rectory. I can't believe he cooks his own meals. I'm glad we don't have to cook while we're here." Then I added, "It'll be like a mini-vacation for us. And to think, we will each have our own private bedroom!" Sr. Judith agreed.

After dinner, we found the furnished rooms for a housekeeper in the back of the house. When we peeked into the priest's bedroom, I noticed how neat everything was. I wondered if he got lonely living by himself. Like his bedroom, his office was immaculate with everything on his desk totally organized. This man must like order in his life. Was he as strict as his letter had sounded?

It was such fun checking out the rectory without anyone there to watch us. As we walked into the spacious living room, we gasped at a gigantic stone fireplace taking up one whole wall. There was even a television set in the corner. I wondered if Fr. Aarden would invite us to watch it. We couldn't have one in our convents, so that would be a special treat.

Just when I thought we had seen all the rooms, we discovered a laundry room. Why not put it to use while we waited for the pastor to arrive? I decided it would be a great chance to iron our wrinkled habits and veils, since we were alone.

"Do you think it's necessary to iron our habits and veils? It's Sunday and we really shouldn't be doing that. Right?" asked Sr. Judith.

"No one is here to see us ironing, Sister! I'm sure the pastor won't be back for quite a while." I dismissed her anxiety, and question, and set up the ironing board and iron. Breaking the rule against ironing on Sunday was my first official act as the older nun in charge of decisions. We were far from the Motherhouse and its rules and regulations. It felt good to go beyond the letter of the law.

I removed my wrinkled veil and modified habit and stood there in my seersucker slip as I ironed. We talked about how exciting it was to be on our own for two whole weeks together. I finished ironing and quickly put the newly-ironed habit and veil back on. The clock struck eight just as I started ironing my spare black habit. Suddenly there was a strange sound outside the laundry door.

I had never heard a garage door opener and wondered what on earth that noise could be. Within seconds, the laundry door sprang open. Filling the doorway was this tall man, dressed in black, complete with his Roman collar. I glanced up and was taken aback with his handsomeness, as well as the quizzical look on his face.

"What? Nuns ironing on Sunday?" he questioned as he pointed to his ironing board.

"Well," I quickly retorted. "We thought we should look well-pressed when the pastor arrived." I glanced up to see his reaction. Lucky for me that he hadn't arrived ten minutes earlier. I would have been in my slip and no veil!

"Well, you certainly have made yourself at home. When I asked Mrs. Moen to tell you to do that, I didn't think it would involve the laundry room." He tried to hide his grin as he walked out. Then he looked back and said, "When you two finish your Sunday pressing, meet me in the living room to discuss your real reason for being here."

Sr. Judith waited until he was gone, then looked at me and blurted out, "I knew we shouldn't have ironed on Sunday, Sister. He didn't look too happy with us." I closed the laundry room door to assure us of our privacy. It definitely wasn't the best way to meet the pastor, but I was sure things would work out despite this first, disastrous introduction.

We found our way to the living room after Sr. Judith reluctantly ironed her habits. The pastor was occupied in his office. I informed him that we were indeed wrinkle-free and ready. Like two schoolgirls awaiting punishment, we sat on the couch and wondered what would happen next. Fr. Aarden walked into the living room.

We both jumped up. "Maybe we should introduce ourselves," I awkwardly burst out. "I'm Sr. Mona and this is Sr. Judith." Bravely I offered my handshake as if it were a peace offering.

Fr. Aarden accepted and asked if we would like a drink. Like a drink? I was the "old" nun in this situation, and had only experienced a small glass of wine on feast days—very special feast days. What should I reply? Act as if this was a question I was asked on a daily basis? Was he testing us? Kidding us? As I tried to quickly think of an answer, I blurted out, "No thank you, Father. We have to work tomorrow."

It looked like a smirk on his face as he promptly sat down on the chair facing us.

"Well, Sisters, are you aware that I will be gone this coming week? We priests will be having our annual retreat at your Motherhouse in Crookston. I'll leave right after Mass tomorrow morning. Mrs. Moen will be here to help you with anything you may need." He then went on to explain that I, Sr. Mona, would be in charge since I was the nun who wrote the letter. I was the older nun, right? I nodded and wondered what other duties would be placed in my lap. Maybe this assignment wasn't going to be as easy as I thought.

Sr. Judith had not said a word in his presence since we arrived. Fr. Aarden may have thought she was mute. As I tried to think of what the older nun would do or say in this situation, I decided to ask to see the place where we would be teaching.

He explained that the rectory was designed and built to be both a rectory and catechetical center. The downstairs catechetical center could be accessed from both the outside as well as from his office. He led us downstairs to the classrooms that we would use. I explained that Sr. Judith would be teaching the younger ones, and I would have the older kids. Were there assigned rooms for different ages?

You could tell that it was a new building because it smelled of fresh paint and varnish. The tables and chairs were brand new. The blackboards were shiny and clean, with almost-new erasers lined up like soldiers awaiting the command to share the word of God.

Tucked in the bookcases, I noticed the lettering on the green and blue paperback books: *Baltimore Catechism*. Trying to avoid the subject of the catechisms, I asked where the paper, pencils, and crayons were. He showed us the supply room containing educational supplies as well as playground equipment. Everything was neatly placed and in order.

"I told my parishioners that Catechism classes would start at 9:00 every day," Fr. Aarden told us. "The children will bring their own lunches. You can dismiss them at 2:30 pm."

Sr. Judith finally piped up and asked what materials he had for the children making their First Communion. What about the formulas to teach them for their First Confession?

"Oh, she does let you get a few words in?" he jokingly laughed. "Sister, we have had some informal sessions during the year to prepare them. Here are the materials I've been using, but feel free to teach the way you think best."

Sr. Judith shared that she had been teaching first-graders for several years, and was happy that she could use materials she had brought with her. Two weeks was such a short time, but she would do her best to have them ready for both sacraments.

"I'm sure you will, Sister," he nodded in approval. "Now it's getting late, and I have to pack and get ready for retreat. I'm sure you two have things to do to get ready for tomorrow's classes. Mass is at 8:00. Do you need an alarm?"

We assured him we were fine, said good-night, and went our separate ways. Just before we went to our private bedrooms, I checked in with Sr. Judith.

"Maybe he is going to be OK," I whispered. "Don't worry. We'll do just fine. We have a whole week to work things out before he returns."

That first week flew by. The kids were eager to learn and well behaved. I was having a ball teaching the older kids, but Sr. Judith was stressed. She had to prepare her students to receive their First Confession and First Communion by the end of the two weeks.

To prepare for Confession, they had to know the difference between right and wrong. How do you help little innocents understand their wrongdoings? These children also needed to learn the confession formula of "Bless me, Father, for I have sinned…" They also needed to memorize all the prayers, such as the *Our Father*, *Hail Mary*, and *Glory Be*, that might be assigned as their penance from the priest. Sister also had to teach them why these two sacraments were so important in their Catholic lives. How do you explain that the host is really the Body of Jesus to little ones?

I remembered my Texas years of preparing the innocent Mexican boys and girls to receive these sacraments. It was a stressful time as these little angels were supposed to think of ways they had sinned. Then they had to memorize the Confession formula. To help them experience what going to Confession would be like, I used to pretend to be the priest.

Horror of horrors, I remembered one of the times I sat in the priest's inner sanctum and slid open the curtain of the grate separating me from the young penitent. I heard a tearful, "Bless me, Father, for I have sinned. I hit my brother twenty times…I sweared forty times…" This was followed by a long, long pause.

Then I heard hysterical crying. Rushing out of the priest's cubicle, I met a river of water escaping from the penitent's side of the enclosed confessional. I pulled back the red velvet curtain to rescue the traumatized innocent who was trying to figure out more sins to tell! Hugging him, wet pants and all, I vowed there must be a better way to bring children to this sacrament.

As this memory of First Confession seized my mind, I had another vision of preparing my Texas young ones for First Communion. It was of Luis, on the day of his First Communion. Even in the 60s, it was drilled into us that we must NEVER touch the host when we received the Body of Christ. In fact, we should NOT even let it touch our teeth—just swallow the host. Trying to embed the seriousness of this, I kept telling my little students how sacred the host was, and to just simply swallow it immediately.

Little Luis was nervous the Sunday morning of his First Communion. He must have been so scared about how to swallow the host that his mouth became as arid as the desert surrounding us. He started to choke and gag after the priest placed the host on his tongue. Before I could get up, his dad rushed to rescue him. To this day, I often wonder if Luis ever went to Communion again after such a traumatic experience.

Thinking of all that was involved in preparing the little ones for receiving these sacraments, I certainly had taken the easy road for these two weeks. How could I help Sr. Judith as she prepared the little ones?

As for my students, I had no such responsibility. They reviewed old prayers and learned some new ones. I decided to teach religion lessons that I had used with my eighth-graders. These involved stories, artwork, and discussions, but no rote question and answer format like the *Baltimore Catechism*. The "Who is God?" question with the memorized definitive answer, "God is a Supreme Being who made all things," was not part of our day. We practiced songs while I played my ukulele so they could teach the younger kids when we gathered together in the church every day before lunch.

"Would you like to help the younger kids learn their prayers?" I asked my students on the second day. Sister Judith had shared the night before that it was difficult to help each child with all the prayers and formulas they had to learn.

"Sure, Sister, it'll be fun to be the teacher," was their response. Our days then became a chance to put religion into practice by helping others in need! It also absolved me of my nun's guilt of choosing to take the easy road by teaching the older kids.

On Saturday morning, we were joined at breakfast by the pastor who had arrived late the evening before. He asked how our week had gone.

"No casualties, Father," I reported. "The parish is still standing. The children were very cooperative and well behaved. We've had lots of fun."

"Fun?" queried the man in black. "What made it so fun?"

"Well, we nuns believe that learning is to be fun," I boldly answered. "So we tried many different strategies to make it that way."

Hoping he would not ask any further questions, much less bring up the *Baltimore Catechism*, I asked him, "So, Father, tell us about your retreat. What new things did you learn? You seem to be in a good mood this morning."

"I'm sure I didn't learn as much as your students, but we had an excellent retreat master," he coyly responded. "These retreats are also great times to get together with fellow priests. It get's awfully lonely when you are in isolated parishes."

He went on to share that our nuns pampered the priests and that the food was always the best. The bakery nun spoiled them with fresh caramel rolls every morning and warm cookies every afternoon.

"Sounds like you were fed well in both body and spirit." I nodded in agreement. "By the way," I asked, "What did you want us to do this weekend since we are not teaching?"

"Well, why not relax?" he answered.

Relax? That was not a word in our vocabulary. There was always work to be done in the convent. I looked at Sr. Judith. She looked puzzled and lowered her eyes.

What would we do to "relax?" We had already walked around the small town after supper most days, and checked the woods for wild berries. Other than that, the town didn't have much to offer for relaxation or entertainment.

Mrs. Moen entered the dining room to tell Father Aarden that she had prepared meals for the weekend. She was having out-of-town company, but would be back on Monday to help. I jumped up and said we would clear the table and gladly do the dishes for her.

Fr. Aarden smiled and said, "Tootsie, that's fine. I'm sure that we can survive. Thanks for all your help. Go home and enjoy your family and company." He then excused himself and went into his office.

After finishing dishes, Sr. Judith asked how we were going to relax like he had told us to do. I replied we should just go out on the steps and think about it. As we sat on the steps, Fr. Aarden came out of the rectory with some letters in his hand. He walked to the mailbox at the end of the driveway.

"Sister," I said, "just look at his strut. He seems to be a very determined man, and serious. Yet he seems to have a sense of humor underneath that serious cover."

"Sr. Mona, we're not supposed to be watching men," said Sr. Judith in a shocked voice.

"Well, I noticed it and I also think he is very good looking. It's not a sin to notice, right?" I responded. She looked at me and just shook her head in disbelief.

"I know how we can relax, Sister," I suggested. "We can offer to wash his car, so he can have time do his priestly duties. I heard him tell Mrs. Moen that was one of the things on his agenda for the weekend."

Fr. Aarden seemed a bit surprised when I told him we would like to relax by washing his car. With a twinkle in his eye, he asked if we had "relaxing" clothes for such a job.

"We can always wash and iron our habits if we get dirty. We do know where the laundry room is," I answered saucily.

Fr. Aarden took us into the garage and gathered the supplies for the job. As we rolled up our sleeves, he backed the car out of the garage. Our "modified habit" still involved black dresses thirteen inches from the ground, full veil, and the old black nun shoes complete with black cotton stockings. It was not the ordinary car washing attire, but we had no substitute.

Before he went back to work in his office, he turned and asked with a hint of humor in his voice, "Do you two nuns want to wax it too while you are at it?"

Our "relaxing" took up the rest of the morning as we labored to wash and wax his monstrous white Oldsmobile sedan. As we worked, Sr. Judith and I laughed and talked about our high school days together and recalled more of our Texas experiences. I said that I never thought we would be washing a priest's car, much less have the experience of teaching together again.

Just as we put the final polishing touches on his vehicle, the pastor called us in for lunch. He chided us for not being able to relax, but that it turned out to be a benefit for him. As he talked, I began to notice what a great smile he had. He did have a sense of humor, as well as a way with words.

"So, Sisters, tell me more about yourselves. Sr. Judith, you must have things to say. Will that be all right with you, Mother Superior?" he asked me with a huge grin on his face.

I blushed and then giggled. I had, as usual, taken over and realized that shy Sr. Judith really had not been given much of a chance to exercise her vocal chords since we had arrived. At that moment his knee touched mine under the table and a shiver of excitement raced through my body. Was this intentional?

Soon he had Sr. Judy actually sharing tidbits about her life. I kept my knee touching his and pretended not to notice the occasional nudging. If he did it, so could I. The longer we talked, the better I liked this man from Holland. He shared how he had left home at age thirteen to enter the seminary.

"Wow, Father, so did we!" we both chimed in. We looked at him in disbelief.

"Tell us how you ended up in the United States from the seminary in Holland," I said.

As he talked, he continued to press against my knee and I enjoyed that just as much as his story of finding his way to the Crosier seminary in Minnesota. He had come to America when he was twenty-one to become a priest. What bravery that took. And to think, he had to learn the English language, as well as study for his seminary classes. This man had amazing courage and determination to follow his dreams.

It ended up being a long lunch. I was puzzled. Why had he written such a terse response to my letter if he was not like that in person? I considered asking him, but decided there would be a better time later.

After Sunday morning Mass and breakfast, Fr. Aarden asked us if we would like to take a drive to his cabin on Midge Lake. I looked at Sr. Judith and asked if she would like to go. She hesitated. I told her that I thought it would be great fun. What else was there to do in this small town? Sr. Judith took that into consideration and nodded yes.

As we got near Fr. Aarden's shiny, waxed car, I immediately jumped into the front seat to sit next to the pastor. Sr. Judith looked bewildered but I motioned for her to come and sit next to me.

Fr. Aarden smiled and broke the ice by saying, "Have you Sisters completed your Divine Office?"

We answered that we had said part of our daily prayers.

"When we priests travel, we can replace parts of the Divine Office with fifteen decades of the Rosary," he shared. "Are you interested in doing that with me?"

Just as we finished the last decade, he stopped in front of a grocery store. He told us to wait in the car while he picked up a few groceries for our meal at the lake.

While he was in the store, Sr. Judith looked at me and asked, "Do you think he's taken other nuns to his lake place?"

"I really don't know, but I think he likes us," I quickly responded. "Let's just have a great time and enjoy this chance to be at the lake. Isn't this exciting?"

On the drive to the lake, I became very aware of the closeness to his masculine body and tried to tell myself that it was not proper for a nun to be thinking such things.

My knee and shoulder touched his and electric shocks went through my body. Why was I so attracted to this man of the cloth? I had started to notice his quick wit, and yet also his gentleness. No, this was not right. I needed to take control of my thoughts and wanderings.

Fr. Aarden drove off the main road to a narrow dirt road that led to the cabin he had designed and built for his refuge. He explained why he had painted it orange, the Dutch color of his homeland. The whispering

Fr. Aarden's cabin in the woods.

pines surrounding the cabin were so inviting. I was carried away with thoughts of my childhood home in the woods. After giving a tour of the cabin and premises, he took us to his boathouse on the shore. There he extracted a two-person kayak he had built.

Fr. Aarden in the two-person kayak he built.

"Either of you been in a kayak?" he asked. With our negative reply, he demonstrated how easy it was to paddle this kayak. "You'll do fine, but..." he added with a playful smile, "If you tip over, I hope you can swim. Those habits aren't the greatest swimsuits!"

Sr. Judith and I climbed into the kayak, thanked him, and said we were sure we could handle it. As we attempted to get a rhythmic paddling going, we headed out further into the lake. The peacefulness of the lake and its surroundings made us just stop and float, lapping up the serenity of such a place.

"Can you believe this?" I broke the silence and asked. "Who would ever have thought we would be kayaking in a lake by the pastor's cabin? I really like this priest. He's so kind and generous."

"Sister, you're not supposed to be thinking about priests. Don't you think we should have sat in the back seat of his car coming here?"

"Oh, Sr. Judith, that would have been so formal, like he was our chauffeur, instead of a friendly pastor. We're fine. Let's just enjoy our time here. We might never get a chance like this again."

At that moment, we heard Fr. Aarden beckoning us to come ashore. "I thought you nuns might like a glass of wine while the hamburgers cook on the grill. I bought some corn on the cob and chips to go with the hamburgers," he cheerfully said. "It's a great day for eating out on the picnic table. Just relax and enjoy yourselves."

As we drank our wine, he told us how he had come to finding this property and how he had spent every Monday (his day off) building the cabin. He now came out on Mondays to enjoy the fruit of his labors, but this week he decided to share it with us on Sunday. The more he shared, the more I was attracted to him. All too soon, it was time to head back to the rectory. I made sure I was in the middle front seat on the way home and began feeling less guilty about rubbing shoulders and thighs.

Monday morning came after a fitful night of confused thoughts and desires. What had happened to me? I had chosen to be a nun and that meant celibacy—no men in my life. Why was I so attracted to this man? I needed to stop this attraction. It could only lead to trouble.

At breakfast Fr. Aarden asked, "So how are the kayaking nuns this morning?"

At that moment, Mrs. Moen brought in our food. She raised her eyebrows and asked, "Did you take the nuns to your Midge Lake cabin, Father?"

"Yes, Tootsie." he said, "I thought they needed time to relax at the lake after a long week of teaching catechism."

I watched Mrs. Moen's face take on a look of concern. Was she upset that he had done that? Maybe he didn't usually take nuns to his cabin. What was she thinking?

Sr. Judith looked at me and I turned to Fr. Aarden and said, "Yes, that was great fun. It would have been quite a scene if the pastor had to jump in the lake to rescue two drowning nuns. Or doesn't the talented carpenter know how to swim?"

His knee gave mine an extra nudge as he burst out laughing. "You are quite right, Sister. I dog paddle, so would not have been able to rescue you."

"That's a great way to get rid of nuns you might not like," I chided him. At that moment Mrs. Moen came back to ask the pastor what tasks he wanted her to work on during the day. She looked at me in a questioning way, and I wondered if she had been listening to our bantering. Was there jealousy in that disapproving look?

Father then told her he would be right with her. As he got up, he looked at us and said, "Sisters, I'll be working in my office today, but will be in and out to see how things are going on the catechism front." He winked and went to talk with Mrs. Moen.

My thoughts went to the catechisms gathering dust on the shelves. Would he notice when he stopped in for his visit?

Just before lunch Sr. Judith and I had all the kids gathered in the church for our daily sing along. We were in the middle verses of the song, *Kumbaya*, when the pastor appeared in the back of the church. Oh, dear, I thought, my elementary ukulele skills were about to be judged. Nervously, I plucked the strings as the pastor sat in the back pew and listened. It didn't matter what he thought. The kids thought I was great! They called me "the singing nun."

As we began our next song, *Michael, Row the Boat Ashore*, he slowly walked up the main aisle, smiling at the students. As he walked in front of me, he winked, bent down and whispered, "Do you know any chords other than C, F, and G?"

Then he walked out the side door of the church.

I was dumbfounded because it was so close to the truth. I was still struggling with the D, A, and E chords. Yikes, I better work hard on those other chords!

I wondered if he would eat with us at lunchtime. I found myself looking forward to meals with him. It was great to have the senior citizens volunteer to watch and play with the kids while we had our lunch in the rectory.

"How are the singing nuns?" he chuckled as we arrived for lunch. "Sr. Mona, do you know any religious songs? Or would they not fit into your catechism program?"

He certainly knew how to wound one's heart. "Sure, Father, but I thought your young parishioners knew all those, so I decided to share some folk songs. I thought God could be praised with all types of song."

"Oh, I thought maybe the religious songs required other chords than the C, F, and G pattern!" he smirked and gave a super big nudge to my knee.

"Well, because the pastor has been so nice to us, tomorrow we could add the song, *Oh, Lord, I am Not Worthy*, or do you have other suggestions?" I inquired.

"Touche!" he laughed. At that moment, Mrs. Moen brought in dessert and asked, with a disapproving look, if there was anything else we needed.

"We need Sr. Mona to learn some new chords. Maybe you could help her with those, Tootsie," he tried to say with a straight face. Everyone but Mrs. Moen laughed. She disappeared into the kitchen shaking her head.

That lunch and the rest of the week were spent in playful bantering, as well as quizzical looks from Sr. Judith. She did attempt to add a few comments as she relaxed a bit more. I found myself playing "kneesies" on a regular basis with this six-foot-four, amazing man. Each day my attraction for this priest grew stronger.

I didn't know how to handle the overpowering emotions. I wanted to ask Sr. Judith, but knew she would tell me I shouldn't be feeling such emotions. After all, I was a nun, and nuns shouldn't be having such thoughts and attractions.

One afternoon later that week, the door of my classroom opened and in walked the pastor. Some of the children were busy creating paper collages while others were paired with their First Communion buddies helping them learn their prayers. I was working with a small group discussing their artwork.

"Sister, I don't seem to see the *Baltimore Catechisms* anywhere."

"No, Father, we haven't had time to find them yet. Students, would you like to have Fr. Aarden tell us what he did during his retreat?"

The children all clapped and said, "Please, Father, would you?" I offered a chair to the pastor and asked the kids to come and sit on the floor around him. The younger children were sent back to their class.

"I'm sure Father will answer any of your questions and also share things he learned at retreat," I assured them. Fr. Aarden gave me a look that told me he would be asking me more about those catechisms still standing untouched in orderly rows.

"What's a retreat, Father?" asked the children. "Can you talk or do you have to be quiet all the time? Who was your teacher at retreat? Did you have only priests there?"

Father patiently answered their questions and then shared that no matter how old you are, you are never too old to learn. Before he could turn the tables and ask them what they had learned, it was time to dismiss the children. I was saved by the bell!

Saturday was spent getting the church decorated for First Communion and calming Sr. Judith down. That evening we gathered in the living room. Fr. Aarden said we nuns deserved a drink for a successful two weeks—even minus the *Baltimore Catechism*. He laughed as he shared how he was surprised, yet happy, that I had not taken the catechisms from hiding. They were filled with such conservative doctrine.

"Then why did your letter stress teaching with the *Baltimore Catechism*?" I asked. "You sounded so strict and conservative. I told Sr. Judith that I didn't like you immediately, after I read your letter. I figured we would do our own thing, in spite of your terse commands."

"It was bad timing. I usually get older nuns who are conservative like the bishop," he explained. "Since the bishop and I don't see eye to eye on doctrine and legalities, I decided I didn't need any more flack. I wrote that letter right after I had been called on the carpet by the bishop for trying to have Saturday evening Masses for the fishermen of the area. We have butted heads on many other issues over the years."

I looked at the hurt in his eyes and my heart melted.

"So," he continued, "it was such a relief to have a nun in charge who thought outside the box—even nuns who ironed on Sunday."

He laughed as he poured himself another drink.

"Well, you certainly are the opposite of the picture you painted in your letter," I answered. "I was afraid these two weeks would drag by. I wondered what we would do, and what the pastor would demand of us."

I looked into his eyes and blushed. Those eyes spoke volumes and I wanted to know more.

We tried to watch a bit of television, but it was mostly snow due to the poor reception in the woods. After shutting off the TV, he returned to his recliner that was close to where I was sitting. His hand suddenly found mine. Shivers went up and down my spine. We needed to talk. Had Sr. Judith noticed? She was sitting farther down on the couch and looked so sleepy. Her week of teaching had been stressful. I told her that I thought it was time for us to retire for the evening. As we left the room, I turned and mouthed the words, "I'll be back."

What was I doing? How bold was that statement? I said goodnight to Sr. Judith and wished her a restful sleep. I then walked into my bedroom, undressed, and put on my modest white nightgown.

Was he waiting for me? I checked and saw that Sr. Judith's light was out in her bedroom. I then quietly tiptoed down the hallway to see if Fr. Aarden was still there waiting. He was.

His surprised look at my nightwear made me wonder why I had done such a thing. Why hadn't I just come back with my habit on? How could I have been so stupid and naïve? Yet, his eyes told me he was glad I came back.

I rushed to the chair next to him and he reached again for my hand. My hand was sweaty with nervousness, and his touch made my heart beat faster than a startled doe in the woods. I looked at him with questioning eyes.

"Sr. Mona, I am very attracted to you. From the first moment, when I came into the laundry room and saw you ironing, I knew you were one spunky nun. I liked that. This past week has created a newness of deep emotions that have caused some sleepless nights for me. I would really like to get to know you better."

He then went on to share that after fifteen years in the priesthood, he was calling it quits. "I'm going to meet with the bishop and tell him that I am leaving the priesthood and explain why. I love this parish and its people, but the writing is on the wall. And now I have another reason to leave—you!"

I looked into his eyes and whispered, "How can one fall in love in a week? I was attracted to you, also, the minute I saw you in that doorway. I was expecting an old crabby priest, not a young, handsome one. I knew from the look in your eyes that you were not serious when you tried to look horrified to see nuns ironing on Sunday."

We both laughed. During the next hour, we shared our thoughts, feelings, and attractions. I wondered if Sr. Judith were really asleep. Maybe she had heard us laughing. What would I do if she suddenly appeared in the hallway?

Fr. Aarden shared that after telling the bishop of his intentions to leave, he would return to Holland to tell his family. Then, after his Holland visit, he would take a few weeks to prepare his parishioners for his departure.

I told him I would spend the first part of the summer at St. Kate's taking college classes. After summer school, I was going to travel with a nun friend of mine for a month on Cape Cod.

Fr. Aarden rose without another word and took me in his arms. We embraced and my heart melted. His mouth found mine and we became one with hungry kisses and emotions that had been locked away for so many years in the vow of celibacy.

Exhausted with guilt and newfound love, we sat and shared a space on the couch to plan a realistic approach to this new discovery of mutual love. How could this have happened so quickly? One week? Was this real? He had been planning to leave priesthood. All I had been planning was a fun time in the North for a two-week catechism assignment. What were we to do?

"Do you want to see me this summer, before I go to Holland?" he asked. "I will be staying with Fr. Reynolds a few days. His parish is only about an hour from the Twin Cities."

"Of course," I replied, "but I can't let the nuns know just yet. This has happened so fast. I really don't know what to say or do."

"Well, we can write to each other. I don't think the nuns would appreciate me phoning you every day," he laughed as he held me close.

As we nestled together, we devised a strategy for the next day. We would drive Sr. Judith to the Greyhound station in Bemidji so she could return to the Mount. Then he would drop me off at my Aunt Ruby and Uncle Howard's home near Bemidji. My cousin had offered to drive me from there to the Twin Cities for my summer college classes.

The clock chimed midnight. Unlike Cinderella, I had no glass slipper but, like her, I had discovered an amazing prince. After multiple hugs and prolonged kisses, we reluctantly said goodnight.

If I had tossed and turned other nights, this was a night I could not even sleep. What had I just done? Was I really in love? Would I think of leaving the convent for this amazing man? What? Why? When? How? These questions bombarded my mind, yet I was filled with an excitement and internal sensations I had never felt before in my life.

I tried to make sense of what had just happened. I had invited it by saying I would return to the living room after Sr. Judith went to bed. That was one big, open invitation if ever there was one. What had happened to my sense of decency? Was it lost in lust? Oh, dear God, I had opened the floodgates of passion, and now had to figure out how to build a dam to control them.

What would Rev. Mother do, if and when I told her? What about my parents? They hadn't wanted me to enter the convent and now, fifteen years later, they had me on this high pedestal that I was about to leap off of. I'd loved my life as a nun, even though there had been some tough times. I realized everyone had difficulties to face, no matter what their vocation was.

What about my degree? I had tons of college credits, but no degree. St. Catherine's told me I needed to complete "student teaching" in order to graduate. To think I had taught for eight years, been a principal, started a new school, and yet never received my degree. If I left the convent, I couldn't get a teaching job without a degree. Another dilemma.

I sat up in bed and blushed as I thought of the intensity of his crushing lips and how I had enjoyed every second. Now that I had tasted of this man's passion, how could I not yearn for more?

Yet, how could I even think about giving up my life as a nun? But, oh, my dear God, I had never felt like this in my entire life. I needed time to pull myself together and face reality, as well as the repercussions of my actions.

The next morning at Sunday Mass, I felt guilty beyond any guilt I had ever experienced. I could barely look at the man saying Mass. I had kissed and hugged this priest over and over again last night. Every time I looked up at the altar, I felt shame; yet, an amazing love engulfed my body. Sinful guilt filled my soul.

At Communion time, I could not bring myself to go up and receive the Body of Christ—I had sinned and felt too guilty. Sr. Judith looked at me with wide, questioning eyes when I sat and let her go up to Communion after her little students had received their First Communion.

I could feel Mrs. Moen's eyes on me. She must have wondered why I had not gone up and received Communion. I felt like Hester Prynne's big letter *A* was stamped on my habit. Why hadn't I just gone up and received Communion? Nuns never skipped Communion. Now people would wonder and begin to ask questions. How stupid of me, but the die had been cast.

Mrs. Moen came over to say goodbye after Mass. She looked at me with penetrating, accusing eyes that told me she was aware of more than I had thought. I tried to be natural and innocent. I thanked her for all her help and then turned away abruptly to say farewell to my students.

Sr. Judith was quieter than usual all the way to the bus depot. When we got to the bus station, I hugged her and wished her well in her summer studies at the Mount. She seemed different and I sensed that she knew more than I thought.

When I returned to Fr. Aarden's car, I wondered what was going to happen next. I would be alone with him again. What had I gotten myself into?

On the way to my aunt and uncle's, he reached over and pulled me close. I was lost again in this new maze of feelings. We were hungry for each other. How he managed to drive and kiss me at the same time without getting in an accident is a miracle.

He missed the turn for my uncle's road and had to stop and ask directions at a café. When he came back to the car, he took me in his arms and smothered me with kisses. He whispered, "I can't think of being without you. I don't want you to leave."

We were already late for my arrival at my aunt and uncle's. When we finally did get there, Aunt Ruby invited Fr. Aarden in for coffee and a piece of pie. He thanked her but said he had an afternoon appointment and couldn't stay.

This meant a speedy farewell. As we said goodbye with a formal handshake, he whispered that he would write to me right away. As he walked to his car, I waited and reluctantly waved as he drove out of the driveway.

As he drove off, Aunt Ruby and Uncle Howard cheerfully said, "We knew Fr. Aarden when he was the assistant pastor here in Bemidji. Everyone loved him and hated to see him sent to another parish. How were your two weeks in Kelliher?"

I tried to pretend that nothing out of the ordinary had happened. "Oh, it was fine." I casually responded. "Fr. Aarden told us the bishop wants to move him again to another parish that needs repairs, because he finished building the rectory and catechetical center in Kelliher. It's too bad he can't stay longer to enjoy the fruits of his labor."

I wanted desperately to change the subject. "Oh, Aunt Ruby, did you make my favorite strawberry-rhubarb pie?"

Since Aunt Ruby loved to have people notice her great culinary skills, she laughed and said, "Vonnie—I mean, Sr. Mona—you always did like my baking. I made this just for you. Let's enjoy it with some ice cream like we did when you were a snotty-nosed kid always wanting to know what I had baked for you."

With that distraction, we sat in the kitchen and ate the pie and ice cream until my cousin arrived to drive me to the Twin Cities. What would the rest of the summer be like?

CHAPTER TWO
Summer of Uncertainties: 1969

That summer of 1969, I was one of the younger nuns from our Motherhouse attending St. Catherine's College in St. Paul, Minnesota. I was assigned to live at our convent-owned house on 239 Summit Avenue, instead of living on campus. This huge, multi-storied, beige-stucco house joined the row of stately homes lining Summit Avenue, reminiscent of the prosperous days of the railroad tycoon, John J. Hill. It was situated across from the cathedral, about fifteen minutes from campus.

Sr. Anselma was a living fixture of the dwelling. She had been in charge of the house, as well as its occupants, since its inception. Sister awaited her summer residents like an army sergeant in charge of boot camp. She certainly did not approve of the new-fangled notion of modified habits; she resolutely clung to her pleated coif and traditional garb. Four of us younger nuns shared a dormitory room: "nun-barracks" with no room for privacy. We were told that beds were to be made neatly on a daily basis and bedrooms had to be presentable at all times.

Sister placed handwritten notes on each bed; the notes featured our name and the household duties we would be responsible for during our summer residence. I envisioned ancient Sr. Anselma bent over her writing desk during the long winter months, gleefully conjuring the minute details for every carefully-scripted task her summer helpers would be expected to perform with perfection.

My note stated I would be cleaning the windows and keeping them clean all summer. The yellow-lined ledger included a specific recipe for the water and vinegar solution; the precise type of cloth and bucket to use; location of the newspapers for drying the windows; plus a time frame for cleaning each set of windows.

Sister assigned two of us nuns the job of driving to and from the college campus. Driving the car was the only sense of freedom I experienced in that "you must obey the rules" atmosphere. We nuns decided on our own that we would leave immediately every morning after our regimented prayers, Mass, and breakfast, no matter what time our college classes started. We also unanimously decided that we would stay on campus as late as possible and arrive back just in time for the 6:00 p.m. supper hour.

In the midst of this "thou shalt not" environment, my mind was totally pre-occupied with a certain Fr. Aarden. Sr. Anselma handled all the mail. When I returned from our second day of college classes, I noticed a letter from Kelliher, MN, on my assigned bed.

Where could I read it and not be seen? Tucking the letter into my notebook, I rushed down the steps to the street and raced to the cathedral. Finding a pew in the corner of the dimly-lit side chapel, I tore open the letter. He missed me! He couldn't stop thinking about me! He wanted to see me again!

When the second and third letters arrived, Sr. Anselma's eyebrows were raised almost to her hairline—if her hairline had been visible beneath her old-school garb. She asked me why I was getting all this mail from this same address? Not only that, it appeared to be a man's writing.

What could I say? I tried not to look into her searing, brown eyes and quickly answered that there were some questions about the summer catechism materials we had used. A little stray from the truth but, after all, Fr. Aarden had mentioned the *Baltimore Catechism* incident again in jest! Right then and there, I knew I had to immediately write and tell him not to send any more letters to 239 Summit. I needed to find a safe address where no questions would be asked.

Sr. Marian, another good friend from my Texas days, was allowed to live on campus that summer. She would be a great choice. I'd have Father send my letters to her address. But…that meant I would have to tell her my secret.

I found Sr. Marian on campus and asked if we could go to her room for a private matter. As soon as I shut her door, I asked her to sit down.

"Sister, I can't go to Boston with you after summer school," I blurted out. "I've fallen in love and I'm going to leave the convent." I told her that it wouldn't be fair to her family, if they found out.

"What?" she screamed. "Fallen in love? Who? When? Where? How?"

I started to cry.

"I didn't mean to fall in love!" I sobbed. "It just happened. I was teaching catechism in Kelliher, with Sr. Judith, and fell in love with Fr. Aarden."

"Nonsense. First of all, you don't fall in love in two weeks," she objected. "You're a nun, for heaven's sakes."

"No, Sr. Marian," I interrupted. "It really was only one week, because he was gone the first week, for the priests' retreat."

"That's even more ridiculous. What do you know about falling in love?" she asked. "What do you know about this Fr. Aarden? Oh, Sr. Mona, be sensible!"

Sr. Marian was sure that by the end of the summer I would come to my senses. I was a good nun, she assured me, and the convent needed me.

We spent that afternoon talking, crying, and even laughing at times as I told her all about my two weeks in Kelliher. In the end, she convinced me that I definitely should go with her to Massachusetts for the month. After all, we already had our plane tickets. We had been planning this trip for months and had all the proper permissions. Her family was waiting for us. How could I be so selfish and disappoint them too?

Before I left her room, I told her that Sr. Anselma was already questioning me about the letters Fr. Aarden was sending. I was worried she might open them. Would it be all right if he sent them to Sr. Marian's campus address? Sr. Marian reluctantly agreed, but didn't think it was a good idea to keep encouraging Fr. Aarden.

As each day went by, my studies suffered more. It was so hard to concentrate. I kept wondering when the next letter would arrive.

My parents had sent me some spending money for the summer, so I had money to buy stamps and stationery. In one of his letters, Fr. Aarden wrote that he was coming to the Twin Cities. Could I meet him for lunch before he left for Holland?

A luncheon date!

My heart raced. Would it be the right thing to do?

As I fleetingly questioned that, my mind conjured up ideas of what I should wear. Should I try to disguise myself so no one would know I was a nun? There was a second-hand store near the college. I rushed over and found a bright orange scarf, the Dutch color that Fr. Aarden always talked about.

The following Tuesday, Fr. Aarden picked me up at the college parking lot. He recognized me. How could he not? Minus my veil—but still wearing my black modified habit with the addition of a blatant orange scarf dangling around my neck—I stood out like an exotic orange-collared blackbird, perched in the jungle of the college parking lot.

"Interesting scarf, Sr. Mona," he quipped as he tried to hide a pleased smirk. "Headed for Holland with me?"

We laughed and quickly hugged before he gallantly opened the car door for me. How could I contain my jitters and excitement for this luncheon date? Like a nervous magpie, I jabbered on and on about classes, the scarf, seeing him again…

When we were seated at the restaurant table, Fr. Aarden immediately grabbed my hand and our knees touched once again. I found my heart palpitating uncontrollably.

I leaned closer as he told me of his unpleasant encounter with the bishop. At the meeting with the bishop, he had shared his resignation plans and reasons for leaving, as well as his plans to travel to Holland for a month. After his return to Kelliher, he told the bishop, he would spend a few weeks with his parishioners to prepare them for his exodus.

"Pray to St. Teresa of Avila, read her life, and meditate on her mystical thoughts of prayer before making any rash decision," was Bishop Glenn's response.

"It's too late for that, Bishop," Fr. Aarden had retorted. "You should have realized, a long time ago, how unfair you have been over the years with my parish placements, as well as refusing my parish requests multiple times."

He told me how he then reminded the bishop of all the times that the bishop had said, "No," to requests to minister in ways that would have been more beneficial to his parishioners. Why had the bishop not allowed him to have Saturday night Mass for the fishermen? Why had he transferred all of the hard-earned funding monies from his Kelliher parish to another parish? Why did the bishop constantly have negative responses to any innovative ideas for making life easier for his parishioners? And now, the straw that broke the camel's back was the bishop's latest order to transfer him to another parish. His new rectory and parish center had just been completed and he did not want to be moved. All of these actions by the bishop were not acceptable.

"It's time to bow out," he angrily told the bishop as he stood to leave. "You'll have to find another handy-man for your building projects!"

As I listened to his story, I felt his struggle, but also his strength. I marveled at this man sitting next to me. What to say in response?

"It's not easy to give up fifteen years of priesthood and not know what the future might bring," he said as he sighed and leaned back in his chair. "It's been a rocky road, but the time has come. I can no longer accept living under such a conservative bishop, especially when my parishioners suffer under his commands."

I looked at the distress, yet determination, in his eyes. He went on to say that it was definitely the best thing to do, and now I was the best thing to ever enter his life. There was no turning back in his mind. He felt certain that his family would accept his decision, but the hardest hurdle would be telling his parishioners.

"Can you come to the airport to say goodbye to me next Tuesday?" he asked, as he drove me back to campus. I melted. Of course, I would find a way. Since I was one of the summer drivers, I would have the car keys. Even if I had to skip a class, I would be there.

The next Tuesday, I arrived at the airport, parked the car, and found him waiting outside the designated airport door. I had, once again, exchanged my veil for his favorite colored scarf. We hugged, kissed, and then made our way inside to the restaurant.

To my utter surprise, there was another priest sitting at the table. Fr. Aarden quickly introduced me to Fr. Reynolds. His priest friend surveyed me up and down and had little to say except a curt, chilly, "Hello."

"Fr. Reynolds," he quickly explained to me, "has been a friend of mine since seminary days. His family 'adopted' me way back then, since I had no family of my own in the USA."

I learned that Fr. Reynolds often traveled with him to Europe. This time, he was going along to buy himself a German-made car that the two of them would drive around Europe, after visiting the Aarden family in Holland. At the end of the trip, he would have his car shipped to the USA.

I had anticipated having this time alone with Fr. Aarden. The atmosphere was stiff, formal, and as uncomfortable as if Sr. Anselma had been asked to join us. Fr. Aarden sat as close to me as he could. We once again shared knees and held hands under the table. The conversation was stilted, and my hand was wet with nervous perspiration.

After an agonizing forty-five minutes, that seemed like years, I said I needed to get back to class. Fr. Aarden said he would walk me to my car. We left his friend behind with a puzzled face and questioning eyes.

"I had no idea you were going to Holland with another priest," I blurted out. "That was so uncomfortable. What have you told him about me?" I wanted to know.

"I should have told you that he would be there," Fr. Aarden quickly said. "But I wanted so badly to see you again before I left for Holland. I'm sorry. I was going to tell him about us on the long plane ride."

"Seeing how distant and cold he was," I said with a shiver, "I'm glad that I'm not the one breaking the news to him."

Was this just a sample of the beginning of our future troubles together? We hugged to try and reassure ourselves. After a long farewell kiss, we promised that we would write as often as we could.

With tears in my eyes, I watched him head back to the airport, and blew him a kiss as he turned and did the same. How could I survive six weeks without seeing him?

Classes dragged by that next week. Every day I met Sr. Marian with the same question, "Any mail for me?" When she finally produced the long-desired, airmail-stamped envelope, my heart leapt like a spirited gazelle. With a pounding heart, I thanked Sr. Marian and rushed off to read my love's message in a secluded corner of the library.

Finally, during the third week of August, exams were finished. I could concentrate fully on my Boston trip, and Fr. Aarden.

I thought of my summer classes. My grades had always been straight As, of which I was very proud. I knew my grades for that summer would not be so spectacular. I had never had the distractions of being in love with a man before. I wondered what the end results would be for both my grades, and the newly discovered distraction named Fr. Aarden.

Two days before we were to leave for Massachusetts, Sr. Robertine rushed up to me to ask a favor. Since we had changed to a modified habit, the Rev. Mother realized there was now a need for a beautician at our motherhouse. Sr. Robertine had volunteered for the job, and was living at 239 Summit while she studied at a beautician school.

"I just need to give one more perm before my exam tomorrow," she pleaded. "I've practiced on all the other nuns here. Please say you'll let me do it."

How could I refuse? After Sister put my hair in curlers, she applied a smelly solution and wrapped my head in a plastic bag. After setting the timer, she became busy with other duties, while I packed for my vacation. As I finished packing, I wondered why it was taking this smelly perm so long, but I was sure Sister knew what she was doing.

Suddenly she rushed into the bedroom. "Oh, Sr. Mona, I'm so sorry!" she panted. "I got distracted with a job in the flower garden! I didn't hear the timer go off. Hurry, we have to rinse the solution."

The perm had worked overtime. My hair was so tightly curled that she could barely get a comb through it. It was a disaster, and there was no time to attempt a "recall" or change. Both Sister and I were in tears. I tried to hide my hair behind the veil, and that looked even worse. When I pulled the veil back a little, the corkscrew curls poked out in funny intervals. I was doomed.

When my sister, Flo, arrived to take Sr. Marian and me to the airport, she took one look at my new hairdo and gasped, "What on earth happened to your hair...the little that is even there?"

My sister was known for her hair cutting skills, as well as giving perms to her friends and neighbors. She stood there dumbfounded, and then tried to perform some magic on the stubborn kinky curls. Nothing worked. She gave up, shook her head, and said it would just take time.

I was devastated, but we had to get to the airport. Flo suggested that maybe I could get a "hair straightener" solution when I got to Boston.

"Maybe you should have resurrected your old nun's habit that covered your entire head," Sr. Marian said with an uncontrollable giggle. This was not a laughing matter. What would her folks think of this curly frizz? But, Boston or Bust, uncontrollable hair and all!

In Arlington, at Sr. Marian's parent's house, I had a unique present on my bed: A twenty-five-pound bag of flour with a big smiley face drawn on it. I heard chants behind me: "We want bread. We want bread!" Sr. Marian had bragged about my bread-making skills to her Boston family.

The next day the kitchen counters were covered with bread pans of all sizes, plus dozens of raised doughnuts waiting to be deep-fried. The family cheered as they tasted the warm, sugared doughnuts and declared that Dunkin Donuts had some serious competition.

Sr. Marian in her "beach clothes" with her mother, Mary.

Since the city was having a heat wave, Sr. Marian's mother, Mary, decided that we should head to Cape Cod for a few weeks. "You two nuns need to change into something comfortable in this intolerable heat," she said, shaking her head. "You look like two sweating penguins strutting about in all that black regalia."

What would Mary say if she knew that in a month I would shed my habit forever? I shivered in excitement, and with fear of the unknown that lay before me. Was I being naïve and simply giving into infatuation, or was this the real thing? When I was thirteen, I had jumped into the convent without taking time to really process what it really meant. Here I was, at age twenty-nine, about to jump into a commitment without much thought again. Was this a pattern in my life? I needed to listen to Sr. Marian and give it more thought. Or did I? Parts of me were so certain—my heart, for instance—but my head wasn't so sure.

Mary rounded up beach clothes—shorts and sleeveless tops—from all the relatives and told us to go and get comfortable. It took less than five minutes and we two nuns were transformed into regular-looking lay people, except for my uncontrollable hair! The shedding of the habits felt freeing, like a snake shedding its old, tight skin, leaving it in exchange for a new liberated layer.

Sr. Marian's cousin, a beautician, was in the room with us as we changed into our borrowed lay clothes. She stared at me, shocked, when I removed my veil. I shared my hair story.

Sr. Mona in "beach clothes".

She took me by the arm and assured me that there was a straightening solution she could apply to help my hair "relax." After she applied the treatment, the solution worked so well that my hair looked like short, spiny porcupine quills. Were there no happy mediums in my life?

We drove to Cape Cod for two weeks of total relaxation. The Cape Cod cottage, which belonged to Sr. Marian's cousin, was situated right behind the grassy dunes on the beach. Rushing down to see and feel the lapping Atlantic Ocean waves, I listened to the squawks of the overhead seagulls and felt Nature's freedom and wonders: Just like Maria had experienced on the mountainside in *The Sound of Music*. The incessant ocean waves became like prayer magnets. They drew me every morning to come and listen to the whispering tufts of ocean grass, feel the coarse sand grains between my toes, and smell the seaweed gathering along the shore. Could heaven be far away?

Visions of Fr. Aarden danced in my head as I lay on the beach. I tried to etch every detail I could into my memory. He seemed like a giant. I was a measly five-feet-four-inches, and I didn't even come up to his shoulders when I stood next to him.

And then there was that distinct wave, on the right side of his parted, dark-brown hair. His prominent, strong nose added to his handsome, domineering features. All these details were softened when he smiled and gave me that special wink with his bluish-green eyes.

I conjured up his trim, well-built frame and melted when I thought of the strength of his embraces. But most of all, I realized what a strong, magnetic personality he possessed, animated by his passion for perfection in all that he did. What a lucky woman I was!

What had made me an attraction for him? I had never thought of myself as attractive, but I knew people were attracted to my personality. Things I said evoked lots of laughter. (Well, there were a few tears too!)

Sr. Marian and I donned our borrowed swimming suits every morning. We walked our whitened bodies to the shore, hoping that the sun's rays would do us justice. We spent our days swimming, sailing, and water skiing, as well as simply lying on the beach, mesmerized by its sounds. The sun's rays managed to quickly burn our fair skin that had been hidden beneath layers of nuns' habits for years.

The phrase, "Life is a beach…" became our new motto with the added byline: "Beware: Women of the cloth."

Alone on the beach, my pen and paper became a constant companion. I shared our newly-found, beach-life freedoms in my love letters to Fr. Aarden. Was this life a sample of what I could expect outside convent walls? Sr. Marian kept telling me to really consider what I was doing. Her advice fell on deaf ears. Little did she know, I had already told Fr. Aarden —in one of my many letters—I would leave the convent and marry him.

It was impossible to stop thinking of him and concentrate on being fully present with Sr. Marian's family. Thank heavens we had so many new places and events to experience. Every day there were always more family members to meet, and that helped keep me distracted from constant thoughts of a certain Dutchman.

I discovered the exact time when the mailman arrived each day, and made sure I was there to meet him. We became daily acquaintances with letter exchanges. Guilt tugged at the recesses of my mind, but I wanted and needed those Holland letters! As soon as the mailman left, I rushed and hid the letter in my suitcase pocket to be read that evening. I needed to keep those letters a secret from Sr. Marian's family.

In one of the letters, Fr. Aarden shared that he had returned from Holland and was back at Kelliher. He had one week left with his parishioners, and was preparing his last homily to tell them of his decision to leave the priesthood. The bishop had tried, once again, to stop him, but it was too late.

The diocese was offering no money, whatsoever, for his fifteen years of service. Fr. Aarden would be penniless, but he had made arrangements to live at Fr. Reynold's rectory near the Twin Cities until he found a job. Fr. Reynolds needed some remodeling done, and would pay him for that work. After that, he had no idea what work he would find. Who would hire a forty-two-year-old ex-priest? But, at least he had a place to stay.

In his next letter, he described how his parishioners had reacted to his decision to leave the priesthood. They wanted him to be their pastor, even if he was no longer a priest. That was impossible. He left for the Twin Cities the next day.

In his letter, he offered to pick Sr. Marian and me up at the airport. He gave me Fr. Reynold's phone number, in case I needed to contact him at any time. I got so excited, I decided to find a pay phone right then and there. How I yearned to hear his Dutch-accented voice!

With trembling fingers, I dialed the number. He answered on the second ring. (Thank heavens that I did not have to speak to Fr. Reynolds!)

"Hello? May I help you?" I heard him say, but I couldn't get anything out of my mouth. All of a sudden, I didn't know what to say! It was so overwhelming to simply hear his voice. "Hello? Anyone there?"

I gulped, took a deep breath, and whispered, "It's me. Sr. Mona."

He laughed and said it was such an unexpected pleasure. I quickly told him it would be great to have him meet us at the airport. Before I finished giving him the airline info, the operator cut in to say I needed to deposit more money. I almost dropped the few remaining coins, but managed to nervously get them in the phone slot before we were cut off.

Just hearing his voice stirred pent-up emotions deep within me. Six more days and I would be in his arms. How could I wait six days?

Finally, August 23rd arrived. We said our fond farewells and thanks to Sr. Marian's Boston family for an amazing four weeks of adventures. As I hugged each one, I wondered what their reaction would be when they learned of my decision to leave the convent.

As we settled in among the clouds, I turned to Sr. Marian and said, "Sister, I just realized: I may not recognize Fr. Aarden in his lay clothes."

She looked at me in the oddest way. "You told me you want to leave the convent and marry him. Now you don't even remember what he looks like? How silly is that?" she questioned. "See, I told you: This is all so crazy." She taunted me as she shook her head. "You better get your head on straight and think seriously of what you have committed to this man you hardly know."

Luck was on my side. When we got off the plane, there was the man of my dreams standing straight and tall, with that special twinkle in his eyes. Sr. Marian and I were back in our modified habits, so I couldn't just rush up and hug him. Instead, I smiled and nervously held out my hand for a respectful handshake and hello.

"This is my friend, Sr. Marian. Thanks so much for coming to pick us up," I said.

My stomach was turning cartwheels and I felt dizzy with excitement. It was so uncomfortable being with him in the presence of Sr. Marian. The fifteen-minute ride to my sister's home was filled with polite conversation, but I was dying to be with him alone. There were a million questions I wanted to ask.

When we arrived at Flo's, Fr. Aarden insisted on carrying our suitcases. When I opened the door, there stood Flo, her husband, Rome, and all five kids. They looked up in total surprise when this unknown, six-foot-four man came in, smiled, and put down our suitcases. I looked at their questioning faces and realized I had some introductions to do.

They all knew Sr. Marian. She had been a fixture of our family for years. I was left with explaining the presence of this smiling man by my side. Suddenly, I realized I had never called him by his baptismal name. In his letters, he had signed them, Fr. Aarden. Or, Fr. Piet Aarden. Or, eventually, just Piet Aarden.

"Flo," I said. "I'd like you to meet Piet." (Which I pronounced Pie–et). "Pie-et, I'd like you to meet Flo". I then turned to her husband and nervously repeated my introduction. "Rome, I'd like you to meet Pie-et. Pie-et, I'd like you to meet Rome."

I was so nervously caught up in the intros, I didn't notice a peculiar smile curling Pie-et's lips. When I finished, there was a deafening silence. Pie-et motioned me to come closer and whispered into my ear, "If this is a serious relationship, maybe it would be good if you knew my name. My name is Pete, not Pie-et." It was a Dutch spelling, and I had never thought that it would have an American pronunciation. I looked at him in shock and embarrassment.

As soon as he said that, I made everything worse by re-doing the introductions, but this time pronouncing his name as Pete.

A veil of deadly silence filled the room and I beheld the shocked, bewildered looks of each member of Flo's family. I could see questions written all over their stunned faces: Who was this man that had brought their sister (or aunt) from the airport? What was he doing here? Their Sr. Mona appeared to be out of control and didn't seem herself. Something was definitely not right.

I turned in utter confusion to Piet, just as he turned to me and asked if we might just take a short ride. We needed to discuss a few important things before he left. I left Flo's family—still standing in disbelief—with Sr. Marian and could not close the door behind me fast enough.

As we walked to his car, "Pie-et" looked at me and we both broke out into nervous, hysterical laughter at my unsuccessful introduction. He drove to a quiet street a few blocks away and parked the car.

"Well, that could not have gone any worse, even if I had planned it," I said apologetically. "Wow, there are so many unknowns between us, I don't know where to start."

"We both have lots to think about and decisions to make. There are not many employers searching for a philosophy-theology major. I still have no prospects for a job," he sighed. "I'm forty-two and might end up being a ditch-digger. I also know that there is an age difference between us. Are you still interested in leaving the convent despite all of that?"

I looked at this serious man and said that I'd leave, no matter what type of work he did. I just wanted to be near him.

"I'm twenty-nine," I shared, "but age doesn't make a difference. I love you, not your age."

We hugged and kissed. I knew I needed to get to my motherhouse immediately, to tell the Rev. Mother that I had fallen in love and was going to leave the convent.

Piet asked if he could drive Sr. Marian and me to the motherhouse in Crookston. I stared at him in disbelief. Oh, my heavens, what would the Rev. Mother say if I arrived at her door with Fr. Aarden? It had been bad enough arriving at the door of my sister's home!

I assured him we already had made arrangements to drive with other nuns the next day, but appreciated his offer. "I'm so mixed up with unknowns. I have no idea what the Rev. Mother will say," I said with apprehension. "Or what my folks will say, either. I'm scared and nervous. Aren't you?"

He held me close and said to take my time with my decision. He had taken the plunge and was not going back.

"Don't feel obliged, even if you said in your letters that you would leave the convent to marry me," he said tenderly. "I'll understand if you're persuaded to remain in the convent. Just know, I'm here for you, and that I do totally love that saucy nun with the orange scarf!"

When we got back to Flo's, I told him not to come in. I had to go in and "face the music" with my family. He was not to worry. I would write, or call, and keep him updated on everything.

As I opened the door to my sister's home, I braced myself for questions. It was not fair to have left Sr. Marian, but I knew she could fend off questions until I returned.

Flo had sent all the kids to bed. She was sitting at the kitchen table with Rome and Sr. Marian. "So what is this all about? Who is this Pie-et or whatever his real name is?" my sister huffed. "Aren't you still a nun and under vows? Does that include being with a man?"

I sat down with a sigh and told my story, starting with my two weeks in Kelliher and falling in love with Fr. Aarden. I also shared how I hadn't wanted to go to Boston, but Sr. Marian had felt it would be the best way to escape and figure things out. "She thought I would come to my senses and see how silly this was. Instead, it cemented my feelings."

"Well, you get your life straightened out and return to your motherhouse. Vows are not made to be broken," my sister preached. "Do you think that I could just pick up and leave my marriage vows anytime I wanted to? Stay tonight, and then you'd better spend some serious time thinking about what you are going to do," she continued in her upset voice. "What do you think my children thought when their aunt, who is a nun, came to the door with a man?"

I had not thought of all the repercussions I would cause. In hindsight, it was not the greatest of ideas to have had Fr. Aarden pick us up at the airport.

I told Sr. Marian, later that night, that I was sorry she had to experience all this. As I tossed and turned waiting for the morning to come, I realized how scared I was. I tried to think of what was going to happen when I told the Rev. Mother, and my parents.

The horizon seemed filled with obstacles. Was I ready to face them?

My family, proudly posing with me after final vows in 1961.
Back row: Mary and Flo
Front row: Sr. Mona, Mom, and Dad

CHAPTER THREE
Rethinking My Vows: 1969

That summer of '69 at St. Catherine's College, I had investigated what classes I still needed to get my diploma and degree. Even though I had taught for eight years, been a principal, and had enough credits for almost a double major in elementary education as well as English, I had never completed the student teaching requirement.

The dean informed me that there were new state requirements for an elementary education degree. I would now need a social studies course, as well as a music and physical education class, in order to graduate.

"During the eight weeks of student teaching, you will not be able to take classes," explained the Dean. "Some of your required courses are in the fall and some are spring, so it would take you a year to finish." She suggested I add some more English courses, to help me get closer to completing that second degree.

When the Dean of the College shared all this information, I had wondered how all this would happen if I left the convent. I had no money and no idea of the cost. I had no car. No lay clothes. I would have to find a place to live.

The day after my fiasco at my sister's home—driving a station wagon loaded with nuns back to the Motherhouse in Crookston—all these thoughts and conversations were swirling in my mind. I was happy to be the driver for our five-hour trip; I could pretend to be concentrating on my driving and not have to talk so much. The other five nuns were filling the air with questions and talk of their upcoming fall assignments. If only they knew what I was planning for my fall assignment.

"I can't believe I'm assigned to our Texas mission," interjected one of the nuns. "What was it like, Sr. Mona? What's wrong? You're so quiet. Are you upset about your fall assignment?" she asked.

I glanced over and caught Sr. Marian looking at me, waiting to hear my answer. My thoughts had definitely been elsewhere, focused on my own questions. What would Rev. Mother say? What would I say? What would the rest of the nuns say? What was going to happen with my fall assignment? Who would replace me?

I came back to reality...

"Oh, I'm assigned back to Mahtomedi. Sorry about being quiet. I was busy concentrating on driving. Sister, you will absolutely fall in love with the Mexican people. I loved my six years there and hated to leave."

Sr. Marian jumped in at that moment and shared some of our Texas experiences and got me off the hook. I gave her a grateful look. At that point, the sisters returned to chattering about the grades they would teach, the other nuns assigned at their school, and how they couldn't wait to be off to their missions for the year. I returned to my churning thoughts as we neared the Motherhouse. My stomach began doing flip-flops and figure eights.

The next morning at the Motherhouse, Rev. Mother Victorine answered my nervous knock on her office door. Her questioning eyes looked troubled as I spilled out my story amidst tears and wonderings of the next step I should take.

"Sr. Mona, I heard about Fr. Aarden's decision to leave the priesthood and the diocese," she gravely counteracted. "There had been rumors of some woman involved. I find it very difficult to believe that you have fallen in love in two weeks, and just like that, have decided to leave the convent."

She went on to explain that this was a life's decision not to be taken lightly. "You don't throw fifteen years of your life away without serious thought and prayer! You need to take time and make a wise decision." She folded her hands, shook her head, and thought for several minutes. "If you insist that you want to leave us, I think it fair—to us, and for you—to take a year's leave of absence," she continued. "A year will give you time to reconsider and think of what is God's will for you."

During this year, she went on to explain, the Motherhouse would pay for my college tuition to finish my degree. It seemed no more than fair, since I had not been in the area to do student teaching during those years. She realized that student teaching was essential to get my degree.

I would be allotted $50.00 a month for expenditures, and I would have to find a job if that was not sufficient. Since I would still be under vows, she expected me to act accordingly. She would arrange a meeting with a psychiatrist she had sent other nuns to in the Twin Cities. It was important to have an objective party listen and give advice.

"Rev. Mother, I have no lay clothes or place to stay," I blurted out.

"You can stay at 239 Summit Avenue until you find a place," she told me. "Sr. Anselma will be informed to prepare a place for you. As for transportation to and from the college, you will have to arrange that."

Thoughts of living in that restrictive environment sent shivers down my spine. How could I spend my year under Sr. Anselma's piercing eyes, questioning my every move? There had to be a better living solution than that. Yet, I had no money, so what choice did I have?

I came back to reality to hear the Rev. Mother saying that the convent had been my refuge and security for fifteen years. If I chose another path, I must be prepared for the consequences that went with it. She wondered if I had discussed this with my parents. If so, what were their reactions to all of this? I explained that I had not, but I was going to do that right after I had met with her.

"So, Sr. Mona, you have one year to decide your vocation," she said as she stood to dismiss me. "I hope you pray long and hard about this. I truly believe you have a vocation to the religious life and belong here."

As I left, she called me back to say that she would simply tell the community that I was going to finish my degree at St. Catherine's and would be on leave for a year. She also pointed out that the teaching position at Mahtomedi would be difficult to fill at this late date. Sr. Agatha would be very disappointed to learn that I would not be there.

I left her office with my mind buzzing with all the unknowns. I needed to call my parents and talk with them. What would they say? Would they be willing to help me? They had not wanted me to join the convent. Now, after all those years, I was going to leave because of a man —a priest, at that.

At least, the convent was going to pay for my year of college to finish my degree. That was a bright light; but what about the other expenses of living on my own? Summit Avenue was not the place to help me make my final decision. I needed to be independent and away from the nuns. How could I find a place to live?

The phone call to my parents filled me with anxious thoughts. I rehearsed how to to tell them of my momentous decision and that I had fallen in love with a priest. I needed to call immediately. College classes started in a few weeks and I needed Mom and Dad's advice and help.

"Hi, Mom, it's me. I don't know how to tell you this. I've decided to leave the convent. I've fallen in love."

"Oh, Vonnie, there was this man who called to ask if you were here. His voice had a different accent," she said in a questioning tone. "I told him you were at the Mount and he didn't leave his name."

"Oh, Mom. He's the one," I stammered.

"Well, just so he's not a priest!" was her response.

There it was. I had to tell her the truth and felt I needed to come home and tell her and Dad the whole story. I asked if they could possibly come and get me. I knew Mom couldn't leave right away, as she still ran the local post office out of their home.

"We can come on Sunday, since the post office will be closed. Can you be ready by then?"

I said that would be wonderful; it would give me two days to settle some of the details of my coming year.

When my parents arrived, they wanted to talk with the Rev. Mother. All the nuns loved my dad, as he was always joking with them. He had always told them, they better be nice to his daughter or he would come and take her back. Ironically, that was happening.

Needing Mom and Dad's help and advice.

"Rev. Mother," my dad began, with tears running down his eyes. "We don't know the whole story. You know we didn't want her to come here, but after fifteen years, we kind of got use to the idea of her being a nun. Guess we'll have to see how this story plays out."

The Rev. Mother said that she was just as shocked as they were. She hoped I would come to my senses, with a year to think and pray.

My parents told her that I had always had a determined mind of my own; certainly she knew that by now. They would take me home and find out what was at the root of all this.

On the seventy-mile ride home, I tearfully began to share what had happened in Kelliher during my two weeks there. Amidst questions and wrenching sobs, I tried to explain how my life had turned upside down after meeting Fr. Aarden.

"I know it all happened so fast, but, Mom and Dad," I gulped, "I can't stop thinking of him and I can't stay in the convent feeling like this."

In the next few days, we talked and tried to figure out the best ways for me to handle my year of absence from the convent. Mom and Dad shared with me they had a little money put aside. I could use that to get started.

Dad found an old Chevy in the village that could be fixed up and running for my transportation. I could stay with them and work out arrangements as best I could before college classes began. A week later I set off for the Twin Cities, despite my parents' worried looks and concerns.

After a few weeks at 239 Summit Avenue, I realized that it definitely was not the best place for me to live while going to college and deciding my life's direction. I felt like I was imposing upon the nuns and not a real part of them anymore.

I needed to find a different place to live, a cheap rental. Where could I find that? Then I thought of Joe and Ruth McCarthy. When I was teaching in Mahtomedi, they lived across the street from our school and convent and had been like family to me. Ruth and Joe, with their seven kids, had supported me in everything I had initiated in my classroom.

They always invited me over for family occasions. Ruth was my "go to" person whenever I had late drives to pick up nuns at the airport or whatever my needs. I decided to go and visit them. Maybe they knew of a place I could live near the college that would not cost a lot of money.

Ruth and Joe greeted me with open arms. They listened compassionately as I shared my love story and its complications. I explained that I needed to find a low-cost rental near the college.

"Oh, I just had lunch with some dear friends who live near there," Ruth jumped in. "They told me about three nuns who had been living in their upstairs apartment, but left for South America last week!"

Ruth said she would call her friends to see if the apartment was available. In ten minutes, Ruth had come to my rescue once again. I couldn't believe my ears. She had explained my predicament and arranged for me to have an interview with her friend the next day. The apartment was available.

The next day I followed Ruth's mapped directions and drove up to the curb on Lincoln Avenue. I opened the door of my ancient Chevrolet. In front of me stood a stately, two-storied, white house with manicured lawns and a large, attached garage. The neighborhood was definitely upper class, and my car definitely was a misfit. I worried I would be, too.

Nervous as I rang the doorbell, I tried to calm myself by replaying the introductions I had rehearsed for this critical moment. After what seemed an eternity, a white-haired, conservatively-dressed woman in a rose-colored wool suit answered the door with a questioning look. I immediately burst out, saying "Are you Mrs. Marzolf? I am Ruth and Joe McCarthy's friend," loudly, as if she were hard of hearing.

She informed me that she might be old, but she most definitely was not deaf. I blushed, apologized, and said I was just so nervous and wanted to make a good impression. I definitely had failed that, but would she give me the benefit of the doubt?

There was a hint of a smile and a bit of merriment in her eyes as she invited me in and introduced me to her husband, George. He was comfortably seated by the fireplace reading his newspaper and smoking his pipe. Slowly taking the pipe out his mouth, he looked me up and down, cleared his throat, and uttered a deep gravelly welcome. I noticed the cane leaning against his chair and walked right over to give him a hearty handshake while telling him how happy I was to be there.

Mrs. Marzolf directed me into a sitting room that harbored a baby grand piano, centered beneath a shimmering chandelier. The upholstered, embroidered chairs were next to expensive lamps. This was definitely unlike any place I had ever lived. It was like coming into a mansion fit for royalty.

She motioned for me to sit on one of the chairs and took her place opposite me. With everything in place, this conservative, devout Catholic woman, began my interview. She informed me she valued the McCarthy friendship, and their judgment of people. According to them, I was still a nun, but on leave for a year. What had caused my decision to leave?

"I've fallen in love. My convent is giving me a year to finish my degree and make my life's decision," I truthfully answered.

The McCarthys had shared with her that I had only a small monthly pittance from the convent during my leave of absence. "You will have to pay for the utilities, and be willing to clean my home every week, instead of paying rent," she explained. "And I understand you are still under vows, so there will be no male visitors allowed in your apartment. Do you understand?"

"Oh, yes, Mrs. Marzolf. I can't believe this is happening," I excitedly exclaimed as I jumped up and hugged her. "I'll gladly clean your home every week. We nuns have been trained well. I know I can do it to your satisfaction. You won't be disappointed, I promise."

She smiled, got up, and said she would give me a tour of the house. She explained what she expected me to do for cleaning her home each week. Mrs. Marzolf went on to say that everything in the upstairs apartment was furnished, even the silverware and kitchen utensils. They had furnished everything for the nuns who had been living there. The apartment was ready for immediate occupancy, and I could move in whenever I wished. When she handed me the key to the house, my hands were shaking and I couldn't keep from hugging her over and over again.

"Thank you, thank you," I cried. "You are like a gift from heaven. I will never forget your kindness. I'll be here tomorrow!"

When I got back to the house on 239 Summit, I shared my good fortune with the nuns. Then I asked to use the phone to call the McCarthy's to let them know I had passed the interview. I couldn't believe my good luck. I had a place of my own to stay! How could I ever repay them?

The next day I thanked the nuns, grabbed my suitcase with my limited wardrobe, climbed into my hiccuping Chevy, and drove from the curb: It was my first real taste of freedom in fifteen years.

CHAPTER FOUR
Learning to Live in the "Real" World: 1969

It was the first week of September. I settled into my new living quarters at Marzolf's. After having a phone installed, I immediately called Piet to tell him of my good fortune. We had not had a chance to communicate since that disastrous day at Flo's which would live on forever in our minds!

Piet answered on the third ring and my heart beat so quickly, I could hardly hold the phone steady. "Hi, is this Fr. Aarden? I mean Piet Aarden?" I nervously blurted out.

"It surely is. Is this a certain Sr. Mona? Or what do I call you?" he asked teasingly. "Since you now know how to pronounce my name, it seems fitting to learn yours."

I giggled hysterically. Here we were, just learning our names, and I had already told him in my letters that I would marry him. This was not an ordinary courtship.

"No matter your name, can I take you out on Friday evening for supper?" he asked. "It can be our first real date, since I'm now free and independent. How about 5:00?" He went on to say that he was going for an interview with New York Life Insurance that afternoon in the Twin Cities.

"That'd be great!" I gushed. "But I need to warn you that Mrs. Marzolf, my landlady, will not allow any men in my apartment."

He paused and then asked what my new address was. He told me that he would park on the street and wait for me to come out, since he could not come in to get me.

"OK," I quickly agreed. "Oh, another thing, my new phone number is 549-6111, just in case you want to call me sometime!" I told him I would look out my upstairs window, around 5:00 on Friday, in anticipation of seeing his white Oldsmobile. "Maybe I can wash and wax it again, to show my thanks," I laughed and heard his deep chortle in response. "Can't wait to see you; you might recognize a certain orange scarf. Love you tons, and see you soon."

As I hung up, I realized how much I had to tell him, and how much I wanted to know about his adventures since he left Kelliher. Friday could not come soon enough.

For our supper date, I found one of my newly-made dresses that would accentuate the orange scarf. On Friday afternoon, I glued myself to the window; I did not want to miss his white car pulling up to the curb.

There he was!

I rushed downstairs, flew out the door, and into his arms. Then I remembered that Mrs. Marzolf might be watching. This was not the way for a nun on leave to act. I quickly pulled away. Holding his hands at a distance, I explained that the windows had eyes. He gallantly opened the car door for me. I felt like a princess being escorted to her first ball.

At the restaurant, when the waitress came to our table, Piet ordered a Perfect Rob Roy with a cherry. I gave the waitress a puzzled look when she asked what I wanted. Piet laughed and said to the waitress, "Make that two!"

We toasted our togetherness when the amber-colored drink arrived. Piet tried to keep a straight face when he asked, "And now for the unveiling of your new name. What do I call this very special woman who accepted my dinner date?"

Giggling, I replied, "Your special woman is now called Yvonne Marie Rumreich. My family calls me Vonnie, but you can choose."

"I think I like Yvonne," he replied, "but Sr. Mona might slip out, if I get too excited and think of my Kelliher days, and all those hot love letters of this summer."

We sipped our cocktails as he told me his interview had gone well. He would start as a New York Life Insurance salesman, the following week. It was not going to be his lifelong job, he assured me, but the flexible hours would allow time to write resumes and go for other job interviews.

I told him I would start classes the next week. My job was to study hard, so I could graduate the following May. I wasn't so sure that the convent's $50 a month would suffice for all my expenses. If it didn't, I would have to look for a part-time job.

We had eyes and ears only for each other. We spent hours talking about all that had happened since our last meeting, not realizing that many couples had come and gone. It took several attempts by the waitress, asking if we wanted anything more, before we took the hint and left the restaurant.

Piet knew the St. Paul area well, since he had gone to the seminary nearby. With his left arm on the steering wheel and the other wrapped around me, he drove to a nearby park. Stopping the motor, he pulled me into his strong arms and gave me a crushing kiss that spoke volumes about his passion and love. I returned it with longing and desire. The Rev. Mother had warned me to not even hold his hand, but I was lost in love and could not think of obeying her commands.

Later, as we drove to my apartment, Piet explained that he did not have much money. He would be busy working with Fr. Reynolds and finding clients for his new job. "Could we try to make Friday nights our date night each week?" he wondered. "It's not the ideal plan for dating, but until things change, we might need to be satisfied with once a week."

"Whatever we can work out," I said, hesitantly. "I wish we could see each other more. But, this way, Fridays will be the best day every week!"

The following Monday, I had my first information session for student teaching. I learned I would be teaching second grade at Hadyn Heights, on the east side of St. Paul, under the tutelage of Georgeanne Williams. Student teachers were expected to spend eight weeks with our Master teachers, and report weekly for a class back at the college campus.

Our supervisor informed us she would visit periodically to check on our progress and determine our grades. Feeling nervous and anxious, even though I had taught for years, I wondered what the Master teacher would think if she knew I was a nun and had already been a principal?

When I presented myself to Georgeanne Williams that first afternoon, she greeted me, "Hello, Mona. My name is Georgeanne and I'm very happy to have you with me for the next eight weeks." She explained that she had been teaching five years and that I was to be her first student teacher.

Totally surprised, I stood and stared at her. "Oh, there's some mistake." I laughed nervously, "My name is Yvonne. Not Mona."

She looked puzzled and pulled out the paper from the college. "Is your last name Rumreich?" she asked as she stared at the paper.

"Yes. I guess they didn't change my nun's name at the registrar's office."

"Nun? You're a nun?" she asked. The color drained from her face into a ghostly pallor.

"Oh, dear, I hope that won't be a problem," I quickly interjected. "I've been teaching for eight years, and was even a principal. I just never had the opportunity for student teaching. I can't graduate unless I do student teaching. PLEASE, I'll work really hard and do whatever you ask me to do. I NEED this, please?"

Trying to recover from the fact that she had a nun as her first student teacher, much less someone who had taught longer than she had, Georgeanne stood up, adjusted her skirt, and said, "Well, then, I shall have to change my planned agenda of teaching you how to teach. How about team teaching together these next eight weeks?"

We laughed. Right then and there, I knew this was going to be a wonderful, fun eight weeks of teaching and learning together.

As the weeks went by, we became best of friends, both in an out of school. She was game to try anything that would make learning fun for the students. We spent lots of hours planning ways to make her classroom more innovative and kid-centered.

With two of us working as a team, the kids flourished, and so did we. My college supervisor couldn't believe the ways we complemented one another. She thought we should publish our ideas to teach others how to team-teach so effectively.

During those eight weeks, when we met for our Friday night dates, Piet's first question was always, "What mischief were you and Georgeanne up to this week?"

My teaching was so exhilarating, I could hardly stop talking about ways we got kids excited in reading and writing. "You should see and hear these kids," I jabbered on and on. "They can't wait to put on plays and share memorized poems with the other students in the school."

Piet shook his head in amazement at my enthusiasm and said, "I sure wish selling insurance was that exciting. Looking through newspapers for a wedding or obituary announcement doesn't quite match up."

His search for other jobs was totally frustrating him. He didn't have the time, or money, to go back to school for a different degree. Jobs weren't exactly abundant for someone with a philosophy and theology degree. I realized how lucky I was to have my motherhouse paying for my college tuition. Too bad the bishop hadn't offered such a gift to Piet!

Piet and I looked forward to every Friday and couldn't wait to be with each other. I also looked forward to being with Georgeanne and her second-graders every day. When the eight weeks came to a close, I didn't want to think of leaving them. With tears in my eyes and a heavy heart, I hugged each second-grader at our Halloween celebration and thanked them for a wonderful time together. Dressed as Raggedy Ann, I hugged Raggedy Andy, my memorable Master Teacher, and hoped that someday our lives would intersect again.

As we hugged and cried, Georgeanne whispered in my ear, "Yvonne, this was the best. Maybe I'll luck out again and get another nun for my student teacher!" We laughed and thought of that first day we met and how awkward that had been.

My $50 convent stipend was not stretching as far as I thought it would. The first utility and phone bill took most of it. Driving to and from the elementary school for student teaching had taken more gas money than anticipated. What was I to do?

The first week of November, at one of my evening classes, I introduced myself to the gal sitting next to me. She told me that she was a teacher at St. Matthew's Catholic school, a few miles from my apartment. She was looking for a place to stay, because her roommate had found a job elsewhere. With her limited income, she couldn't afford to live alone. Worst of all, she had to be out of her apartment the following week.

I stared in disbelief. I had just written a notice to pin on the bulletin board seeking a roommate to help me with expenses. After class, I learned that Rita had been a Notre Dame nun who had left her convent two years earlier. She was taking classes to get her Master's degree.

The more we talked and learned about each other, the more I knew Rita would be a great person to share my apartment with. She seemed quiet, but enthusiastic about life, learning, and teaching. Her contagious giggle and bashful blushing gave her an aura of innocence. I learned that she came from a conservative German farming family from North Dakota. Having twelve brothers and sisters, she shared that two of her sisters had also entered the Notre Dame convent in Mankato, Minnesota.

Rita was thrilled about the possibility of sharing an apartment. I explained that we needed to get Mrs. Marzolf's approval for another roommate. That Rita had been a nun should make it easier. After all, Mrs. Marzolf had a soft heart for nuns.

When I shared Rita's story with Mrs. Marzolf the next day, she told me that St. Matthew's Church was the church she attended. She would be happy to interview Rita if I wanted a roommate. After all, the apartment had been the home for three nuns before I had moved in, so there was no question about enough space.

Rita had her interview with Mrs. Marzolf and moved in the following week. Now I had someone to help with the utility bills and my car expenses. It was fun to have someone to share my day's experiences with and learn about hers.

Since Rita had no car, we worked it out that I would drive her to and from school every day. If that didn't work out on certain days, the apartment was near the bus route. Every morning, we hoped that my car, nicknamed Lizzy, would start. Then we chugged down the street praying it would last through the winter.

One late-fall morning, when my car wouldn't start, I ran into the house to ask Mr. Marzolf if he could please help me. He hobbled outside with his cane, jump-started my car and gruffly said, "You're going to need to think about replacing that battery pretty soon." Then he looked at the tires. "Then you better think about getting some new tires. They look pretty bald to me. You'll need good tires for the winter."

Yikes! I hadn't thought of all the expenses an old car could bring.

I needed to be practical and miserly with the money I had. Rita and I shared the cost of everything, but my expenses still amounted to more than my monthly stipend of fifty dollars. Now I needed to think of replacing the car battery and tires. I knew I also needed a coat, gloves, and boots for the cold Minnesota winter ahead, as well as textbooks for the winter quarter. Was there no end to the expenses?

In the convent, everything had been paid for. If I had a need, I simply got on my knees in front of my Superior and asked. I had not handled or been responsible for money in years. I would not ask my folks for help.

If only I could get a little extra spending money.

Rita helped clean Marzolf's home every weekend, so I had some extra time. I found an ad on the college bulletin board asking for a cleaning lady, and it was not too far from my apartment. Hopefully, I could clean her home on the days that I had the fewest classes.

I wrote down the address of a Mrs. Steinmetz, found it on the city map, and set off to seek my fortune. When I found the house, I nervously knocked at the door and wondered what would happen next. A well-dressed woman with coifed hair, looking to be in her late forties, answered the door. "I'm sorry, but we don't take solicitations in this neighborhood," she said, curtly.

Just before she slammed the door, I blurted, "No, I'm here to answer the ad you placed at St. Kate's. You are Mrs. Steinmetz, aren't you?"

"Oh…you should have called to set up an appointment," she frostily said as she glanced at her watch. "Well, since you're here, come on in. I have a few minutes before I leave for a meeting."

She explained she had a cleaning lady, but that this person was getting older and needed some help. What were my past experiences and what references did I have? I explained that I was taking college classes and cleaning another home. I was sure Mrs. Marzolf would give a good reference. As we talked, I was thinking, "Oh, if only she knew that she was talking to a nun on leave!"

After several more questions, she stood. "I'll give you a trial run and see how you do," she said. "I can pay you $1.00 an hour."

"Oh, no," I interjected. "I need more than that. I couldn't clean for less than $2.00 an hour. I have lots of expenses and need the money."

With raised eyebrows and an open mouth, she told me that I was quite brazen, but she liked the spirit of my response. She would call Mrs. Marzolf the next day, and if she were satisfied after speaking with her, I could start the next week.

"Oh, if it all works out," I interrupted, "I hope you can be flexible. I have classes every day, but could clean on Wednesday and Friday afternoons." I also said I would need cash each day after I cleaned for her. Once again, she raised her eyebrows but gave a nod of agreement as she closed the door to dismiss her on-trial, outspoken cleaning lady.

When I got back to my apartment, I told Mrs. Marzolf about my interview in Highland Park. This time it was Mrs. Marzolf who raised her eyebrows. "My dear, that is a very exclusive Jewish neighborhood. What would she say if she knew you were a nun cleaning her home? Are you sure you want to do this?"

"Oh, yes! I really need the money, and she's going to call you as my reference. Please don't tell her I'm a nun. I might not get the job!"

Mrs. Marzolf never shared what transpired, but I got the job. The house of my new employer was a beautifully-furnished mansion with adjoining living quarters for her ailing mother, Mrs. Abramson. I was expected to clean whatever the other cleaning woman did not get done.

A few weeks after I started, Mrs. Steinmetz led me upstairs and opened the door to her private, opulent bedroom, with velvet drapes and matching bed accessories. She asked me to organize her walk-in closet and multiple dressers. What a stark contrast from the four nails in the Texas closet I had shared with three other nuns! Never in my life had I seen so many pairs of shoes or matching outfits hanging row after row in her cavernous closet. Overwhelmed, I looked at her in amazement, never thinking one person could have so many clothes to choose from.

After a month of cleaning on Wednesday and Friday, Mrs. Steinmetz told me that she needed to talk to me when I finished my assigned chores.

"You know, I've been watching you. I could use your help in other ways than cleaning," she said. "You're older than most college students. I've wondered if you might have a story to share with me."

I decided it was time to tell her who I was, and why I needed this work so badly.

"Oh, my goodness, I knew there was something different about you!" She shook her head in disbelief. "I'm Jewish and never dreamed I would ever hire a nun to clean my house!" she said in a dazed voice. "I wish I had known this before. Of course, you're qualified for what I was going to ask you to do!"

She shared that her mother had been living with them since her father died several years before. Recently her mother, Mrs. Abramson, had been diagnosed with shingles and needed more attention and care than ever. Since I was a college student—and now to add to that, a nun—would I give up the cleaning job and be a companion to her mother?

We went to the mother's room. As I was introduced, the mother quickly said, "Just call me Anna. Now sit down and tell me all about yourself. I get so lonely here by myself. My daughter keeps herself so busy, we don't have time to talk, much less discuss books. I certainly hope we can spend time doing that, if you choose to be a companion for me."

I liked Anna immediately. Seeing Robert Frost's poetry books on her bed stand, I thought how fun it would be to read poetry and discuss it.

Before I could suggest that to Anna, Mrs. Steinmetz interrupted us. There was another thing she wondered about. Her son was having difficulty in school. Would I be able to help tutor him some of the afternoons, after spending time her mother?

There was no mention of a fatter paycheck, but, at least, I wouldn't have to be on my hands and knees cleaning her house every Wednesday and Friday.

The next Wednesday, I met with Anna, who turned out to be a delightful world traveler in her late seventies. She was filled with questions about nuns and my life. Despite her pain, she kept her sense of humor and passion for life. We shared stories of our lives and read the classics and poetry together. Those afternoons quickly flew by.

Working with the son, Josh, was another story. He was a teenager, and the idea that he needed a tutor did not sit well with him. His sullen moods were a stark contrast to time spent with his Grandmother.

Josh kept me on my toes, trying to think of ways to reach him. Some days were better than others. The moodiness and negativity became his trademark, until I discovered his love of science fiction. I knew nothing about sci-fi, and that became the catalyst for creating a teachable bond between us. Not every session went picture perfect. On the off days, the broom and mop I'd left behind looked pretty inviting. But I was a teacher, and I would continue to search for ways of capturing his interests, no matter how long it took! It took many weeks of building trust before he opened up and let me help him.

Thanksgiving was around the corner. Mrs. Marzolf approached me to say she had been watching me every Friday when this certain man came to get me. She wanted to know more about him. As we talked, she listened and nodded frequently. She said he certainly sounded like a gentleman and, having been a priest, he must be a very good man. "I think it would OK to invite him to your apartment for Thanksgiving," she said with a smile. "I know I said in the beginning that you couldn't have any men up there, but I am going to make an exception."

"Oh, Mrs. Marzolf!" I jumped up with excitement, "That would be wonderful."

I couldn't believe my ears. Wait until I told Rita and Piet. We could celebrate together! That night, I called Piet to share my good news. I hoped he would be available to come and celebrate with Rita and me. "Couldn't think of a better place to be!" he answered. "You are the best thing that has happened in my life, and I'd love to share my thankfulness with you."

It was set. He said he'd bring the wine to celebrate. Rita and I planned the menu. As we were planning, our phone rang. It was Rita's sister, Beasy. Could she join us for the holiday? She had a job interview in the Twin Cities the day after Thanksgiving.

Our party was growing, and the more the merrier.

After Rita hung up, she asked if we could talk. If her sister got the job, would it be all right if she lived with us? We had an extra bed, and she knew her sister would be so happy if she could. Of course, I agreed. We talked about how the three of us could share all the expenses, and Beasy could help us clean the house as well. We certainly had the room, and it would be fun to have another roommate. Rita and I were so compatible with our opposite personalities, and it would be interesting to add a third to the mix. Now, all we had to do was to ask Mrs. Marzolf's permission to add another roommate. She could meet Beasy when she came for Thanksgiving.

Thanksgiving Day arrived.

"Hey, here comes the man of the hour," Rita kidded me as she glanced out the window. "Can't wait to meet your prince. Wow, is he ever tall! I'll run and get the step-ladder so I can shake his hand, or else try to give him a five-foot hug."

The doorbell rang and I rushed downstairs just as Mrs. Marzolf opened the door to see who was there. Piet bowed, took Mrs. Marzolf's hand and gave it a princely kiss. He told her he was so thankful to be invited upstairs for this special day. He also promised he'd behave in a very gentlemanly fashion. Of course, she melted and turned around to look at me with an approving nod. "Have a wonderful Thanksgiving," she said with a satisfied smile. "George and I will be at our daughter's, so enjoy your time together. I can smell that turkey already!"

I led Piet up the steps into the "forbidden" apartment. Before we reached the top step, he drew me into his arms for an embracing hug and kiss. We heard a slight cough and then another—poor Rita wondered when we would be coming up for air. I laughed and introduced my new roommate to the man with whom I hoped to be sharing my next apartment, and the rest of my Thanksgivings.

A half-hour later, a taxi drew up to the curb and out bounced Beasy. She was laden with two suitcases and a smile that could have lit up the east side of St. Paul. Piet, the true gentleman, rushed downstairs to be her porter. More introductions as Piet poured wine and we settled into the only four chairs in our apartment.

"Piet, are you not the lucky one to have three admiring women at your side?" I coyly asked.

"Couldn't ask for more," he joked. "Do all of these women have a convent history?"

Beasy quickly jumped up and protested, "Not me! In my family of thirteen brothers and sisters, the convent took three of them. I'm the baby and objected to any hint of me going there."

Rita quietly spoke up, "They had me for ten years, but I decided it wasn't for me. Now here we are each with a different story to tell. Would you go first, Piet?"

Our Thanksgiving meal flew by with each of us sharing parts of our life's story. The room filled with laughter as our hearts exploded with thankfulness. I wondered where would we each be the next time this holiday rolled around. This was certainly one of the best Thanksgivings I had had in many years!

Beasy, with her bubbly personality and excellent references, got her job as an insurance company's bookkeeper. Mrs. Marzolf agreed to let her live with us, since she was Rita's sister and seemed to be a very decent young woman, even if she hadn't been a nun.

As for Piet, every Friday when we met for our dinner date, my first question to him was, "Did your papers from Rome arrive yet?"

Every Friday, the same answer, "Not yet."

"I can't understand why," he said with a discouraging shake of his head. "I signed the application forms in September and they thought maybe eight weeks at the most." He said he was going to call the Archbishop's office weekly to ask about his papers. He went on to say that he was also going to make a personal visit to see what he might possibly do to speed up the process.

It was during these Friday evening dates that we shared stories of our lives before we met each other. Piet explained that he had NEVER wanted to be a farmer like his father, and definitely did not want factory work like some of his older brothers. Instead, he had longed to go to America where his father's brother was a priest. His ticket to a future life in America was further education. When his mother told him that she expected him to be the priest in their family, he left for seminary boarding school at the age of thirteen.

"How interesting that our lives took their future directions when we left home to begin a religious life, at the same age," I interjected. "Your mom determined your vocation, but a visiting nun determined mine."

Piet then winked his special wink, took my hand and laughingly said, "Yes, but when I set out for my vocation, you were just a baby entering this world. Who would ever have thought that two people so different in age and culture, once separated by an ocean, would one day be sitting at a table discussing a future together?"

In early December I visited with the psychiatrist. That had been one of the Rev. Mother's requirements during my year of absence. In the hour and a half session, the psychiatrist shared with me that it was totally up to me to make the decision of staying or leaving. "You might be the next Mother Superior if you stayed," he said with a straight face. "Or, you could be the wife of a certain ex-priest whom you have talked about. It is totally up to you. Whatever you decide, you have the spirit to succeed."

He then told me that he would call the Mother Superior to share the results of our meeting, and that I would not have to come back. Shaking my hand, he wished me the best, no matter what my decision might be.

During Christmas vacation, after long Friday talks with Piet and lots of evening discussions with my roommates, I decided that I would not take the whole year to cut my ties with the convent. If Piet got his papers, I wanted to be free to say, "Yes." I knew I would marry him, no matter how little we had to live on, or where.

A few days before New Year's, I gathered my courage and decided it was time. I called the Rev. Mother to ask for my laicization papers. "Rev.

Mother, I've decided not to wait the full year," I bravely said. "I want to apply for my dispensation."

There was a long pause. "Are you sure, Sister?" she questioned. "This is a huge decision, and I'm not sure you should be so hasty. Why are you in such a hurry?"

I explained that I wanted to be free of my nun's vows and be free to get married when Piet's papers arrived.

"Sister, pray more; give it more thought," the Rev. Mother responded. "If you still think the same way, then I will send you the application form. Realize that you will be totally severed from us if you do this."

I said I did not need more time. Would she please send the form? Because we were not a diocesan order, the papers had to be sent to Rome to get Papal permission. She did not know how long that would take. As far as monetary help, she explained that my tuition had been paid for the year, but the $50.00 stipend would end when I signed the papers.

"Thank you, Rev. Mother," I said with relief. "Please send the form and I will sign it." With tears running down my face, I hung up and realized I had just opened another new chapter in my life.

The next day, I stopped in to have lunch with Sr. Myra, one of the nuns from the Motherhouse who was doing her residency at a St. Paul hospital. She had been very kind to me and had even sewed a few dresses for me the two weeks I had stayed at 239 Summit at the start of my leave of absence. As we talked, I mentioned that I needed yet another part-time job to meet my expenses. I had borrowed money from my roommate to get new tires and a battery for my car, and needed to pay that back.

"Well, I just saw a notice in our lounge that they need a part-time cafeteria cashier on weekends," she shared. "Would you be qualified to do that?" I laughed and said I had been a clerk in my Uncle's store. I wondered if that counted as being qualified? "Let me get the information for you," she said. "Wouldn't hurt to try. We nuns are always up to a challenge, right? I'll put in a good word for you."

We finished lunch, and I left with the phone number to call and a question buzzing in my head: "What if I was hired? I had never been a cashier before, but why not give it my best shot? I had nothing to lose, but a possible job to gain.

The next day I called and was so surprised when they asked how soon I could come in for an interview. That afternoon worked for both of us. "We are short-handed and our head cashier has to have surgery next week," the manager of the cafeteria explained. "Sr. Myra assured us that you are a very capable and responsible person."

When asked if I had ever been a cashier, I answered in the affirmative. After all, I had used the adding machine in my Uncle's store. It never occurred to me that my interviewer was speaking of a computerized machine. Nor did I realize I would have to memorize the menu and prices to efficiently carry out the job. I was hired on the spot, due to my friend's recommendation, but mostly because they were desperate for a cashier.

On Friday, the head cashier took me through the paces so I could start on Saturday. She gave me a copy of the menu and a strong suggestion that I study it carefully to memorize as many prices as possible.

She explained that once a month the National Guardsmen were in the immediate area. They had an arrangement to eat at the hospital cafeteria those weekends. My first weekend was one of those weekends. The tricky part was that I needed to make sure that the military food trays did not tabulate to more than $3.50. That meant some quick revisions of cost for what was actually on the tray. She would demonstrate and I was to watch carefully. Then it would be my turn.

While I tried my best, it didn't help to look up and see the line snaking down the hall and beyond. I heard upset people shouting out, "Don't tell me, another NEW cashier! We'll be in this line forever!"

It was, for me, a baptism by fire. I was scorched with feelings of inadequacy and failure at the end of the day. Could it get any worse?

As the weekends went by, the job got easier. I was paid over and above what I was making elsewhere, so I repaid Rita for the car expenses. I was even able to open up a bank account for the first time in my life.

I continued working with the Jewish family because I knew Mrs. Steinmetz's mother looked forward to our time together. Josh, the son, told me that school was improving for him since we had started working together. He admitted that he even looked forward to our time together—some of the time!

The cafeteria job brought me a new set of friends from many walks of life. One Saturday evening after work, I mentioned to my fellow workers that my old Chevy was on its last leg. It was so unpredictable that it had been stolen the week before, but immediately abandoned only a few blocks from my apartment. That was a definite sign that my Chevy was falling apart!

As I shared my story, Sheila, one of the gals, spoke up. "Hey, Yvonne, I'm in the market for a new car and would be willing to sell you my Mustang convertible at a reasonable price."

A convertible? I had never dreamed of driving a convertible. Since I knew nothing about cars, I asked her how much and told her that I would have Piet check it out for me.

On our next Friday date, Piet drove me to Sheila's place to see if the car was worth the $1500.00 she was asking. He checked it over, looked at the mileage, took it on a test drive, and told me that it was a bargain.

Sheila agreed to let me pay her in monthly installments. I couldn't believe my luck. The day before I signed the papers for the Mustang, my Chevy literally died. It had to be towed away to a car graveyard. The towing fee matched what I got for the parts—$50. Even trade!

I now sported a flashy, white convertible. It drove like a charm. Rita, Beasy and I felt like homecoming queens when, one unexpected warm day in January, we put the top down and experienced the wind blowing through our hair. The next day, snow fell and we had to wait for June to relive the liberating experience.

During those winter months, my love for Piet grew by leaps and bounds every time we were together. I could not imagine a life without him.

CHAPTER FIVE
Discovering Each Other's Past Lives: 1970

That January of 1970, Piet still could not figure out why his dispensation papers had not been processed. After all, he had signed them in August, the year before. When he inquired at the bishopric, he was told that the procedure had been stopped. His friend, Fr. Reynolds, had told the bishop that he was sure he could get Piet to change his mind, so the bishop went ahead and halted the paperwork.

"How could you stop the papers without meeting with me?" Piet angrily asked. "I requested them, not Fr. Reynolds!" This was an inexcusable act and needed to be reversed immediately. Piet informed the bishop he would stay right there until this disaster was resolved.

Leaving the bishopric, Piet immediately called Fr. Reynolds. He was furious and in disbelief, "How could you do this to me?" he demanded. "What kind of friend are you?" Didn't Father Reynolds know we were planning on getting married as soon as our Papal papers were approved? Now, with this delay, who knew when the papers would come through?

Piet was angry and disappointed. He decided he could no longer live in the same building as Fr. Reynolds, so he immediately searched for an apartment in the Twin Cities. There was a reasonably priced, one-bedroom apartment on the east side of St. Paul. Fr. Reynolds, hoping to make up for his interference in the Papal papers, offered to lend Piet money to furnish the apartment and get started in his new life. He shared with Piet that two of his elderly aunts had died and left their inheritance to him, so he had extra funds.

My dispensation papers arrived in February. I was free to get married, but Piet was not. We wanted to do the right thing and have a Catholic wedding, so we decided to play the waiting game. March and April passed. Still no papers from Rome. Piet made weekly phone calls to inquire about the status of his dispensation. What was taking so long? Every week, it was the same reply. "Be patient. Rome wasn't built in a day and things move very slowly at the Vatican. They are currently swamped with requests such as yours," replied the bishop.

We agonized over the delay, but kept a glimmer of hope: Any day now, the papers might arrive.

Piet was not happy with his life insurance job. He was pounding the pavement trying to find new clients, and hoping some big breakthroughs would come through. We had little time together; his work and my college classes kept us too busy.

During those months, we continued our Friday night dates, but now met for dinner at his new apartment. I discovered he was a great cook and it was so much cheaper than eating out. The stories of our individual lives kept unfolding as we got to know each other more intimately.

During those evenings we dipped into the past. Piet shared that during his grade school years, his mother, Anna, reminded him over and over that he was named after Heeroom (his uncle), who was a priest in the U.S.A. She was sure that he would follow in those footsteps and become a priest as well.

When Piet graduated from grade school (Grade 7), he had to make a choice: farming (which meant walking behind a horse pulling a plow and doing follow-up work of harvesting and all sorts of sweaty stuff) OR go to school at a seminary. Going to ULO or MULO (higher education beyond grade school) for a farm kid was not heard of in his family circles. But the entrance into a seminary was definitely a welcome invitation. It offered an escape from the family workshop.

At that time, Piet's family was living in Aarle-Rixtel, a small village rather close to Uden, where there was a minor seminary run by the Crosier Fathers. It was a feasible starting point for somebody aspiring for the priesthood. Did he want that kind of lifestyle and dedication? He didn't know, but he certainly didn't want to be a farmer. The idea of him becoming a priest had been repeated in his presence over and over again by his mother. So, why not try it?

His uncle—Fr. Peter Aarden, pastor at Georgetown, Minnesota in the U.S.A.—was willing to sponsor Piet's education. His parents were not financially capable of sending him to a boarding school, so they were very happy and thankful for this financial arrangement.

Another brother of Piet's father lived in Holland and was willing to carry the financial burden until Fr. Peter could reimburse him. This proved to be a very important financial arrangement in the WWII years, when no payments could be made from the U.S.A.

Piet's family was barely able to keep their heads above water during the war, since his Mother possessed a great spirit of charity. People from

Helmond and Eindhoven (nearby cities) flocked to buy eggs and grain from Piet's folks because they were available at very reasonable prices. If these people were caught bringing back the eggs and grain, heavy fines were levied on the seller.

Piet said it was amazing that his family never got caught in the transporting of grain to or from the mill. To get their milling done, they needed to show the required coupon which stated how much grain could be milled. They were usually over their allotted limit. Piet's mother was always helping those who needed extra grain to feed their large families.

In September of 1941, Piet found himself at the doorstep of the Collegium S.S. Crucis in Uden, a city about thirteen miles from his home. The transition from his small country school in Beek en Donk to the Crosier seminary boarding school repertoire was too much of an academic challenge for Piet. After two months of desperately floundering, the faculty decided to move Piet with another fifteen students into what they termed "Preparation Class" for the rest of his first year.

That year, the Germans soldiers developed a military airport in the neighboring town of Odiliapeel. After building the airport, the German soldiers decided that the Crosier boarding school would function beautifully as their barracks. All the seminarians were sent home at Christmas time.

After a month and a half of being at home, the seminarians were notified to return to Uden. Piet was given lodging with an elderly couple. He and the other seminarians were served meals at a farmhouse and sent daily to classes in a schoolhouse that had been abandoned.

In September of 1942, Piet reported to Zeland, a province west of Noord Brabant. There, he was part of a class of thirty other seminarians. They slept in a school attic and had classes and meals in a grade school.

Each fall brought a new location for their seminary schooling. In September of 1943, the class reported to Vorstenbosch, a city about fifteen miles away, where an old church had been converted into a grain warehouse. The attic served as their dormitory and they shared a local grade school classroom with the elementary school children. Their meals were prepared and eaten in the school's home economics room.

During those years of German occupation, the Crosier Fathers would bike from one town to the next to teach their particular subject of expertise. One of the Crosier Fathers, whose academic subject was a daily requirement for the seminarians, became the person to stay at that location to eat, sleep, and recreate with the young seminarians. Other priests would bike to different locations on different days of the week to teach their subjects.

It was in this setting that Piet said he could remember one incident as clear as if it had happened yesterday. After lunch, the students had approximately thirty minutes during which most of them clustered together as they walked in circles around the playground. Suddenly, an English fighter plane came flying by. Since their school location was close to the German airport, it didn't take long for one of the German planes to arrive on the scene.

In broad daylight, they were treated to a dogfight overhead. It only lasted for a couple of minutes. The German fighter plane went tumbling down, with the pilot parachuting to safety. Piet's whole class applauded and shouted at the top of their lungs congratulating the victorious English pilot. The Crosier Father in charge, however, put a damper on their jubilation. They were under German domination and never too sure what the German reaction might be. The German reaction hadn't crossed their young minds.

In September 1944, seminary classes never started. The English and Americans chased the Germans from southern Holland, but got held up by the Rhine River. The occupying forces naturally took over the airport in Odiliapeel, as well as the school facilities. Since a great number of the seminarians lived in the northern part of Holland, they were unable to travel south for school. Classes were discontinued for that school year.

(I listened to Piet's childhood stories in awe. I was born the year the Germans invaded Holland. While Piet was experiencing the agonies and hardships of WWII in Holland—the shortage of food, lost money, the dangers of being bombed or punished if Nazi directives were not heeded—I was safe in my mother's arms, isolated on my reservation.)

I wanted to learn why Piet decided to come to America, so he shared more of his life's story. In September of 1945, after Holland was liberated from the Germans, classes resumed in Uden in the usual setting and conducted under regular academic circumstances. Classes were going smoothly and sports activities of soccer, field hockey, basketball, and volleyball were in full swing for Piet.

During this time, thoughts of the future were beginning to occupy Piet's mind. A future with the Crosier Fathers seemed to be a good possibility.

There was one point of contention for Piet. He often observed that the Prior, William Van Hees, would come to the college and stand by the window to read the outgoing mail. Seminarians were not allowed to seal their letters, and the Prior was a voracious reader. This seemed like an enormous invasion of privacy, and it caused Piet to decide against joining the Crosiers. He was not ready to turn himself over to a religious order that would demand he give his whole self, body, and soul, to the one in command.

Piet decided the secular clergy would be his choice. The problem with that choice was that if he joined the secular clergy in Holland he would have to repeat the sixth academic year he had already completed. He was not willing to do that. France was looking for seminary students and would not make him repeat his last school year, so that was an option.

There was also the possibility of moving to the U.S.A. In his correspondence with his priest uncle in Minnesota, Piet broached the subject. His uncle thought that idea was splendid, but if Piet was going to come to the United States, the sooner the better. He told Piet that he would have a better chance of learning the English language during the first two years of college, rather than waiting until later years of seminary.

During Piet's senior high school year, things started moving into place. He began his first year of college in Uden, and by December of 1947, all was ready for his transfer. This included a study Visa, as well as passage on the *Nieuw Amsterdam* that was to sail from Rotterdam to New York on January 2, 1948.

On December 1, 1947, Piet said his farewells to his classmates and went home for a month's vacation to stay with his family. The hardest part came on January 1, 1948, when he had to say goodbye to his family. Unbeknownst to him, he would not see them again for the next eight years. (I, at this time, was in my second year of elementary school!)

Leaving Holland (1948). Piet's family (L to R): Cor, Piet's Dad (Jan), Hein, Johanna, Piet, Karel, Piet's Mom (Elizabeth), Gerard, and Martien

The ship's voyage was quite smooth with Piet being seasick only for half a day. There were no language problems because Dutch was the prevailing language on the ship. Upon arrival in New York, the ship's financial manager gave him $25.00 for personal expenses (compliments of his uncle). He was to get a taxi to take him to the railroad station. His train ticket had already been sent to him before he left. The ticket was for his travel from New York directly to Moorhead, Minnesota where his uncle was living.

With only two years of textbook English under his belt, Piet had no desire to explore the Big Apple. He only wanted to get away from that BIG city. With help at the train station, he was able to exchange his ticket for a night passage. In the morning he found the train dining area. He wanted an orange, but didn't know the English word for it. The Dutch word, "sinasappel," was such an easy word. How did they expect him to know that in English you called this fruit by its color?

Late afternoon the following day, Piet arrived in St. Paul and had to call his uncle in Georgetown to let him know that he would be arriving in Moorhead around 5:00 the next morning. With the help of a gracious lady, he was able to make the telephone connection. After all, he told me, I had to understand that he was a real country bumpkin coming from a farm in Aarle-Rixtel, where at that time, you could probably count on two hands the families that had a telephone in their home.

When he arrived in Moorhead, his uncle (whom Piet had not seen since he was probably eleven years of age) was waiting for him on the train platform. It was early in the morning. Not many people were getting off the train, and there was only one person in clerical attire! Recognizing his Uncle was easy.

Piet lived with his uncle for three weeks and then had to report to the Junior College at Crosier in Onamia, Minnesota, which was almost 200 miles away. Attending school at Onamia was a natural transition since it was run by the same religious order as the one in Holland. In fact, there were three priests on the faculty who themselves were Holland transplants.

On Piet's first day of classes, he had one of those Dutch priests teaching Latin. At the end of the class, the instructor gave his students the assignment to translate one page from Latin. He then looked at Piet and said, "Into English, young man!" Piet remembered that the Latin text was not too difficult, but translating into English was an animal of a different color. In the following year and a half, he wore out his college English dictionary!

During walks on campus, Piet learned to become a great listener. At least once a week, he would sit down with one of his classmates and read out loud so he could have his pronunciations corrected. He claims he may not have learned an awful lot of new things, but translating from Latin, Greek, and German into English taught him a lot. By the beginning of June, he felt like he had mastered the language, and he was ready for a summer break at his uncle's parish house. His uncle had been given a new assignment in Bagley, Minnesota. Piet helped him move to his new parish and offered to repaint the outside of the rectory.

It was during these summer months that Piet first got to meet Bishop Schenk of the Crookston Diocese. His uncle mentioned to the bishop that he had a nephew from Holland who was studying for the priesthood and probably would want to join the diocese. Bishop Schenk indicated that he wasn't interested. The diocese did not have the funds to be transporting seminarians from another country.

When his uncle said, "Ok, I'm sure he'll find another diocese somewhere." Bishop Schenk then asked, "Where is this nephew of yours?" With the answer, "He's around the corner painting my rectory," Bishop Schenk's reaction changed. "Oh, well, then, he is from within the diocese. We won't have to pay extra."

The bishop walked outside to meet this possible new addition. After that short introduction and talk with the bishop, Piet officially became a seminarian of the Crookston diocese.

Piet's second year at Onamia College was a breeze. At the end of the school year, his uncle ended up in the hospital in Crookston for a stomach ulcer operation. Piet was able to visit him, but didn't think his uncle ever knew it. Within a day, his uncle died and they placed him to rest in the Catholic cemetery in Crookston. He had left Piet $10,000.00 in savings bonds. All his uncle's other personal belongings were willed to Fr. Miller, who for years had been his neighboring priest and friend.

Since Piet had made arrangements with the prior at Crosier to work for them during the summer months, he returned to Onamia after the funeral. He spent the following two months painting and even operated the farm while the farm brother took his vacation.

There was another seminarian working at Crosier that summer. Stanley and Piet spent their free time together, whether it was on the lake or going downtown in Onamia. One evening they were coming back from a movie and were met by the prior. His question was, "Where are you two coming from?" Piet replied, "Oh, we went to a movie." The prior then asked them, "Did you have permission for that?" Of course, their reply was, "No." The prior told them that from then on, they needed to ask permission before leaving the premises.

With that last directive, Piet knew it was time for him to pack his bags and look for another living space. He wrote to the rector of the St. Paul Seminary to see if it would be possible to send his personal belongings there in advance of the Fall semester of his upcoming school year. The rector answered and asked if Piet would be interested in becoming the Chapel sacristan in payment of board and room for the remaining three weeks of vacation. Piet took him up on the offer and said farewell to Crosier.

When Monsignor Victor Cardin, the treasurer for the diocese, learned of Piet's inheritance money, he told Piet that he must pay for his own education at the major seminary in St. Paul. Later, Piet found out that the diocese paid for all the other seminarians' education. So, when he left the priesthood, he did not have a guilty conscience because the diocese never spent a nickel for his education.

He then added that as good or bad as that decision of leaving the Crosier seminary may have been, he had ample opportunity to get acquainted with the city of St. Paul. Getting to know the dean of his building was another story.

The dean ran the dorm as if it were a military barracks and chose Piet as his target. The first two weeks of classes, he found fault with every minor detail. Didn't Piet know how to make a proper bed? Where had he been trained? Lights were to be out by ten o'clock. Did he not know a flashlight was a light? No talking was allowed during study time. Why was he whispering to his roommates? After the first two tortuous weeks, Piet made sure he did not offer the priest one more opportunity to discipline him. He had learned his lesson.

Studies kept Piet occupied during the seminary school years. He spent his summers employed with different kinds of work. The first summer was spent as a farmhand on a farm in Stewart, Minnesota. During his second year at the St. Paul Seminary, he was looking for a means of transportation, but seminarians were not allowed to have a car. Therefore, he decided to buy a Harley-Davidson that he kept in a classmate's home garage about ten blocks from the seminary. Donning his leather jacket, helmet, and goggles, he could safely meet any of the seminary professors without them recognizing him.

He spent his second summer selling subscriptions to a farm magazine while living in a motel. The third summer, he worked at the Grain Belt brewery throwing beer kegs around, while the fourth summer he cut re-bar to the proper size at U.S. Steel.

Piet's Harley-Davidson transportation.

Those last two summers he lived and batched at a fellow seminarian's cabin at Lake George, about ten miles outside of Anoka. It was a primitively furnished cabin, but quite livable. The cabin did not have a refrigerator, but at the back entrance, it had an icebox.

Piet started by getting a square block of ice at a dispenser in Anoka, wrapped it in a pouch, and carried it on his lap out to the cabin at the lake. This was cumbersome and freezing cold. He quickly built a plywood box to the dimensions of the ice-block and fastened the box to the metal carrier on the back of his motorcycle. That box also served him well when he went grocery shopping. His Harley-Davidson transportation was the best investment Piet could have made.

Seven years after leaving Holland, on May 30, 1955, Piet was ordained a priest in the St. Paul Cathedral. He celebrated his First Solemn Mass on June 5 at the Church of St. Olaf in Minneapolis. The holy card sharing this information had the photo of Pope Pius XII with the prayer:

> "I recommend to Thee, O God, my family, relatives and friends, and all whose prayers and sacrifices have led me to thy Holy Altar. Mary, Mother of Priests, help me and all priests in the service of God."

His first assignment in the Crookston diocese was to be the assistant pastor in Bemidji, Minnesota effective June 29, 1955. (At that same time, fifty miles away, I was enjoying my first summer at home after having spent my freshman year at the convent boarding school.)

Piet had a student visa and wanted to get permanent residency. He was told that this was not possible because of quota restrictions. At this time Hubert H. Humphrey was a U.S. Senator from Minnesota. He became an important person in Piet's struggle to achieve his dream to live in the U.S.A. Following are letters that Piet archived:

> United States Senate
> June 16, 1955
>
> The Reverend Petrus Aarden
> % Frank J. Reynolds
> 3646 South 13th Avenue
> Minneapolis, Minnesota.
>
> Dear Father Aarden,
>
> Mr. Thomas Hughes, Secretary to Governor Freeman, has forwarded to me your letter regarding your difficulties in obtaining permanent residence. I have also had a letter from the Bishop of Crookston, and I promised him I would give you every possible assistance.
>
> In order to prevent your immediate deportation, I have introduced a private relief bill in the Senate to provide for your permanent residence. I have no doubt the bill will pass, but our real problem is to get it passed before this Congress recesses. I am not at all sure we can accomplish this in the short time that remains,

inasmuch as the bill must be passed by both Houses of Congress. However, I shall certainly do all I can.

I have also written to the Immigration and Naturalization Service to see if some way can be found to solve the problem administratively. Before the McCarren Act went into effect, a minister was entitled to non-quota status, but that privilege was not extended under the provisions of the McCarren Act.

A copy of my bill is enclosed, and the Immigration Service will be notified of the introduction. This will prevent having to leave the country while it is pending before the Congress. In the event it is not acted upon before we recess, it will be carried over to the next year to allow us the opportunity to pass on it. I shall keep you informed of developments.

Sincerely yours

Hubert H. Humphrey

P.S. Before I could mail this letter to you, I received the attached report from the Immigration Service explaining what occurred with regard to your request to adjust your status to that of a permanent resident. I understand now what happened. There still may be a possibility of your adjusting your status under Section 245 if you re-apply after the first of July. I understand the new quota allocations for the fiscal year go into effect at that time. I suggest that you again contact the Immigration Office and then let me know what develops.

U.S. Department of Justice Immigration & Naturalization Service
1014 New Post Office Building.
St. Paul, Minn.
June 15, 1955

Honorable Hubert H. Humphrey
United States Senate Washington, D.C.

My dear Senator Humphrey:

A receipt is acknowledged of your letter relative to an inquiry made by Francis J. Schenk, Bishop of Crookston, regarding the problem of one, Petrus AARDEN, a citizen of Holland.

While Petrus Aarden was still in student status, he came to this office to make inquiry regarding the possibility of applying for adjustment of his status to that of a permanent resident. At the time of this interview, it was explained to him that he was ineligible for the reason that a non-preference Netherlands quota number was not available to him at that time, according to information received from the Visa Office of the State Department. It was suggested to him that he wait until after he had been ordained as a priest and then make an application for adjustment of status under Section 245 of the Immigration and Nationality Act as an alien entitled to first preference (Section 203 (a) ((1) of the same Act) under The Netherlands quota.

Soon after Reverend Aarden was ordained, he came to this office to make inquiry regarding procedure for adjustment of his status under the first preference status mentioned, but in the meantime this office had been notified by the Visa Office of the State Department that this category under Netherlands quota had been closed, a matter over which this office had no control. For this reason alone, he is ineligible at the present time for adjustment of status to that of a permanent resident.

At no time has Reverend Aarden been eligible for non-quota status inasmuch as the law requires that, under Section 101 (a) (27) (F) (i) of the Immigration and Nationality Act, he must be "an immigrant who continuously for at least two years immediately preceding the time of his application for admission to the United States, has been and who seeks to enter the United States solely for the purpose of carrying on the vocation of minister of a religious denomination and whose services are needed by such religious denomination having a bona fide organization in the United States".

Very truly yours,
J..D. Perfetto
Acting Officer in Charge

The Bill that H.H. Humphrey introduced was as follows:

84th Congress: 1st Session

S. 2235

IN THE SENATE OF THE UNITED STATES

June 14, 1955

Mr. Humphrey introduced the following bill; which was read twice and referred to the committee on the Judiciary

A BILL

For the relief of Petrus (Piet) Aarden.

Be it enacted by the Senate and House of Representatives of the United States of America in Congress assembled, that for the purposes of the Immigration and Nationality Act, Petrus (Piet) Aarden shall be held and considered to have been lawfully admitted to the United States for permanent residence as of the date of enactment of this Act, upon payment of the required visa fee. Upon the granting of permanent residence to such alien as provided for in this Act, the Secretary of State shall instruct the proper quota-control officer to deduct one number from the appropriate quota for the first year that such quota is available.

The bill was passed and Piet did not have to be deported! The following June he traveled to Holland to celebrate his accomplishment of becoming a priest. The little village of Aarle-Rixtel was ready to welcome him home with a parade through the village streets. The whole town came out to celebrate. Piet proudly celebrated his First Mass on Holland soil for family and friends.

Piet's homecoming as a priest, with his dad and mom. (1956)

When Piet finished telling me of the grand Holland reception that happened in that year of 1956, he brought out an old photo album. I met Piet's family for the first time through those long-ago photos. I could hardly wait to meet them in person. We decided right then and there to put aside money every paycheck to be able to travel to Holland for our honeymoon, after we were married.

As Piet shared more of his stories each time we met, I realized more and more what strength of character and determination he possessed. How fortunate I was to have found a person like him! When I asked him about the process of becoming a United States citizen, there was another amazing story to be shared.

He said there was a document that H.H. Humphrey had sent to him. It was titled, *Our American Government: What Is It? How Does It Function?* It contained 175 questions and answers and was a comprehensive story of the history and functions of our American government. Piet studied this diligently. In July of 1961, when he was an associate pastor at East Grand Forks, Minnesota, he became a citizen. This brought about a barrage of letters from members of the Congress of the United States: His favorite was from Hubert Humphrey:

> United States Senate Washington, D.C.
> July 12, 1961
>
> Mr. Piet F. Aarden
> 222 South 3rd Street
> East Grand Forks, Minnesota
>
> Dear Mr. Aarden:
>
> Congratulations on becoming a citizen of the United States of America.
>
> The vast majority of our people obtained this privilege of citizenship by birth. You have obtained your citizenship by hard work, study, and personal desire and decision. It takes a great deal of effort to fulfill the requirements demanded by our naturalization and citizenship laws. You have every right to be proud of your accomplishment.
>
> As your Senator and fellow Minnesotan, I want you to know that my office is always ready to serve and assist you. In order to keep my constituents informed of activities and developments here in Congress, I send out a newsletter from time to time. I would be happy to add your name to my mailing list if you will fill out the enclosed card and drop it in the mail.
>
> I am taking the liberty of enclosing a copy of House Document No. 386 which I believe will be of interest to you.
>
> Again, my best wishes and congratulations.
>
> Sincerely yours,
>
> Hubert H. Humphrey

I learned it was when he obtained his U.S. Citizenship that he had his name "Petrus Aarden" officially changed to "Piet Francis Aarden." "Piet" was the name commonly used when he was growing up in Holland while the Latin name, "Petrus," was used just for official records. He did not have a middle name, so his good friend, Francis Reynolds, asked him to take his name for that purpose. What a story of accomplishments!

Every Friday evening, as Piet and I shared more of our life stories, I fell more in love. The question foremost in our conversations: WHEN would those papers from Rome arrive so we could go forward with our wedding plans?

In early May, I interviewed with St. Paul Schools and was offered several different teaching jobs. There were a plethora of teaching positions. Each offered different opportunities for teaching styles and philosophies such as team teaching, schools without walls, or traditional classrooms. I chose Battle Creek Annex, a K-1 school on the east side of St. Paul, a few miles from Piet's apartment. The Annex staff was all female, and the school was a series of portable buildings to house students from the overcrowded main school. Situated in a scenic, wooded setting, I was taken with the atmosphere and camaraderie of the staff. It felt like a great place to start my career as a public school teacher. I was living for the moment when I could have my future students address me as Mrs. Aarden!

Finally, May 30, my graduation day, arrived. My folks drove to the Twin Cities to share in my celebration along with Piet, Rita, and Beasy. Mom and Dad's twenty-nine-year-old daughter was finally getting her long-awaited degree. The Marzolfs told me that it was fine to have a big celebration in our apartment for the special occasion.

Piet said he would drive us to the college for the ceremony. On Graduation morning, he arrived early. "Can we go for a brief walk?" he asked. "There is something we need to talk about."

He looked so serious. I wondered what had happened. Did they refuse his dispensation? Was he quitting his insurance job? My head was buzzing with so many questions. As we walked, he held my hand and asked how I was feeling about the coming ceremony. Then he stopped suddenly and took a small box out of his pocket.

As he opened the box, Piet said he had a special gift for my graduation and hoped I would accept it. Would I do him the honor of marrying him? As I jumped up and down for joy, I hugged him uncontrollably. Who could ask for a better graduation gift?

He grasped my left hand to slip the ring on. "If you say yes, I promise to be yours forever. You will have made me the happiest man on earth!"

"Yes, yes, a thousand times, YES," I shouted for the whole world to hear.

The ring magically fit.

"Well, I've already talked with your folks and have their permission," he continued. "So my dream has come true. Now, if only those papers from Rome would arrive, we could set the date."

That day of May 30, 1970, was the happiest in my life. I had won Piet's heart, received an engagement ring, and a promise of marriage, not to mention my degree. I knew my folks admired and liked Piet already, and they hardly knew him. Life was good.

After the graduation ceremony, we returned to my apartment. At our celebration luncheon, my mom asked what my summer plans were. There was a need for a Head Start teacher in Naytahwaush, my hometown, starting the middle of June. She was sure I would qualify and had a phone number to call if I was interested.

Wow, I had been so involved in finishing my exams and getting ready for graduation that I had not given any thought to what else I was going to do for summer employment. I would not have studies to complete and the cashier job at the hospital was only part-time. My Jewish family would not need my tutoring services during the summer and the grandmother was recuperating very well. This Head Start job would be a great way to earn money that Piet and I could certainly use for our future life together—whenever that would materialize.

My parents said they would be very happy to have me live with them if I got the teaching position. They left the next day. I told them I would call and find out more information and thanked them over and over for checking out this amazing possibility for me.

The next day, I discussed the pros and cons of the Head Start job with Piet, as well as Rita and Beasy. If I were to leave, my roommates decided they would stay on in the apartment and continue cleaning for the Marzolf's. Piet said I should do what I felt was best.

I decided to call the number for the Head Start job. The phone interview went well. I was offered the job and would need to start June 15. The salary for teaching was far and above what I was making with all my jobs together. All I had to do now was to give my two-week notice to the cafeteria manager. When I talked with Mrs. Steinmetz, she understood why I needed to leave. All seemed to fall into place.

On June 13, my white Mustang convertible and I headed for Naytahwaush and my new summer job. As I drove, my thoughts conjured up memories of the many twists and turns my life had taken since I made that abrupt decision to leave Naytahwaush when I was thirteen to become a nun. I was caught in the web of memories, going way back as if it were yesterday. My early life's decisions played out like a movie in my mind.

In 1954, what does a thirteen-going-on-fourteen-year-old girl, tucked away in a remote Ojibway Indian village, know about making a decision that will transform her life? It all began with me rushing home during the second week of summer catechism classes with the nuns. "Guess what, Mom? You won't believe this, but Sr. Kathleen just told me I have a vocation to be a nun! I can't believe it!"

In the past, the nuns dressed my older sister as a nun when they came for the two weeks of summer catechism. They always seemed to ignore me. Now they noticed me and even wanted me as one of their own!

Looking at me closely, my mom placed her worn hands on my shoulders. In her patient voice she replied, "Vonnie if you truly have a vocation, it will still be there when you turn eighteen and finish high school. No thirteen-year-old knows if she has a vocation or not. Tell Sr. Kathleen that your parents appreciate the fact she thinks you might have a vocation, but that you will make that decision when you are much older."

Before catechism started the next day, I rushed up to Sr. Kathleen to tell her what my mom had said. Sister kindly told me that girls do in fact have vocations to the sisterhood at an early age. She assured me that she knew I was one of them.

I could hardly wait to share my latest talk with Sister. "Mom, guess what? Sister is sure I have a vocation and they have a special girls' boarding high school in Crookston, Minnesota. I can go there this fall to be an aspirant—those are young girls who learn all about being a nun while they go to high school classes!"

As I looked into Mom's worried face, she sighed wearily, shook her head and told me that she was not convinced. Taking her time, she sat me down and then explained that we could not afford a private boarding school. I was to take the idea of being a nun and tuck it away in the back of my mind until I was eighteen, and that was that.

"Sister, my Mom says we don't have money for me to go away to your school, and I should wait until I graduate from high school."

"Mom, guess what? Sr. Kathleen says they have scholarships for girls like me who can't afford it, and that I could get one of those. Oh, Mom, PLEASE ... "

"Vonnie", my mom replied, "you are TOO young to leave home. Besides, you are just learning how to be our new organist. The church needs you here, not far away in some girls' boarding school learning how to be a nun." Mom assured me that Fr. Gus would not approve of this, either. I was to just tell that Sr. Kathleen to stop filling my head with such nonsense. "Your vocation right now is to be of service to our little Indian village and do your church work right here, not seventy-five miles away. We need you. I need you. No, Vonnie, my answer is NO."

Once Fr. Gus learned what was going on, he became angered that the nuns were trying to take away his newly-trained organist. He spent hours trying to talk sense into my head. My mom cajoled and did her utmost to make me realize that vocations don't just flit in and out of your head.

September 1954 came, and with it a new beginning for a certain thirteen-going-on-fourteen-year-old girl who was firmly convinced that her vocation needed to start that freshman year at Mount St. Benedict Academy with the Benedictine nuns. Sr. Kathleen had won the match. Or had she? As I lay crying homesick tears into my pillow night after night, I began questioning: Was this truly the right choice? The best choice? Were the tantrums, crying fits, and stamping of feet the proper reactions of someone preparing to become a nun? What lay ahead? Would I learn to regret my decision to only listen to Sr. Kathleen? (At the same time, Piet was finishing his last year of seminary and became an ordained priest the following year.)

In 1957, what does a seventeen-going-on-eighteen year old girl, tucked away in an all-girls' boarding school, do to celebrate New Year's Day in her senior year? Was she about to make a decision that would transform her life once again? Kneeling on the cold, brown-tiled floor in the sisters' stark refectory with my arms extended in a crucifix position, I heard the echoes of my trembling voice, "I humbly beg, for Jesus sake, to be admitted as a postulant and to learn the ways of St. Benedict during these next six months of training."

The sisters who were about to approve or disapprove of me as a postulant had no idea what this very girl, asking for their approval, had done the night before. This candidate had decided to "live it up in the worldly sense" by having her last fling before officially entering the convent as a postulant.

My white poodle skirt, pink-sequined sweater, and high heels—worn at the previous night's New Year's Eve dance—were a stark contrast to the black net veil, black pleated dress with matching cape, black cotton stockings, and old women's black stodgy shoes that I was wearing a few hours later. Doing the jitterbug on the dance floor at the stroke of midnight was not fitting into this scene of austerity and silence.

Yet, the past four years of convent boarding school had magnetic attractions that could not be cast aside, despite the questions of my family and friends back home. Was I ready for this? Hearing the Rev. Mother's voice brought me back to reality: "Yes, Miss Yvonne, you are now accepted as a postulant in our Benedictine community."

In 1958, what does an eighteen-going–on-nineteen, recent high school graduate do just before July 4? If you were Miss Yvonne, you dressed in a previously-owned white bridal gown and veil and marched down the chapel aisle to become the bride of Christ. The outfit was complete with new rimless glasses (replacing the fancy cat-eyed, black frames that were given up as being too worldly). The chapel was filled with nuns, as well as my family and the family of the other postulant, Marguerite.

As rehearsed, when the Rev. Mother stood to beckon me to approach the altar to make my commitment to becoming a novice, I walked forward to accept my new nun's garb, the next step in becoming a nun. This upcoming novitiate entailed a year of silence and contemplation, as well as a year of total separation from my family.

The Rev. Mother had given us postulants three choices of names that we would want to be called as a nun, since we were to give up the worldly, baptismal name given to us by our parents. She would then choose, from those three options, the name she felt was most fitting. Since Fr. Gus Augustine had done so much for our St. Anne's parish in our small Indian village, I decided to honor him and simply wrote down my three choices:

> Sr. Augustine
>
> Sr. Augustine
>
> Sr. Augustine

As the Rev. Mother held out the new nun's habit that I would soon be wearing, she leaned over, blessed me, and said, "From this day forward, you will no longer be Miss Yvonne, but your new name will be Sr. Mona."

What? Had I heard wrong? I was supposed to be Sr. Augustine. Those were the three names I had given for my choices!

"Excuse me, Rev. Mother, but that is not the name I chose."

She looked at me with disbelief and repeated her words. "From this day forward you will no longer be Miss Yvonne, but your new name will be Sr. Mona."

I looked up into her distressed eyes and said again it was not what I had chosen. Exasperated, and not quite knowing what to do with this unyielding new novice-to-be, she leaned over once again and sternly said, "You do not look like an Augustine. We have a Sr. Monica already, named after the mother of St. Augustine. Mona is the closest I could get to Augustine. Go and get dressed, Sr. Mona!"

With a heavy heart and a new name that I had NOT chosen, I obediently walked from the altar and proceeded downstairs. There some nuns would help me don the layers of clothing underneath the black, floor-length habit covered by a long, modest, black scapular. My face would be enclosed within a white, pleated coif and a heavily-starched headband that connected to a long, flowing black veil.

As I slowly walked down the steps, I heard Marguerite's footsteps behind me. I tearfully turned around to ask what name she had been given. (She had taken my advice and had asked for Sr. Stanislaus three times, to honor her parish priest, too.)

"I got the name Sr. Mona, what did she give you?"

Marguerite broke into tears and cried, "She gave me Sr. Isabel, in honor of her favorite niece. I bet Mona is not the prostitute in your Indian village like Isabel is in mine!"

With that news, I suddenly did not mind my new name at all. In fact, it had a rather nice ring to it.

(During my convent years, Father Aarden served as an assistant priest in Bemidji from 1955-58; Thief River Falls from 1958-61; East Grand Forks from 1961-66. From 1966-1970 he was pastor of the parish in Kelliher.)

That summer of 1970, driving home to Naytahwaush, I was totally absorbed in my memories. I didn't pay attention to the posted speed limit while driving through St. Cloud. Suddenly, I looked in my rear-view mirror and was jolted back into the present by whirling lights and a siren screeching behind me. I pulled over to let the policeman go past me to catch his victim. It startled me that he pulled up right behind me.

"Ma'am, do you know what the speed limit is?" the stern patrolman asked. "I clocked you going fifty in a thirty-five-mile hour zone."

Unprepared for this encounter, I apologized profusely and began to cry. I explained that I was on my way to teach little Indian children on my reservation. I was so sorry I had not seen the speed limit sign.

Twenty minutes later, I left the scene with a $75.00 ticket, and no money to pay for this newly-acquired debt. How would my folks react to this transgression? I didn't want to begin on the wrong foot and have to ask if I could borrow money for a speeding ticket, but I would have to.

My eyes carefully watched the speedometer as I continued the rest of my journey to Naytahwaush. I wondered what it would be like to live with my parents again. In all those years of being in the convent, I had only been able to go home every three years, for two weeks. This would truly be a gift to have two months to spend time with them.

I looked to see what might have changed over the past sixteen years. What would be the same? What would be different? The dirt roads were the same, but our little, white, wooden St. Anne's church had been replaced by a modern-looking wooden structure across the road. The brick public school on the corner looked the same.

As I drove down the hill past the school, my heart quickened as I saw our small, white house with the hand-painted sign on the new addition: Naytahwaush Post Office. The American flag was proudly waving at its side. I knew my parents would be inside, busily handing out mail to their daily customers. A sense of belonging and comfort settled within me. I was home. I was also feeling secure knowing I was deeply loved, and looking forward to this special time with Mom and Dad.

I parked the car behind the house and rushed in to feel the warm, embracing hugs of Mom and Dad. Afterwards, I shared my speeding mishap and waited for my dad's little sermon about the need to drive within the speed limits. He asked how much damage the ticket amounted to and said they would lend me the money until I got my first paycheck.

My first week of work was occupied with meetings, paperwork and learning the ropes for this new assignment. Marilyn Goodwin was to be my assistant. She was several years younger than I, but her sister and I had been childhood friends, so I knew her family well. Marilyn was eager, constantly had a smile on her face, and shared how excited she was to work with me. We developed an immediate sense of partnership and couldn't wait for our fifteen preschoolers to arrive the following Monday.

That summer became another summer of love letters filled with the constant question: When would Piet's papers come through? We decided to proceed with wedding plans, and have everything ready for the day the papers would arrive. Piet even applied for our marriage license.

In one of his letters, Piet wondered if it would be possible to spend some weekends together at his Midge Lake cabin. It would be a five-hour drive for him, but only an hour or so from my parent's home. We could have from Friday night to Sunday afternoon together, as well as have a relaxing place to make our wedding plans.

My heart said, "Yes," but my mind was filled with so many questions: What would my parents think? Was I putting myself in temptation's way? When would those papers come to free us to get married? Should we wait?

During those weekends together, we decided to hold off our wedding until the papers arrived. Hopefully, that would be sooner rather than later.

In early August, Piet interviewed at the Stillwater State Prison in Minnesota and was offered the job of social worker for the inmates. He had two weeks before he would begin his new job, and wondered if he could come to the reservation and visit with me at my parent's home.

When I asked Mom and Dad, they hesitated and then said, "Sure, BUT, he will be sleeping on the porch—not with you!"

I was ecstatic and couldn't wait for my Dutchman to arrive. When he did, he wondered if there was any work he could do for my folks during his visit. My folks told him he was our guest and did not have to repay them in any way.

If he did want to make some money, my mom heard that my cousin, who owned a resort nearby, needed some painting done on his buildings. The resort was only a few miles from my parent's place. Piet jumped at the chance. While I taught my Head Start classes, he painted and earned some extra cash. It was a great time for my folks to get to know Piet. As for Piet and myself, we no longer needed to write daily letters. We could just bask in each other's love and presence.

My sister, Flo, and husband, Rome, and their children were enjoying their yearly vacation at that same cousin's resort where Piet was painting. One night they came to my parent's home for supper. As tradition would have it, my dad took charge after supper and set the table for a game of poker. No one ever refused.

"OK, everyone, come on, feed the mahogany," my dad directed, as he shuffled the cards. All of us, except for Piet, obeyed and sat down at the table. Dad told everyone to ante up for the first game, Seven Card Stud. He noticed Piet had not joined us at the table.

"Piet, get over here and show us some of that money you've been earning this week," my dad laughed.

"I don't play cards," Piet answered in a definitive tone. "I've never enjoyed cards, even when I was a kid."

There was silence in the room.

"What do you mean, you don't play cards?" my dad asked in a huff. "Every priest I ever knew was a card player."

"Well, not this one," Piet politely responded.

At that, my sister's husband, Rome, broke the icy silence and said, "Piet, I've been with this family for ten years. I really don't care for cards either, but I have never had the guts to tell my father-in-law. Maybe you want to reconsider—you don't have his daughter's hand in marriage yet."

Everyone laughed. After Rome's speech, Piet reluctantly sat down to learn the Rumreich ritual of poker playing. Piet was baffled because every hand was a new, unknown game: "South Dakota," "Jacks are Wild," "Night Baseball." The evening could not end soon enough for him.

The two weeks sped by. Piet needed to return to St. Paul to start his new job. When he left, my parents told me I definitely had found an amazing man to share my new life with. "Even though he doesn't like cards!" my dad added.

Piet had won their hearts, as well as mine. I thanked my parents again and again for opening their hearts and home to him. As we talked, I shared how eternally grateful I was that they had accepted my decision to leave the convent.

The following week, one of Piet's daily letters arrived telling me about his new job in the prison:

> My precious doll, Yvonne:
>
> I realize this will not arrive until Friday morning, but no matter when it does arrive I want you to know that I LOVE YOU!!! I wish I could sit down with you and talk things over with you. I MISS YOU!!!!!
>
> The last three days they have been adding names after names to our caseloads so now we have all we are supposed to carry. I haven't had time to sit down and add up the number of inmates that are assigned to me. It looks like I won't have enough time to do all I am supposed to for the time being. As time goes, on, I'm sure, a person will become more used to it and be able to do some of these things in half the time it takes now. But you get interrupted so often that you just cannot get any place. If I had been driving my own car today, I would have stayed a couple of more hours – the inmates certainly would not interrupt during the supper hour and probably not too much during free time.
>
> Not much else happened since I wrote you last night. Oh, yes, I did get a bed lined up for myself at the prison for August 17th. Of course, I hope that nothing is going to happen to me – I want to live a long time with you – but since I started work for the State, I picked up another $15,000 worth of life insurance to which I made you the beneficiary, but I gave 2040 Hudson Road as your address. They would have a tough time finding you if something did happen before you moved in. Oh, I'm planning on staying alive but just in case.
>
> I LOVE YOU MUCH!! And MISS YOU TERRIBLY. I'll see you Friday evening. Can't wait. Take care of yourself.
>
> Love from your dreaming lover, Piet

The two summer months had gone by so quickly. One Friday afternoon, in the middle of August, I packed my belongings and said a tearful goodbye to my parents as I left for the long five-hour trek to St. Paul. It was time for me to prepare for my new job, a new apartment, and a new life of being with Piet—but not totally.

My teaching job was to begin the last week of August. Piet offered to let me live in his apartment. Since he still did not have his dispensation, we couldn't be living together without being married. It was definitely not the thing to do in the 70s, especially with our backgrounds.

Until the papers arrived, he would have his cot in the attic within the prison walls and would suffer the hardships and inconveniences related to that sacrifice. I would have the luxury of living in his modest apartment. Since we did not have the money, it was not even thinkable to each have an apartment of our own. We would have to make the best of our situation as we played the waiting game.

Graduation and engagement day. May 30, 1970. Dad, Me, Mom, and Rita.

CHAPTER SIX
Wedding & Building of Home: 1970-1972

In the fall of 1970, as we were making wedding plans, the topic of children came up. I eagerly announced that I wanted a big family and was thinking of at least six children. Silence filled the room. Piet sat and stared at me in disbelief. He then calmly and cooly shared his views.

"Yvonne, look at us. I am forty-three and you are thirty. Even if we started a family immediately, and had a year or two between children, do you realize how old I would be when they become teenagers? I want to be able to really spend quality time with our kids, and actively participate in their growing years. Two is the maximum, in my book."

I stared at him in disbelief. How could he only want two children? He had grown up with six other siblings. I had always wished that I had grown up with lots of siblings. "But, Piet..." I began.

He took me in his arms and as he cradled me, he whispered in my ear, "And I want you to get an appointment with your doctor to get birth control pills. We just can't afford to think of starting a family until we get on our feet, financially."

I jumped up and said, "Piet, I don't know a thing about birth control. That was not discussed in the convent!"

He laughed and told me it was easy. I just had to get a prescription for the pills from my doctor and follow the printed directions.

The next week saw me walking with trepidation into the clinic and feeling embarrassed when the Filipino doctor asked why I was there. With hesitation and not wanting to look him in the eyes, I said I needed to get some birth control pills. He asked me how old I was and if I was Catholic and did I really know what I was doing? Nervously, I told him I was thirty, a Catholic, and that my future husband told me to do it. The doctor then proceeded to give me several reasons why I shouldn't: #1 I was an older woman. #2 I was Catholic. #3 I needed to think about possible side effects. The doctor said I should go home and think it over, as he did not agree with my decision. I told him that I couldn't leave without a prescription. He reluctantly acquiesced and I rushed out of the office hoping to never see him again.

By early November 1970, we had reached the end of our rope. Papers or no papers, we decided that the time had come: We would get married. Piet and I were totally frustrated, trying to be together without sharing a conjugal bed.

The directives from the bishop had stated that even with the laicization papers, we would have to be married in the catacombs of the cathedral. It was not to be a public event.

Piet and I totally disagreed. How could the church tell us to go underground to proclaim our marriage vows to each other? That was sheer nonsense. What did we have to hide? Were we to be branded for all eternity because we had done such an unthinkable misdeed—that of falling in love with each other?

Since Piet's family all lived in Holland, we decided to have a small wedding the day before Thanksgiving, November 25, 1970, with just my family present. We chose that date because we would have a long, holiday weekend for a short honeymoon at Piet's cabin. Our extended honeymoon would be a trip to his family in Holland, the following summer.

It was time to ask a favor of Father Reynolds. Would he marry us even if the papers had not arrived?

When Piet met with Fr. Reynolds that first week in November, he agreed to marry us in his parish church in Buffalo, Minnesota, about an hour from the Twin Cities. We were surprised when he offered to have the women's guild in his parish prepare our wedding meal. Fr. Reynolds was bending over backwards, and ready to do everything he could to make up for his horrible mistake in trying to stop Piet's request for laicization—even marry us above ground and without the Papal papers!

Practicality and minimal expense were key factors in planning our wedding. Flo and Rome agreed to be witnesses to our marriage. Another unexpected surprise was that Flo said she would sew my wedding dress. Piet was to wear the grey suit he had purchased for job interviews. A white shirt, complete with cufflinks and a gray-maroon striped tie would complete his wedding outfit. Since this was the era of mini-skirts, I decided I wanted a practical dress that could be worn for other formal occasions. Flo found a simple A-line pattern that she decorated with a simple gold neck trim. After all those years of wearing a veil, I opted to dispense with that item. This ex-nun would walk down the aisle in a dress above the knees, minus both a veil and a bouquet of flowers.

For Piet and myself, the important aspects of our marriage ceremony were the preparations for the actual liturgical ceremony itself. Flowers and veils were insignificant. We had spent the summer and early fall creating a wedding booklet that Piet had printed for minimal cost at a friend's publishing company. Our booklet contained songs to be sung by all those attending the ceremony. Piet would lead everyone with his amazing, melodious voice. No instruments other than the human voice were needed.

That fall, we had also designed and created a unique wedding banner for the altar that symbolized our love and future life together. It contained a triangle with each angle containing one of the words, "God Is Love." In the middle were wedding rings with our names intertwined. Grapes and wheat were added to symbolize the love of the Son of God for mankind. This same design became the cover of our marriage booklet.

When I requested the Wednesday before Thanksgiving as one of my vacation days, I learned that my school district would not grant me the request since it was the day before a regular holiday. I would have to take a day without pay. That seemed immaterial at that point; we were finally going to be married.

Our wedding day arrived, snow and all, November 25, 1970. Piet dropped me off at Marzolf's that morning because, Beasy, my former roommate, had offered to be my hairdresser. As soon as she finished, I donned my short wedding dress and matching shoes. My prince, in his white Oldsmobile, appeared at the curb dressed in his wedding suit. The Marzolf's hugged and wished us well. I thanked them for their support when I had so desperately needed a place to stay. They had become special friends. I owed them thanks, as well as the McCarthy's, who had helped me find them.

Wedding day. November 25, 1970

It was actually happening: We were going to be married in a few hours! Since we could not afford a professional photographer at our ceremony, Piet and I spent the early afternoon posing at a photographer's studio. We would have some professional photos as official proof of a day forever etched in our minds and hearts.

Our wedding ceremony went off without a hitch. Our vows to each other cemented our union:

Piet's Prayer: "God, we are starting now a way of life new to both of us. We realize that every person is different and the two of us will have an ocean of discoveries to make in each other. With the blind man of the Gospel, I call out to you, "Lord that I may see"; help me to keep looking for and find the good qualities in Yvonne. I beg you, Lord, help me be a good husband and father if you so will. Never let the day come that I take my wife, Yvonne, or my family for granted, but let me keep loving and cherishing her as much as I do today."

Yvonne's Prayer: "Father, Son, and Holy Spirit: I, as Piet's wife, thank you for the love you have brought to us and ask in all sincerity that with your guidance, I may become an understanding and devoted wife and mother. Grant to me the insight and concern needed in this new life I have vowed today and may our love grow deeper by being blessed with children. Help me to be ready to sacrifice myself totally for Piet and our future family. I am eternally grateful for this love you brought to me and may the rest of my life be one of sharing your gift of love to all those I encounter."

After the Mass that united us in the Sacrament of Matrimony, we walked down the aisle singing, "God Is Love, and he who abides in love abides in God and God in him." Our new life had begun as man and wife.

Wedding ceremony and banner. (L to R) Fr. Reynolds, Rome, Piet, Yvonne, and Flo.

The Thanksgiving meal prepared by the women of the parish was delicious and greatly appreciated by all. Fr. Reynolds had even ordered a two-layered wedding cake, adorned with a silver cross, bearing two wedding rings, intertwined. After the meal, we opened gifts. With lots of laughter and tons of hugs and well wishes from our family and guests, we set off for our short honeymoon at the cabin, a good five-hour drive away.

As we drove, we laughed and thought it quite amusing as we recalled that the same cabin Piet had introduced to Sr. Judith and me over a year and a half earlier was to become our honeymoon cabin within a few hours. We had SO much to be thankful for and our dream had come true. We were now married and had done it all above ground!

With his knack for practicality, Piet had carefully planned all our meals for the long weekend. All the groceries were loaded in the trunk as we set off for our honeymoon. The snowdrifts that greeted us in the cabin's driveway couldn't put a damper on our happiness. Laughing, we leaped over snow banks and entered a freezing cold cabin. While the heater attempted to raise the room's temperature, we had good reason to keep hugging and kissing while dancing around the room to get warm. Such minor details—we were actually married. Could it get any better? Could anything break this bubble of total love and happiness?

What a wonderful change it was to return to our apartment after the honeymoon and realize that Piet no longer had to leave each evening for his prison cot! The last months of 1970 were spent in blissful thanks for all that had happened to bring about the circumstances that had brought us together. We were like little kids lost in a candy shop, making up for all those years of not knowing what it was like to experience the sweetness of married lovers.

In January of 1971, Piet's limited wardrobe for work gave us cause to go shopping, only to realize that buying clothes for a six-foot-four-inch tall man was not within our budget. I boldly decided, right then and there, to become his seamstress. This was despite the fact that I had always tearfully taken my torn habits to one of the older nuns and had never attempted to sew for myself. Piet said he had a sewing machine if I was serious about sewing, but his machine turned out to be archaic.

Searching the newspaper, we found a place that took trade-ins if you bought a new sewing machine. Knowing absolutely nothing about sewing machines, we found this "Mom and Pop" store where the owner started quizzing me about the type of sewing machine I was looking for. When it became immediately apparent that I had no idea about machines, he started asking what I planned on sewing. I proudly said I was going to sew all my husband's clothes, even though I had no experience.

With a shake of his head and questioning eyes, he said I might want to start with a simple, inexpensive machine and try that out first. No, I told him. I was really serious and needed a good machine, so I could be successful with my sewing. I was bound and determined to become a seamstress. We walked out of that shop having made a down payment on a new, top-of-the-line Elna machine. The look on that man's face still makes me smile. I proved later that we had made the right decision.

The week after our big purchase, I enrolled in a Stretch and Sew class. Someone should have warned me not to start with men's trousers, but that was the article of clothing that Piet needed the most.

Polyester plaids were the fashion of the 70s. I quickly learned that the plaids MUST match at all the seams. One of our assignments was to study men's clothes (and matching seams) we noticed in public, and especially take note if the plaids on the fly of men's pants matched! Did they not know I was just freshly out of the convent? Now I needed to be on the alert and notice the seams on the fly of men's pants?

Needless to say, I warned Piet that this was a very difficult class. If the zipper ended up in the back instead of the front, that would be his worry, not mine! After six weeks of class, Piet proudly wore his first home-sewn pair of beige plaid pants, with all plaids matching—even the fly! This began my tradition of sewing clothes for the Aarden family.

Since Piet no longer needed to spend hours every evening searching the newspapers for future insurance clients, he was free to help me. The evenings of our first year of marriage were spent together coming up with themes and artistic creations for my classroom bulletin boards.

After tediously creating the monthly bulletin boards, we went to bed where we read a book I had discovered in a bookstore called, *Everything You Ever Wanted to Know About Sex but Were Afraid to Ask*. Now that was a bit different than my nighttime convent reading!

One day in April, the phone rang. It was the bishop's office. The phantom papers had finally arrived from Rome. Piet was free to get married! April 21, 1971, became the OFFICIAL laicization date—five months too late for us! Piet drove to the Bishopric for the official signing of the long-awaited document:

THE ARCHDIOCESE OF SAINT PAUL AND MINNEAPOLIS
240 Summit Avenue
Saint. Paul, Minnesota 55102

ACCEPTANCE OF LAICIZATION, AND DISPENSATIONS

I, the undersigned PIET FRANCIS AARDEN, residing at 2040 Hudson Road, Saint Paul, Minnesota, 55119, herewith signify my free and willing acceptance of the document wherein I am given membership in the lay state with all of its rights, privileges, and responsibilities, and I acknowledge and accept the dispensation from all of the obligations arising from the free acceptance of Sacred Orders (and from religious vows), and particularly the dispensation from the obligation of celibacy.

This action and dispensation are taken in the light of the response of Pope Paul VI dated March 5, 1971, Correspondence Number of the Sacred Congregation for the Teaching of the Faith S.C.D.F. #3492/69.

In accordance with the guidelines issued by the Congregation on January 13, 1971, I wish to state positively my intention of building the Church of Christ among men, so far as possible, by my own example of a devout Christian life in the midst of other men.

Recognizing the sensitivities of some towards the very fact of this dispensation granted me by Pope Paul VI, particularly with regard to the questions of residence, celebration of marriage, and participation in the life of the Church in its liturgy and in its teaching function, I express hereby my readiness to abide by the guidelines and directions issued by the Bishop of the place where I am residing, in each of these matters. In a general fashion, and deferring to these uncertainties which some may yet feel with regard to these dispensations, I recognize that my permanent status as an ordained minister of God should, in general, be held in some confidence; with regard to a marriage, I shall decline widespread publicity, against the possibility of this misunderstanding and misreporting, and surround the ceremony with some privacy, but without any implication of secrecy.

With regard to future functions of ritual and ministry, and of association with religious education, I recognize in the first category that by my petition and this return to the lay state, I may exercise no specific function confined to Sacred Order, with the exception of absolution from Church penalties and from sin, in a circumstance of danger of death. Furthermore, I recognize that, in accordance with the guidelines of the Sacred Congregation, I may not take any part in liturgical celebrations such as that of lector, where my status as a priest is known. I am aware, however, that it is the function of the Bishop to dispense from the prohibition contained in the guidelines of the Doctrinal congregation regarding the teaching of religion in Catholic (or in non-Catholic) schools, and I shall abide by the decision of the Bishop in these individual matters.

With regard to financial relationships to the Archdiocese arising in my former status as a diocesan priest, I shall recognize and abide by the disposition contained in the Retirement Plan for Priests, particularly with regard to those priests who will have left the ministry, and their proportion of a vested interest in their retirement Plan.

In all of this, it is my hope and aim that I might take an active part in the life of the People of God, in a fashion appropriate to this new state of life, and that I might be a source of edification—of a building up of Christ among his people—and that I might show myself in all things as in this, a devoted son of the Church. I accept this dispensation and recognize its effectiveness as of the moment of this signature, given at Saint Paul, Minnesota, on this 21st day of April 1971.

 Piet F. Aarden
 Terrance W. Bernston

When Piet brought his laicization papers home that evening, I found mine to compare the differences:

> SACRA CONGREGATIO
> PRO RELIGIOSIS
> ET INSTITUTIS SAECULARIBUS
> Prot. N. 273/70
>
> Beatissime Pater, Soror Ivona Rumreich, professa votorum simplicium perpetuorum in Conventu Sororum Bemedictinarum Cong. S. Gertrudis in loco v.d. Crookston (USA), a Sanctitate Tua humillime implorat indultum saecularizationis, ut in saeculum legitime reidre valeat, ob rationes allatas.
>
> Et Deus, etc.
>
> Vigore facultatum a Summo Pontifice tributarum, S. Congregatio pro Religiosis et Institutis saecularibus, attentis, expositis, annuit pro gratia iuxta preces, ita ut oratrix maneat soluta a votis ceterisque obligationibus suae Professionis, et deposita exterior forma habitus religiosi, in usu Sacramentorum saecularibus assimmiletur, testituta ei dote, aut servato praescripto can. 643 &2, si casus ferat.
>
> Praesens rescriptum nullius roboris esto si abo oratrice non fuerit acceptatum intra decem dies ab eiusdem recepta communicatione.
>
> Contrariis quibuslibet non obstantibus.
> Datum Romae, die 16 Ianuarii 1970
> D. M. Hust, e.m.m.
> Subs

> Sisters of St. Benedict
> MT. ST.BENEDICT
> CROOKSTON, MINNESOTA 56716
>
> I, Sister Yvonne Rumreich, O.S.B., do hereby accept my Dispensation from Perpetual Vows. This Dispensation is on file in the Archives of Mount Saint Benedict Convent, Crookston, Minnesota.
>
> I absolve the Community of Mount Saint Benedict Convent, Crookston, Minnesota, from all further obligations.
>
> Signed: Sister Yvonne Rumreich, O.S.B.
> Yvonne Rumreich
> Witnesses: Sister Myra Shmeig, O.S.B.
> Sister Anne, O.S.B. Date: February 4, 1970

Piet wondered why I was called Sister Yvonne Rumreich on my dispensation papers, when I had been given Sr. Mona the day I made my profession of vows. It was interesting that the convent had me return to my baptismal name when I took my leave of absence. I explained to Piet that the nuns had been given the choice to return to their baptismal names by 1970, so the convent must have changed my name when I was on my leave of absence. We put those papers in safekeeping and celebrated the late arrival of Piet's papers that had caused us so much pain and anxiety. Free at last, according to Church laws!

That winter and spring, we decided to purchase some land and have Piet design and build our home. Since Piet had been so successful with carpentry during his priestly career, he could "easily" now build our dream home. Piet suggested that we go to real estate open houses in the area to get ideas of the type of home we might want, as well as ideas for designs and layouts.

At a sewing class in the summer of 1971, one of the gals told me that she and her husband had just purchased land across the river, in Wisconsin. Land there was so much cheaper than Minnesota. She shared that the developer was opening up more lots and gave me his business card. Since the lots near the Twin Cities were too expensive, we decided to look in Wisconsin.

We set up an appointment with the realtor and headed for Hudson, Wisconsin. About four miles outside the city, we followed a dirt road that seemed to be in the middle of nowhere. At the end of the road, we met up with the realtor. The three-hundred-acre area had belonged to a local farmer who decided selling land was more lucrative than farming it. The realtor was experiencing bankruptcy in some Colorado land deals, and needed fast cash. He explained that no lot was less than five acres and that each lot was numbered. Why didn't we drive around and see which lot appealed to us?

As we drove, we decided not to tell which lot appealed the most to each of us. After viewing all of them, we would make a decision between our two favorite lots. When we had viewed all the lots, Piet asked which was my favorite. Lot #22 was totally wooded with birch and oak trees and covered with massive underbrush. "Number #22," I said without hesitation. He whooped with joy. That was his pick also!

The realtor told us the acreage was priced at $800.00 an acre. Piet tried to get it for a lower price. The realtor quickly rebutted, "This price is the lowest it will ever be. Prices will only increase as I sell more lots."

Right there on the spot, we excitedly told him we wanted to claim Lot #22 as ours. Our dream of having a place of our own, surrounded by trees, became a reality that afternoon. We made an appointment to meet the following week to do the paperwork and pay for the lot.

As soon as we got back to the apartment, Piet called Fr. Reynolds to ask for a $5,000.00 loan. Piet explained that we would pay monthly on the loan at the same interest rate Reynolds was currently getting for that money in the bank. When Piet hung up the phone, the loan money was ours. In total jubilation, Piet smiled like a Cheshire cat. The following week, Piet and I signed legal papers that made the property our very own. We were now proud Wisconsin landowners, only a half hour from our apartment in Minnesota, separated by the St. Croix River!

Those late summer months and early fall of 1971 were spent exploring our new purchase. We found the boundary markers and tied bright red plastic ribbons on them to determine how deep and wide our land extended. It was difficult walking through the woods; the underbrush was so thick and high beneath all the trees.

On one of our many explorations, we discovered this huge, beautiful oak tree that seemed to overpower its surroundings. Gazing at it, we decided this would be a great symbol of beauty and strength to serve as a landmark for our future home.

The next time we explored our five acres, we searched and searched for our unique oak tree. This time, Piet was armed with a machete in hopes we would find it. Once the favored tree was found, Piet cut a swathe through the brush, back to the dirt road where we had parked. I was ecstatic and shared how romantic it would be to have this winding road lead to our future "castle" in the woods. My prince said he would do his best to fulfill that wish when it came time to create our road.

Our goal for that fall was to get the area cleared so that bulldozers could prepare the land for pouring the foundation the following spring. Every time we drove out to our land, we worked like the early pioneers to clear a homestead. With the machete, Piet cleared a wider walking path to the majestic oak. The lot was filled with trees that needed to be cut down. The buzzing sounds of a chainsaw filled the quiet woods. Trees fell to their demise. Piet would cut off the branches that I then hauled to a designated spot to be burned. Then he cut the fallen trees into sections that I was able to carry to another area—our future firewood!

After many long weekends of dedicated teamwork, over twenty-five trees had been cut to make space for the foundation.

That winter of 1971, Piet hunched over blueprints as he meticulously drew plans for our home. Building his cabin at Midge Lake had forced Piet to learn how to create blueprint plans. Now he was using this expertise for building a home for his future family. It was unfathomable to me how mere inches on that blueprint could represent an entire room.

The Minnesota State Prison had an auction every spring of used cars and trucks. We badly needed a truck to carry the lumber and materials for building our home. Due to our limited finances, Piet decided to try and get a good deal at the auction. That is how we became the proud owner of a red pickup. Not being able to afford three vehicles, Piet sold his famous white Oldsmobile to one of the workers at the prison. I had the Mustang convertible and he had the pickup for transportation. Fair trade, I said!

A year and a half after we purchased our property and had begun planning our future home, we decided to try to get pregnant. It must have happened over Christmas vacation, but I was not sure until I had missed a few periods. In February of 1972, Kitty and Dennis, our downstairs neighbors, were up in our apartment for the evening. I started to experience the most horrible cramping. I rushed to the bathroom and quickly called for Kitty to come. Blood was gushing down my legs. What was happening? Kitty, who was an experienced mother of two, looked at me. She yelled for Piet to come. "Yvonne is hemorrhaging. You need to get her to the hospital immediately."

The next thing I knew, I was in the ER and heard Piet saying, "You are going to be OK, but we lost our baby. I baptized it when they showed me the fetus."

I started crying hysterically and clung to Piet. Why did this happen? Would we be able to have other children? Was something wrong with me? He quietly and gently embraced me and said this happened when something was vitally wrong with a fetus and, of course, we would have more children. I just needed to get some rest and the doctor would explain more of the details later.

That spring, bulldozers prepared the land for our road and building site. It was a rainy spring and the workers were delayed in trying to get up the hill to excavate the area for our house. As the bulldozers plowed into the hillside, we became aware of how steep that hill really was. It would require a retaining wall, but we would have to cross that bridge at a later date. We had our special oak tree as our guardian in the front!

Getting all the permits for the building took time. We learned that the Rural Electric of Wisconsin needed to dig in the area to place underground wires. They came to do this when we were not there to supervise. Due to the muddy, rain-soaked earth, their equipment got stuck. The men decided to put a chain on our huge oak tree to help them dig out. This left a huge gouge in the tree trunk. When we came out the next weekend to work on the property, I could not believe my eyes. Our precious tree had been severely damaged. The electrical workers had simply placed a chain on the tree and not used anything to protect the

Above: Piet unloads lumber from his "new" truck.
Below right: Tin pail short order cook!

bark of our special oak. How could they be so stupid? Why could they not have used another tree? When I called the company, they said if the tree died, they would try to do something for remuneration. Where were the environmentalists when we needed them?

Now that Piet had the pickup, it was time to put it to good use. We were miles from any toilet, so Piet built the first important structure on our property: Our very own outhouse! The oak planks that he bought for the outdoor toilet assured us that no winds would ever blow it over, no matter how hard they puffed. Piet playfully asked, "Will you do me the honor of sitting on the planks so I will

know how large to cut the hole for the queen's throne?" Laughing, I agreed. How thoughtful that he made it in the shape of a heart, and just the "right size."

Those weekends of going out to our property to prepare the land were filled with long hours of exhausting work. Yet, it was also very exciting to get closer and closer to building our dream home. For our evening meals, I cooked hamburgers on top of a primitive tin pail with a wire grate that covered the top. After the charcoal pieces inside the pail became red hot, I placed two hamburgers on the "grill" to cook. They always managed to get slightly burned, but that seemed of little importance. Our picnics of hamburgers, chips, and a beer tasted woodsy as we sat on our log chairs listening to birds chirping. We were home!

With the approach of summer 1972, Piet had the foundation poured and became a well-known name at the local lumberyards. My dad turned sixty-five that year. He said he would be willing to come and live with us that summer to help in the construction. Mom agreed to this, but she needed to stay in Naytahwaush to tend to the Post Office.

Since my dad loved to sleep until late morning, our schedules worked out beautifully. I had signed up to teach morning summer school. Each noon I came back to the apartment to make lunch for Dad and myself. After lunch, we set off for our half hour drive to the Wisconsin property. Piet had carefully outlined the jobs we were responsible to accomplish each day.

On weekdays, Piet would join us after his work day, and the three of us worked until dark. This became the daily summer routine, and we worked long hours every weekend making the four-level house that Piet designed. Checking the famous blueprints and then measuring, sawing and finally pounding the nails were always part of the routine. Dad did not mind our simple meals in the woods. During our suppers, he and Piet strategized about their next job in constructing our home.

Mary and Dan (my sister and her husband) came on different weekends to help us, even though they lived four hours away and had a two-year-old son. Dan was a jack-of-all-trades—like Piet and Dad—and knew a lot about building structures. He and Dad asked why Piet had designed so many gigantic windows in his house. Piet told them to look around! What amazing scenery we would spend our lives looking at! Small windows would not do it justice.

Piet was a perfectionist in all things, and building our home was one of his passions. Every minute detail from his blueprints was followed as he meticulously built each room. The living room fireplace was going to take a lot of time and effort, so Piet decided to do a good deed and hired a prison parolee to build it. Toby, the inmate, had told Piet that he knew all about building fireplaces. He even offered to get the rock and all the supplies to build it.

Since Piet was so busy that summer trying to construct the rest of the house, he didn't have much time to supervise Toby and his workmanship. When Toby finished the fireplace, he lit a newspaper and a few small pieces of kindling to show that the fireplace really worked. Then Toby got paid and quickly disappeared.

Summer melted into fall and we were still busy trying to construct our home so we could move into the basement area before winter. Watching the framework take the shape of a real house was like a minor miracle unfolding before me. Each week it grew in dimension and form, with Piet taking photos of each new section as it progressed.

Dad and Piet were great building buddies and worked together like finely tuned clockwork. When Dad would offer what he called his "two-bits worth," Piet listened. Piet's shirtless, six-foot-four body became bronzed and muscular. My Greek Atlas! Dad's striped coveralls, denim striped cap and work shirts with sleeves were a stark contrast as I watched them working side-by-side. By the end of summer, I had mastered hitting those nails on their skinny heads in one blow, but still experienced a few "ouches" as the hammer thought my finger was the nail! I was not trusted to work in any area that needed expertise, but I was kept busy.

If I had a hammer, I would hammer in the evening...

In July of 1972, I once again had missed two periods; I was very anxious and wondered what would happen with this pregnancy. At three months, I went to an OBGYN doctor and everything looked fine. I LOVED being pregnant! My growing belly, with this live baby within, was truly a miracle I never thought I would ever experience. I was so fortunate and did not experience morning sickness and seemed as healthy as an ox! As the pregnancy continued, I felt great. Piet and I checked out so many books from the library, the librarian probably thought we were teaching classes to pregnant women. The baby was due at the end of February.

In the fall, my fellow first-grade teachers told me about Lamaze classes, and how much the classes had helped them for the birthing process. Of course, Piet and I immediately signed up. We fervently did our homework like good students, working together on the breathing techniques and strategies for having as natural a delivery as possible.

Piet had experimented with an old Dutch tradition of determining the sex of the baby by using a water glass and a piece of string tied to his gold wedding band. With one hand hovering the ring over the water glass and the other hand on my pregnant belly, he watched the ring swing back and forth and proudly declared, "It's a boy!" Not really believing this to be true, I stated we needed to be prepared with both a girl and a boy's name, just in case!

We bought a book overflowing with pages of only baby names, and their derivatives, and after days of discussion, we finally decided on a name. If the baby were a boy, we would call him "Bret" with one 't'—a short name so there would be no nicknames.

As for the possibility of this baby being a girl, Piet and I found no common ground for a girl's name. Weeks led to months of searching and discussing names, to no avail.

Coming home from teaching one September afternoon, I combed through the baby name book for the zillionth time hoping a name would jump out at me. I closed the book in total frustration. At that moment, Piet came rushing into the apartment with a grin on his face. With a triumphant whoop, he told me that he had found a girl's name. IF our baby somehow defied his prediction and appeared in a feminine torso, she would be called: PYRA.

"What??? Pyra???" I uttered in total disbelief. "Whoever heard of that name? How on earth did you find a name like that?" With that special twinkle in his eyes, he pulled me onto his lap, gave me a huge hug and kiss and proceeded to share how he had "found" the name.

"It's really the best," he beamed, proudly. "I made it up: P for Piet; Y for Yvonne; R for Rumreich; A for Aarden! She will have each of our initials. Pyra is a Greek derivative of fire. The baby really was created in our FIERY passion of lovemaking!! See, isn't it just the greatest name ever??"

That night I woke with a start. Thinking of the name, I grabbed Piet's shoulder to awaken him and ask if he was really serious about the name. Groggily, he assured me that it definitely was the best ever. Then he turned over and immediately went back to sleep. I, on the other hand, tossed and turned and tried to come to grips with the name, "Pyra." Yes, it was unique, but…

Things did not get any better when I shared this news with the four other first-grade teachers the next day. "Pyra??? What kind of name was that?" After I explained the reasoning behind the name, my colleagues then offered a few of the possible nicknames she would endure: Pyrea,- Diahhrea, Pyromaniac, Pyrex, and Pirate (to recall a just a few). Undaunted by all of this, Piet insisted "Pyra" was the name of all names. I really hoped and prayed that the Dutch ring trick was accurate in its prediction of a male baby.

By the time the trees took on Mother Nature's rainbow hues, we made plans for moving into the basement. We had enough furniture for the three rooms, but would have to find kitchen appliances, as well as a washer and dryer. In the evenings, we searched the newspaper ads for used appliances. Our first call was to a commercial kitchen that was getting rid of a white-enameled, double sink, with extensions on each side and lots of shelving space underneath. $50.00 and it was ours if we would come and get it. The red pickup was there the next day and we now had a place to wash dishes and future babies!

Another ad was for a double-oven stove that was advertised as "almost new." This time Dad, Piet, and I drove to the house to look at it. The dear old lady that met us at the door was weeping and saying her husband had died and she had to move to a small apartment. To help with her expenses, she was selling her appliances. We felt sorry for her, but were thrilled when we saw the stove. We would take her washer, dryer, and refrigerator, as well, and the slop sink in the basement. The prices were right. We decided to transport the double-oven stove first and come back for the other appliances the next day.

The weeping woman held the door as Piet and Dad lifted the huge stove and carried it outside. Just as Dad stepped down, he missed a step and the stove hit the cement and chipped and dented one side. Now there were two weeping women to contend with. "OH, no!" cried the woman, "It was like new, and now look at it." I tried to control my sobs when I saw the stricken look on my dad's face. Then I tried to console him as well as the former owner. It was a quiet ride back to Wisconsin.

We now had the appliances we needed to live in the basement, and all at a terrific bargain. Our purchases fit snugly in the room that we would come to call the kitchen, laundry, and dining room. Piet found a cheap, white-metal cabinet to place over the sink to hold dishes. Dad took on the role of plumber and Piet became the electrician as they connected all the appliances. We added our dining room table and chairs to complete the multi-purpose room. It did not require many steps to complete the meal, wash the dishes, and put in a load of laundry. The dining room table converted into my sewing area after the evening meals. Small, ground-level windows on the north and east sides brought in natural light. Cozy and efficient were definitely words to describe this useful room.

The room that served as our bedroom didn't have windows. (It would later become the cellar for canned goods and Piet's winemaking.) Our queen-sized bed barely fit, with a little room to squeeze in a small dresser. Piet constructed a rod to hang our clothes. It was tight quarters, but we had a place to sleep, and never had to worry about being awakened by the sun's light.

The middle room in the basement was our living room. It contained furniture from our apartment. At least it had a ground-level window on the west wall so we had some of Mother Nature's lighting. As for the bathroom, we walked up five cement steps to reach it on the first landing. Piet had designed a tuck-under garage, positioned underneath our future master bedroom. The inside door of the garage led into a hallway on the right and a small bathroom to the left. When you entered our house from the garage, you could go down five steps to the basement, or up ten steps to the future kitchen and living room area.

The wide hallway on ground level became a storage area for everything we couldn't fit into the three basement rooms. In the bathroom, Piet installed a white, metal, enclosed shower, a toilet, and a sink with a medicine cabinet above it. In the corner next to the shower stall, he placed the oil heater for our hot water heating system throughout the house. Piet had done his homework and said heating with hot water was much more efficient and economical than forced air or electrical.

When we moved to Hudson, Wisconsin, in the fall of 1972, we decided to not share the story of our past religious vocations. We wanted people to get to know us as Piet and Yvonne—a social worker and a teacher. We just wanted to be ORDINARY people and not singled out as, "Those two: Ex-priest and ex-nun."

It wasn't that we were ashamed of our past, but we had already experienced strange reactions when people learned we had been a priest and a nun. People would put up their guard and say such things as, "Oh, oh, don't say that around them. Remember who they were!" Or, "I'd say something, but you know who is here: The exes!"

In Hudson, we attended Saturday evening Mass at St. Patrick's Catholic Church. We discovered there was nobody in the parish to lead the singing. It seemed logical that we would offer our music leadership for this new parish, like we had done in St. Paul. We talked with the assistant priest, Fr. Doohge. He couldn't believe his ears and asked when we could start.

Piet and I became the Saturday evening Mass music providers. Several months later, the pastor, Fr. Anton, asked Piet if he had ever been a lector. With Piet's affirmative answer, the priest asked Piet to take over the readings. A few weeks later, they needed another person to distribute communion. Had Piet ever done that? Affirmative answer. Before we knew it, Piet was leading the singing, distributing Communion, and serving as a regular lector. Not only that, but Father Anton would never turn down an invitation to come to our place for a home-cooked meal. Bea, his sister and housekeeper, came as well, along with Fr. Dhooge. Naturally, we felt extremely comfortable with all of them. We shared food, drink, and stories, but the topic of our past never surfaced.

From our home in Hudson, I drove a half hour every day into St. Paul to teach my first-graders, and Piet drove twenty minutes into Stillwater to work with his inmates. We had joined the Wisconsin "bedroom community" of commuters living in Wisconsin who crossed the St. Croix River every day to work.

Orval Iverson, our school principal, infrequently visited our little Battle Creek Annex school, located about ten minutes from the main school building. He realized he had very efficient teachers and staff to run it. That was his reason for seldom interfacing with us. This situation was a delight for us all. We were very capable women and knew we ran the school extremely proficiently and successfully, without a principal.

In early December, Orval appeared at our school. After he came into my classroom, he asked if he could talk with me during recess. After much hemming and hawing, he finally said, "Mrs. Aarden, when is your baby due?" Being so excited about my pregnancy, I told him that my baby was due to arrive in February. He stated that I was definitely looking very pregnant, and that I should take maternity leave at the first of the year. "That way the children would not be asking lots of questions, and it would be an easier transition for them to have a substitute when they returned from Christmas vacation." Case closed.

I could not believe my ears! I was so healthy and feeling great. Piet and I had already decided that when the baby was born, I would quit teaching and stay at home to raise our children. It would be a sacrifice to live on only one paycheck, but I had not planned on having this happen so soon. But this was the 70s and one did not question administrative decisions.

(Right) Wild berries were a major benefit of our homestead. They were great in jams and jellies, and Piet later utilized the local fruit for wine-making purposes.

(Below) The winding road up to our home in the woods.

Piet worked tirelessly on the construction of our home. My dad was a big help, too!

CHAPTER SEVEN
Working on our House and Having Babies: 1973-74

My unemployed life began a week before Christmas. I busied myself with Christmas preparations, sewing Christmas gifts, and preparing for motherhood with Lamaze classes. I spent hours reading parenting books and enjoyed having the leisure of preparing our evening meals.

In 1973 Piet was able to contract a forty-hour week, with ten-hour workdays, four days a week. This gave us long weekends to work on our home, without major interruptions. My outside world experiences had switched to inside world experiences of basement living. Since our acreage was part of a new housing development, I knew no one.

Our volunteering at St. Patrick's spread to other areas in the parish when they learned I was on leave. The parish needed people to teach catechism to the senior high students. January of 1973 saw us meeting with the students in a dingy church basement. The kids wanted a meeting place for social activities, as well as doctrine instruction. They wondered if we could fix up the basement to become a teen center for them.

The next thing we knew, we were involved in getting parishioners to help with the project of creating a space that would meet the needs and wants of the high school crowd. People came to help paint, and others donated furniture and decorations to make the space inviting and relaxing. We even had a phonograph and lots of lamps to create a cozy atmosphere. A celebration party for the teens—complete with pizza and pop donated by a local business—topped the evening when we finished.

As January progressed, with no neighbors and no one to talk to, the days dragged by in the basement. Talking to family and friends was long-distance calling, and that cost too much money. So I spent my time talking and singing to my child in-utero, and being amazed at all the latest kicks and movements within my pregnant body. January became a long month of waiting—waiting for the baby to be born, waiting for Piet to come home every afternoon, waiting for the snow to stop as it covered the window openings... I couldn't wait for February to arrive.

The month of February came and went and no sign of the child within wanting to come out. Piet worked every day after supper on the upper levels of our home. We knew the construction of the kitchen needed to be complete before we tried to move upstairs. That was far from finished.

Our baby would have to sleep in the basement living room for several months, but we could live with that. The baby wouldn't know the difference. With one more person downstairs, it would just make it that much cozier!

On the morning of March 1st, Piet asked how I was doing. I mentioned that I felt somewhat different and had a few cramps. He assured me he was only a phone call away if anything further developed.

That afternoon I began having some severe contractions. I called my doctor to see what to do. After describing the frequency of contractions, he said it would be wise to get myself to the hospital. My heart beat rapidly as I nervously called the prison to tell the latest news to Piet. Before I could explain anything, the prison operator told me that they could not accept any outside calls. The prison was being shut down due to a riot. With that, she hung up the phone.

I looked outside. Snow was falling heavily and trees were swaying in the wind. What must it be like out in the open areas? I couldn't have this baby out in the woods all alone. Just as certainly, I couldn't be driving with these frequent contractions. Not being able to think of any other possible solutions, I grabbed the phone and impatiently dialed the prison once again. As soon as the operator answered, I screamed, "This is Piet Aarden's wife and I'm having a baby. HELP! I'm alone in the woods with nobody to help me. I need him right now!"

The operator told me to take it easy. She was not sure where Piet was, due to the riot, but she would try to track him down. What seemed like ages—and several contractions—later, an excited and nervous Piet came to the phone. He told me to hang in there. He would be home in less than a half hour. I was to have my things all ready for the hospital.

I timed each contraction and thought Piet would never arrive. As I heard the crunching of car tires in the snow, I waddled up the stairs to meet Piet as he opened the hallway door. Falling into his arms, I cried and begged him to help me into the car and drive as fast as he could. I didn't want to have the baby on the way to the hospital. With near-blizzard conditions and a wife moaning with each contraction, Piet managed to get us to Miller Hospital in St. Paul in short order. I hobbled out of the car. Piet rushed to help me. I was sure this baby would be there any minute.

As we went through admission procedures, I asked them to please hurry: This baby wanted out! My doctor examined me, smiled encouragingly and said, "My dear, you are only dilated to three. You need to walk the halls. I'll come back in a few hours to check on you."

WHAT?? Only three centimeters? Oh, no, that couldn't be. But it was. I called my sister, Flo, who was an OBGYN nurse who had given birth to five babies of her own. She laughed and said, "Just keep walking; it'll be a while. Listen to your nurses and doctor."

Hours and hours later, I lay in the birthing room with Piet writing down every contraction as it began and ended. Finally, he said, "Yvonne, my hand is sore. I've filled two pages back and front writing down the times. Can't I stop doing this?"

Exhausted and weary from experiencing what seemed like a million contractions, I still had the strength to tell him where to go. Did he have the audacity to complain about writing down the contraction times? Did he have no sense of compassion? How could he complain about a little cramp in his fingers when I was birthing his child?! How was I to know that it took so long for a birth to happen?

Eleven hours later, at 1:27 am on March 2, 1973, our first child emerged into this world. All pain was forgotten upon seeing this amazing miracle materialize. Piet's Dutch ring trick had worked: We indeed had a boy and his name was BRET! He was a healthy eight pounds and eight ounces, measuring twenty-one inches long, with lusty lungs.

(Bret was our big news, but the newspaper headlines for March 2 were the return of U.S.A. servicemen from Vietnam known as MIA and POW's. Two totally different "homecomings!")

Life took on a different form when we brought our new baby home and settled into learning how to become loving, doting parents 24/7. I wanted to breastfeed and do everything the "natural way." I discovered a LaLeche group of women, in the nearby town of River Falls. Attending weekly meetings, I learned how to nurse on demand and soon our chunky, ever-hungry baby was keeping me busy with his demands night and day. Being a full-time mother was my new occupation and kept me not only busy, but also contented and thrilled to be a mom.

On March 17, Fr. Dhooge baptized Bret in St. Patrick's Church with my sister, Mary, and her husband, Dan, as his godparents. Piet and I recycled our wedding banner by sewing the baptismal candle symbol onto our wedding rings. We added the name of Bret beside the candle to symbolize what an integral part of our lives he had become. A parishioner volunteered to hold Bret during Saturday Masses, so Piet and I could continue leading the singing.

Piet played with Bret after coming home from work, daily. After supper, Piet worked into the night, trying to get the upstairs ready for occupancy. Bret's crib was in our living area, since there was no room for another bed in our crowded bedroom. We decorated the wall behind Bret's crib with nursery rhyme pictures. Piet's homemade wooden mobile animals with bright colors swirled over Bret's crib. The rhythmic sounds of Piet's pounding nails and buzzing of saws became Bret's lullaby. He slept peacefully with a cherubic smile on his face, as if he was truly aware of how much he was loved and cherished.

With the severity of the cold Wisconsin winter, and the gigantic snowdrifts surrounding our home, I realized I had to create my own indoor activities. We were warm and snug in the cocoon of our well-insulated basement. I passed time in my isolated world by listening to music, reading books, cooking, and sewing. I missed teaching, but the joys of holding my new baby and seeing him develop each day were like watching a miracle unfold in front of my eyes.

I was so scared I would do something wrong when I had to clean the little belly button appendage and his circumcised penis. Never having had a brother, I was wading into new territory. Nervously, I changed his diapers and hoped he wouldn't unexpectedly spray me, or that I wouldn't accidentally prick him with the big safety pin. Bret was a wiggler and must have sensed my newness in motherhood. Cleaning messy cloth diapers and folding his tiny clothing were part of this new motherhood experience.

That March, shortly after Bret was born, my parents came to visit us. Near our home, they stopped to help a young woman having car trouble, and they learned that she and her husband and baby girl had just moved into the basement of their home, also. Her name was Becky and her husband's name was Dave. Mom learned that Dave had grown up in Erskine, Minnesota on the same Indian Reservation I had. He, too, was building their house, as they could afford it. Their little girl, Amy, was three months older than Bret. Becky told my parents that she was experiencing loneliness living out in the "boonies." Mom and Dad got her phone number and told Becky they were sure I would be calling her soon. That was the start of our lifelong friendship!

Bret now had a new "girlfriend," as did I. Amy and Bret were such compatible babies. They laughed and cooed as Becky and I spent hours sharing our life stories. We took turns visiting each other in our basement homes. We tried to help one another as first-time mothers. This brought both laughter and tears.

On April 6th, Bret and I visited my former first-graders, so I could show them the pride and joy of my life outside of school.

That spring, Piet decided his new son needed a pet in his life—a dog. One of the prison guards had been telling Piet about the litter of pups his favorite dog had just given birth to. Was Piet interested? These puppies needed good homes. A few weeks later, a mutt named Price became Bret's constant companion—outside of the house, that is. My mom had never let us have animals in our home. I was definitely going to keep up that tradition. Besides that, our basement home did not need another addition. So, Piet built an insulated doghouse from our left-over lumber. It was fit for the prince called Price. Why hadn't Piet called him PRINCE? Instead, he chose to call him Price, because that was the name of one of his favorite dogs when he was a priest.

Since it was a warm spring, we were able to let Bret sit in a portable swing outside many afternoons. Price became Bret's bodyguard and stood like a proud sentinel watching his "prince" swing back and forth. As soon as the swing stopped, Price licked Bret and Bret tried to return the favor. There was a special boy-dog bond that developed between the two and lasted until the dog's dying day.

The first week of June, Bret learned how to turn over in his crib. From then on his movements were a delight to behold. Added to that, he began to laugh aloud that same week.

In August of that year, we moved our beds upstairs. On August 18th, Bret began to crawl. We needed to look at "baby-proofing" our home. A gate had to be placed on the steps going up to the bedrooms.

The master bedroom was unfinished, with open studs for the walls, but it was filled with sunlight and a view of the beautiful wooded environment surrounding us. The change from crowded, windowless quarters to spaciousness was a gift in and of itself. We had floor-to-ceiling windows on two sides that overlooked our guardian oak tree and the rest of Mother Nature's green-leafed forest. No window coverings were needed, and each season brought its colorful beauty as we peered out the windows each morning and evening. It was like living in a national park without the visitors! The sounds and sights of Mother Nature were ours to enjoy night and day.

We moved Bret's crib into his new bedroom that also had unfinished walls with open studs. In between the studs, there were sheets of spun glass insulation. Since the bedrooms were small, I had placed Bret's crib close to the wall. I thought nothing of that location until one afternoon, when I went to get Bret from his nap. He was happily tearing off a piece of insulation and putting it into his mouth. I screamed and grabbed him while trying to get the fiberglass out of his mouth. Needless to say, everything was all right, as he had not finished chewing his new "snack," but I moved the crib to the center of the bedroom. Our next project was to drop everything else and install the paneling in his room! The 70s were the era of wall paneling, so we decided to panel every room rather than sheet-rock and paint the walls.

Our kitchen sported all new appliances. Having a flat, CorningWare counter-top stove and built-in double ovens were a luxury. Piet decided we should make the kitchen top-of-the-line, and installed a powerful, Nutone, built-in food center—no cords for all my appliances such as a blender, food processor, meat grinder, juicer, and mixer. It was pure luxury, and so appreciated as I cooked and baked to my heart's delight with an uncluttered countertop.

Our entire home was built with ceiling-to-floor windows in every room to reflect the changing scenes of our picturesque outdoors. The three-season porch changed to a four-season room, separated from the living room by sliding glass doors. Each week brought new advancements as we added insulation in the inner walls, paneling, bathroom fixtures, ceilings, or whatever was part of Piet's plan for the week. Gradually our home began to take on the features of a "real" home, and I was pregnant once again.

One Saturday in early September, Becky and I decided to pick apples at a local orchard. After we had picked our bushel of apples, we stood in line to pay. Suddenly, I had severe cramping and blood began oozing down my legs. We panicked and left our bushels of apples right there. Becky drove full speed to get me home. She said she would take care of Bret and not to worry. Piet needed to get me to the River Falls hospital immediately; the hemorrhaging wouldn't stop. We lost another child that evening. I was two months along with this pregnancy, but my life had been endangered by the severe blood loss. Transfusions were necessary, but I would be all right with some bed rest. Questions were whirling in my head. Would we be able to have more children? Why was I having another miscarriage? What was wrong with me? Would we not even have the two children Piet wanted?

The doctor warned us it would be wise to wait several months before trying to get pregnant again. (I don't think the doctor knew of our past history: We had a lot of "catching up" to do.) We did not heed his words very well. In November we were once again expecting another child.

Bret took his first steps at my parents' home that Thanksgiving. To celebrate his first Christmas, Bret "baptized" the Baby Jesus—in the manger under our Christmas tree—with my unfinished cup of coffee he found nearby. He also scattered all the Christmas cards around the living room floor. There were a few more lessons on baby-proofing his surroundings that we needed to learn, including: NOT to touch the hot glass of the fireplace; NOT to try to climb up onto the recliner; NOT to open all of the cupboard doors and spill out all their contents... How to put all those negative commands into positive, kid language?

No place was safe anymore. In one of the many parenting magazines, someone suggested dividing a child's toys into seven containers, one for each day of the week. Wanting to establish the best environment I could to encourage creativity, I prepared seven grocery bags and labeled them for each day of the week. Each bag contained different toys and books. Every morning I emptied the contents of that day's bag into the empty seasonal room, played stimulating music, closed the sliding glass doors, and watched the "magic" take place. That gave me time to complete a few household chores as our son discovered that day's treasures. Operation successful! How would this work when Bret's sibling arrived?

So we could enjoy walks in the winter wonderland surrounding us, Piet built Bret a wooden sled with protective sides that could be pushed by one of us. Price loved walking beside his little master and licking his face whenever we slowed down. Bret's giggles only encouraged the dog, and a playful banter followed at every stop along the walk. The months flew by. All was progressing well with our home as well as with our baby who turned a year old in March.

Fr. Dooghe, the assistant priest, started coming more frequently to our home and we became close friends. During one of his visits, the talk turned to theology, and he wondered where we had received our background knowledge. Piet looked at him and laughingly said, "You really haven't discovered our backgrounds after all this time?" Father looked at us and said, "What have I not been aware of?" With that, we poured out our story. He sat there with his mouth gaping open. He just shook his head in bewilderment.

His immediate response was, "Whatever happens, we can NOT let Fr. Anton know this. He would never let you continue helping. He can't accept the fact that priests leave, much less that they marry nuns. This has to be our secret. I do not want to lose the two of you!"

That spring, Piet and I decided it was time to visit his family in the Netherlands. The best time for Piet to take a vacation was in June, but by then I would be seven months pregnant. Would the doctor allow me to fly at that time? "Only if you promise to get up and waddle down the airplane aisle every forty-five minutes," was the doctor's response. He then added that Holland was a very safe place to have a child, so if the baby came early, the doctors there would take good care of me.

It was the era of charter flights. They were the cheapest way to fly, but had flights only on certain days to different areas. Room was limited on the plane, and Piet's long legs were scrunched tightly, while my pregnant belly took up most of the space in front of me. In these cramped quarters, we took turns holding Bret on the eight-hour journey.

Since Bret had not paid for his ride, the attendant explained that they did not have a food tray for him. We must share our food with him. Bret was was like a bottomless pit, and he managed to eat most of our food. All we could do was grin and bear it. We could eat when we got to his family, a three-hour ride from the airport.

Piet's brother and dad met us at the Brussels airport. We were soon squished into the back seat of his brother's small car. Ten minutes outside the airport, it began to rain. As Piet's brother tried to turn onto the main road, there was a horrific crashing sound as his car collided with another.

Damaged, the car could not be driven. We were all OK but shaken up by the accident. We had to wait hours for a tow truck. In the meantime, Bret began to cry with hunger.

A small Tupperware container filled with soda crackers was the only food we had. I rationed those and hoped Bret would soon fall asleep in exhaustion. The tow truck finally arrived. I was too scared to sleep.

Piet's brother had to get in the truck with the driver to give directions to the little village that was our destination. That meant Piet had to steer, while their dad sat calmly and quietly next to him. Since his dad knew no English, I had no one to talk to. Bret devoured the crackers and soon after we were being towed, he fell asleep. It was a quiet, long ride as Piet had to concentrate on steering. He had to try to figure out when the tow-truck would make sudden turns to get on and off the highway. The driver did not use his turn signals very often.

The truck driver suddenly began to speed up. I was totally uncomfortable and nervous. Those lurching movements made me wonder if I would be adding to all the excitement by having our baby right then and there.

Five hours later, the tow truck dropped us at his brother's doorstep. The worried family members filled the street, rushing outside to find out what had happened. There had been no way to let them know about the car accident. Martien's wife was distraught with worry. We were all OK, but totally exhausted. What a way to start our Dutch visit.

Piet, Bret, and I must have been quite a sight for the Dutch people as we rode our bikes around the village. People would come out of their homes to watch the American couple bicycle past. Piet's baby-back carrier was a novelty for them. Add to that picture, a very pregnant woman with her unsteady, slow biking, trying to keep up with her skillful, Dutch husband with the baby on his back.

Bret's babbling was as foreign to Piet's family as their Dutch was to him, but he won their hearts, especially that of his Opa. Piet's dad had his own cows. He made a rich vanilla pudding every day for himself, since he had some stomach issues. After

Bret and Piet's Dad

offering some of his pudding to Bret at our first visit, Opa soon learned he had to make a double batch. His new grandson could never seem to get enough of this tasty substance. It became a ritual of beginning and ending the days with Opa's specialty pudding. To watch the pleased smile of Piet's dad as he gazed on this firstborn child of the son whom he had lost to American soil, was a sight that remains forever in my heart and mind. While Opa lived, he always had extra pudding for his American grandson.

When we returned home from Holland, we continued working on the house and preparing for our next baby. In August, the wild berries were in full bloom. Piet helped me pick them so I could make jam and jellies for our larder. Since there were a plethora of berries, Piet decided to try his hand at converting some of the berries into wine. I had been using our former downstairs bedroom as my cannery. Piet said it could serve as a multi-purpose room: A winery, as well as a cannery.

He checked out different ways of making homemade wine and decided to try the old-fashioned method of placing balloons on each bottle. After filling them with the berry juice, yeast, and sugar mixture, the balloons expanded as the sugar turned to alcohol. The released gas filled the balloons. When the fermentation was finished, the balloons would deflate. This took about six weeks. Sometimes the wine was quite tasty, but other times it was less than tolerable.

Being a perfectionist, Piet decided to deepen his research into the art of winemaking. Soon, new plastic trash barrels were filled with brewing berries. Piet employed scientific, precise methods by using special wine tablets and precise directions for achieving drinkable results. One day he discovered a rhubarb-wine recipe and hit the jackpot. No longer did he spend unending hours meticulously picking tiny, wild grapes. The berries were replaced by rhubarb. Nearby farmers grew the perennial, red and green rhubarb, so there was never a lack of this prolific plant. They gladly let Piet pick it for them regularly during the summer. He used our powerful food processor to chop rhubarb stalks into pieces. These were put into the plastic containers, along with all the ingredients needed for fermentation. (When the smell of his fermenting rhubarb mingled with the smell of my fermenting cabbage, it was wise to avoid entering the room containing our products.)

Piet's homemade rhubarb wine became his trademark. His Aarden wine specialty became white and rosé wines, resulting from the rhubarb's color. The white resembled a Chardonnay, and the red a mild rosé wine. He never had undrinkable wine again, as he constantly perfected his art of winemaking.

To store his hundreds of bottles, he built angular shelves in our canning/winery room. (Neighbors collected their used wine bottles so he never had to buy bottles—just the corks!) Frugality was definitely another of Piet's trademarks. As for the Aarden's, we never bought a bottle of commercial wine again while we lived in Wisconsin. Piet loved making his wine and everyone loved drinking it.

Late in the afternoon of August 18th, I began having contractions as I was boiling berries for jelly. Piet was in the woods picking more berries. I remembered how long it had taken for Bret to be born, so I decided to finish my task of making twenty jars of chokecherry jelly. As I was finishing up, the contractions were coming much more frequently, so I went outside to try to find Piet. Yelling loudly that our baby was coming, I saw him emerge from the woods with his bucket of berries.

I called Becky to ask if we could leave Bret with them. Piet was nowhere in sight. I found him downstairs in the basement kitchen cleaning the berries. How could he not realize how little time we might have before this baby arrived?

I quickly showered only to come into our bedroom to find Piet picking burrs off his stockings. Honestly, there wasn't time for such things. Shouldn't he be ready to race me to the hospital? Was he thinking of that long evening of contractions when Bret was born? He decided he would have time for a quick shower too.

My contractions started coming harder and with more frequency. I grabbed Bret and waddled downstairs to get in our car. Beeping the horn, I yelled that I just didn't think we had much time. Piet arrived on the scene with an unbuckled belt and shoelaces dangling from his shoes. Bret was totally unaware of why we were acting so strangely. We dropped him at Becky and Dave's with no time to spare, according to my contractions.

When we arrived at River Falls, WI, hospital, I just knew this baby was probably going to be born any second. Doctor Hammer examined me, smiled, and said it would be a while. Why didn't we just relax and call him when I was fully dilated? Piet, who did not care for card playing, readily agreed to play cards with me, rather than write down the onset of every contraction. It had been eighteen months since our Lamaze classes. I had forgotten many of the breathing techniques. Hours passed with our card playing being interrupted frequently by my contractions. No complaints from Piet about having cramps in his fingers this time!

Finally, I yelled that I felt like pushing. The nurse came running and saw the baby's head trying to enter this world. The doctor had just been leaving the hospital, but he came rushing back. He told Piet to quickly put on the hospital gown. We hastened to the delivery room. Exhausted from pushing and hours of contractions, I heard the doctor and Piet say together, "It's a girl!"

"Do you have a name for your baby girl?" asked the doctor, very innocently.

Piet immediately interjected, "It's PYRA." Too weary from delivering this feminine bundle of joy, I sighed and lay back in the delivery bed. We were proud parents of a beautiful, healthy girl who would forever be called Pyra. She was an eight-pound girl who arrived at 11:05 pm on August 18th. Bret had a sister to enjoy and cherish.

When Pyra arrived on the scene in 1974, the family that took care of Bret during Saturday Masses did not hesitate to take care of both children. We were busy, but happy on all fronts.

Bret loved his new little sister and gave her constant hugs and kisses whenever anyone was holding her. He, at eighteen months, was definitely her protector! Life with two little ones took on a new routine and busyness that kept us hopping. I was thankful each time I could place Pyra in her crib and have her stay there as I chased her big brother around the house. Bret's love of books and interest in building blocks kept him occupied while I made meals and did household chores. What a joy these two innocents had brought into our lives.

In the fall of 1974, the upstairs bathrooms were completed, and finishing touches around the window frames were added. The tongue-in-groove cedar ceilings in the kitchen, living, and four-season room were added as we could afford the lumber. Getting real carpet was our next big purchase, after the woodwork was finished. We went with the orange and brown shag carpet of the 70s. It matched the burnt orange refrigerator and countertops in the kitchen!

That fall, I sewed oversized, beanbag chairs. We had visions of curling up in them in front of the fireplace to enjoy the warmth and sight of flickering flames. I also envisioned lovely romantic music playing softly in the idyllic background, as we sipped a glass of wine while sharing our day's adventures. Right after we squatted comfortably onto the beanbags, Piet set a match to the carefully placed logs in the fireplace. Smoke engulfed the room. My dream quickly vanished and became a nightmare. What was wrong? Why was there all this smoke?

Piet discovered that Toby had used an eight-inch flu instead of the twelve-inch that Piet had ordered. Since our home was tucked into the hillside, the draft was poor and we now had an unusable fireplace. By this time, Toby had returned to prison and was unable to to fix his errors. The fireplace was the only thing that Piet had not done himself, and it was a disaster. Toby was in deep trouble, if he ever got parole again!

About a week later, Piet came home with the good news that Toby, our famous bricklayer, was once again on parole. Piet told Toby how upset he was with his fireplace miscalculations. Toby promised to come out to try and solve the problem by building up the outside flu bricks. He even offered to build some stone window boxes for us. We graciously declined and said the fireplace needed his attention. Needless to say, that fireplace never had a good draft. Piet ended up creating a firebox in front of the opening and later was able to build a fan and different apparatus to give us the pleasure of actually seeing logs burn. No matter, the glass required constant cleaning with the sooty deposits.

(Toby ended up back in prison as a lifer and was definitely never again part of our lives.)

Pyra began walking at eleven months and her babbling took on both a Dutch and English mixture. She was a happy baby who loved being around people. After learning to be an independent mover, she followed her brother constantly, and wanted to do whatever he did. The four-season room still held no furniture and made a lovely play space for Bret and Pyra as they explored the "new" bag of toys and books every day.

At age two, Pyra was singing the ABC's in rare tunes and sequences and loved trying to play her big brother's ukulele. Music was definitely a key part of the Aarden family life. Bret had become a constant question mark at age three, and Pyra had become an "independent live-wire" who kept us laughing and enjoying her antics.

Life was good.

Bret and Pyra.

CHAPTER EIGHT
Rejected by the Church: 1976-1977

Our lives changed with a phone call. It was one October evening in 1976. I called Fr. Anton to tell him that our Women's Guild wanted to have space in the weekly bulletin to advertise a rummage sale for the parish. As soon as Father answered, he said, "You know, Yvonne, it's providential that you called. I just received a letter from the bishop, and you can't be active in our church anymore."

I let out an earth-shattering yell, "WHAT??"

The pastor had learned of our past, and he was totally upset. I dropped the phone, crying. Piet rushed over and said, "Who is this? What is wrong?"

Fr. Anton reiterated that he was holding a letter from the bishop stating we could attend St. Patrick's Church and contribute money, but that was the extent of our permitted participation. Piet told him that this was not acceptable and that we needed to talk and see the letter.

"I don't have time to see you, but I will send the letter so you can see for yourself," was the answer.

"No," interjected Piet, angrily. "You will see us in person and discuss this face-to-face. We have been volunteering our time and talents every time there was a need, for the past five years. You do NOT dismiss this with a phone call and a letter."

The priest hung up and we were left in a dazed bewilderment. How could he do this to us? We had our papers to prove we had all the rights of lay people. What had happened? We needed to get to the root of this.

Fr. Dooghe came over the next evening. He told us a wealthy and conservative contributor to St. Patrick's Church had relatives who were members of St. Paschal's in St. Paul, where we had volunteered. Somehow the Aardens came up in their conversation. It was shared that we had been a priest and a nun. The Hudson parishioners then asked Fr. Anton if he knew that he had an ex-priest and former nun active in his church.

At the same time, the bishop of our Wisconsin diocese visited the parish for Confirmation. Fr. Anton shared his new information, and wondered what he should do. Rather than offering to talk to us and find out our story, the archconservative bishop said he would write a letter telling this couple they could no longer be active members.

We explained to Fr. Dhooge that Fr. Anton would not take the time to meet with us. Fr. Dhooge reiterated how conservative the pastor was, and how difficult it was to live with him in the same rectory. He told us to continue our attempts to set up a meeting with the pastor. A few days later, when I went to the mailbox, I found an envelope addressed to Mr. & Mrs. Piet Aarden from Fr. Anton. There was no explanation, only the following letter inside the envelope:

> OFFICE OF THE BISHOP Diocese of Superior
> 11201 Hughitt Ave.
> Superior, Wisconsin 54880
>
> October 18, 1976
> Reverend Alex Anton St. Patrick Parish
> 321 St. Croix
> Hudson, Wisconsin 54016
>
> Re: Exclusion of Dispensed Priests from Functions in the Church
>
> Dear Father Anton:
>
> Last Saturday, when Father Hoffman and I stopped to visit you, Father Keilen and your sister, Bea, you asked about the participation in the liturgy by a priest who has been dispensed from the obligations of celibacy and who is married to a former nun, properly dispensed from her vows. They live in your parish and are active in your liturgies, he as a lector and she as organist. It now has become known among your parishioners who they are, and as a result, you have received some strong reactions from some of your parishioners about their participation in liturgical celebrations. I agree with their position and protests. They conform to the official position of the Church.
>
> I am enclosing a copy of a document to that effect which a dispensed priest must sign. I do knot know if all bishops and major religious Superiors of men require that such dispensed priests sign a document like this, but all should know the official position of the Church and convey it at least orally to the dispensed priest. Even if that is not done, the dispensed knows about it because there have been news articles in the past ten years on the problem. Even if a dispensed priest should happen not to know about these restrictions on his participation in various capacities within the Church, he will have to accept them when he is informed of them. If he is a man of understanding and goodwill, he will do so. He should acknowledge that he can never be a divisive force within the Church which has granted him a dispensation for his personal and spiritual good. As the recipient of a special favor from the Church, he should acknowledge that he can never inflict himself on a particular parish and its parishioners if his presence and participation cause the parishioners to

become disturbed about his participation in the life of the parish or to defect from the Faith. I could enlarge on these points, but I am sure you know what I am trying to say. Briefly, what I am saying is this: "If you wanted a personal favor for yourself and if it is granted for your spiritual good, be content with your new condition of life subject to the restrictions of the Church. You have no other choice if you were conscientious in presenting your petition and in accepting the dispensation. You will have to live according to the directives of the Church."

Whenever I face a situation which is divisive, and there are many, I cite a quotation from the Gospel of St. John, Chapter 17, verse 12, in which at the Last Supper St. John quotes Christ as follows: "As long as I was with them, I guarded them with Your name, which you gave Me. I kept careful watch and not one of them was lost, none but he who was destined to be lost in fulfillment of the Scripture."

I have found this quotation to be very effective because if any sincere person, even if he believes he is right, will yield to my obligation to preserve the faith of everyone and not to cause anyone to defect from it.

I could write more, but I hope that what I have written will be helpful to you in terminating this particular priest's participation in your parish liturgies and other parish functions.

There is no restriction placed on dispensed nuns. However, in this case, since she is married to a dispensed priest, she will not be able to continue as organist or in any other parochial function. That is my decision. Because of her marriage to a dispensed priest, she has to accept the restrictions which have been placed on him.

With kindest regards and best wishes, I remain,

Very sincerely in Christ,
George A. Hammes
Bishop of Superior

Upon reading the letter, we were stunned and furious and demanded a session with Father Anton. He refused again and again. We decided to write to the Apostolic Delegate in Washington, D.C. to explain our situation and hope to put an end to the banishment we were suffering. In early November we received his response:

APOSTOLIC DELEGATION UNITED STATES OF AMERICA NO. 3347/76
3339 Massachusetts Avenue
Washington, D.C. 20008
November 5, 1976

Mr. Piet Aarden
Rural Route One
Hudson, WI 54016

Dear Mr. Aarden:

I wish to acknowledge and thank you for the kind letter of October 31st, 1976.

> It is regrettable that your status as a laicized priest was not clearly known to the Bishop and certain permissions obtained prior to your participation in the local Parish and its liturgical celebrations. I share this because I believe such an action would have avoided much subsequent pain and embarrassment. However, I must inform you that the Bishop is fully within the limits of his jurisdiction in the restrictions that he has imposed on you and your wife.
>
> The difficulty and frustration that is yours can be appreciated. To protest the decision most likely will only cause further tension and exacerbate the situation. It is my suggestion, tendered with heartfelt concern for you and Yvonne, that your service to the Catholic Community be more in the line of attending to the social needs of the poor and distressed rather than strictly liturgical or catechetical functions. So much needs to be done in this area. Such activity can also be most rewarding.
>
> Be assured of my prayers on behalf of you and your wife.
>
> With cordial and kind regards, I remain.
>
> Sincerely yours in Christ,
> Jean Jadot
> Apostolic Delegate

Another slap in the face. This Apostolic Delegate did not know us, or all the social work we were already doing in our community, much less the fact that Piet took a lesser-paying job to be able to work with prisoners. There seemed no other recourse than to present our case before the parish council. Our many friends and neighbors were willing to attend and testify, if needed.

The night we were to present our case, Piet was called for an emergency meeting at the prison, and I was left to take over. We had written our testimony, so it was only a matter of reading it.

When my cohort of friends and I arrived at the meeting, I was told that we were last on the agenda. I waited and listened as the parish council spent forty-five minutes discussing whether to remove the current communion rail or leave it in its place.

When my turn finally arrived, I looked at Fr. Anton and the parish council. I said how amazing it was to listen to the lengthy, heated discussion about the removal of an inanimate structure, such as a communion rail. Compare that to a hasty, spur-of-the-moment decision by Fr. Anton and the bishop to remove two people from the parish who had given of themselves and their talents for the previous five years. This was done without asking us for any information. We were not invited to give our side of the story, or a chance of rebuttal. Talk about injustice!

I then shared our written rebuttal which told our side of the story. It outlined our connections with the parish: Piet and I never refused when we were asked to do more than what we were already volunteering to do. We freely gave hours every week helping with the liturgical music on

Saturday evenings, and for funerals, or whenever needed on special Sundays. Piet and I developed catechetical lessons for the senior high students and helped them totally renovate the old church basement into an instructional and fun area. We had created opportunities for weekend retreats for the high school kids, as well. Was the Parish Council aware of my involvement with the Women's Guild, and that I had taken on officer positions and leadership roles? Did they know that we sacrificed our time to help the elderly in the parish?

We had given freely and never asked for anything in return. Yet, we were removed from the parish without any explanation or discussion. Fr. Anton had discovered, from a wealthy family within the parish, that a former priest and nun were performing liturgical services under his very nose. He never so much as came to our home to inquire if this was true, though he had certainly spent many evenings enjoying meals and conversations at our home. Whenever he needed something, we were always there for him and the parish.

With that, Fr. Anton rose up in anger and said I had no right to be there. The council called for dismissal, despite the fact that many of our friends wanted to speak. I left in tears, not believing what I had just heard, seen, and experienced. This was Christianity in action? I could not accept such behavior. How I wished Piet had been there with me to witness this horrific meeting! Were Piet and I wearing a huge "A" like Hester Prynne? Was this the very same Church for which we had each given fifteen years of celibacy, work, and dedication of our total selves? Was there no justice—much less love, and compassion—in this institution called the Catholic Church?

The days following the disastrous meeting with the Parish Council, Piet and I called Fr. Anton several times. Finally, he agreed to a meeting at the rectory. The meeting was not amicable. At the onset of the meeting, he stood up, shook his finger at Piet, and yelled, "Once a priest, always a priest!" He would not back down on anything he had said or done. If we chose to leave the priesthood and convent, then we needed to abide by the bishop's decisions, and that was that.

We learned from Fr. Dooghe that Fr. Anton had even gone to the meeting of diocesan priests in the area to warn them about the Aardens who just might try to become active in their parishes. We could not believe what we heard. We composed a letter for the local newspaper to publicize the injustices we were experiencing. The local, conservative paper refused to publish it.

During this time, we had several Protestant pastors visit and invite us to be active in their churches. Piet was ready, but I was not. I shared how the Catholic Church had been such a part of my roots. I knew this was not my Church speaking, but a few conservative clergymen. If they chose to be so prejudiced and narrow-minded, we needed to be bigger than they.

We decided to attend Mass at the Newman Center located at the University of River Falls, about ten miles from our home. Piet, as usual, sang with all his might and gusto. Three Sundays in a row, the officiating priest stopped by the pew to say what an amazing voice Piet possessed and how they really could use a song leader for Saturday night Masses. After the third request, we decided we needed to talk with the priest to explain why we were not volunteering to help with the singing.

As we shared our story, the priest smiled and said, "Don't you think I know who you are? I think that what happened to you two is the most unChristian action I have heard of." Piet and I stared at him in disbelief. He then continued, "Please know I do not approve of the bishop's action. We are liberal in our thinking here at the Center, and would love to have you two take over the liturgical music on Saturday evenings."

Could we be hearing correctly? We stood staring at this priest and realized we now had a new church to attend and share our talents with. Participating in the university surroundings would be both inspiring and liberating.

About a year later, this priest was suddenly removed from his post without any warning. We arrived on a Saturday evening for Mass and were greeted by a new priest. He told us that he knew who we were and about our participation in the liturgies at the Newman Center. Then he went on to say that he felt it was his duty to obey the bishop. We were no longer to be a part of the Newman Center liturgies.

The writing was on the wall. The Catholic Church was rejecting us once again. What should we do? We began to look at other possibilities with other religions. Piet then heard that one of his fellow seminarians was now pastor of Guardian Angels Church in Woodbury, Minnesota. Maybe we could attend Mass there and see what might happen. At that point, we were willing to give it one more try before abandoning the Catholic Church totally. Guardian Angels Church was located in the Minnesota St. Paul Archdiocese, so Bishop Hammes had no jurisdiction there. It would require a half-hour drive, but it was worth the try.

As we entered the church, I felt dubious, but I did not want to give up hope that we just might find a fit on the Minnesota side. The music was vibrant and led by a young man with an amazing voice. The words of the hymns were displayed on the walls with a projector, and people attending Mass were very engaged and enthusiastic. Fr. Ken came down toward the people to give his homily, and it seemed as if it were created for us—refugees searching for a safe haven where everyone was welcomed.

At the Kiss of Peace, I turned to shake hands with the person behind me. Startled, I took a second look. It was Fr. Mielke. He had been the assistant pastor at St. Jude's in Mahtomedi when I taught there! Shocked, we shook hands and said we would talk after Mass. He couldn't believe this was happening. Neither could I. There we were, almost ten years later, greeting each other as lay people in a different church.

After Mass, as Piet and I were talking with Don Mielke and trying to catch up with each other's lives, Fr. Ken came over to greet us. He had noticed Piet during the liturgy and wanted to know all about his current life. Before we knew it, he was asking us if we were planning on joining his parish. Piet immediately shared our Wisconsin church rejections and said we could never go through that again.

Hearing our story, Fr. Ken told us that we would definitely be most welcome in his parish. In fact, there were several ex-priests and nuns active in his parish. It was a large parish and offered many opportunities for everyone, and it would be an honor to have us join and participate in any liturgical function we might choose. He suggested we attend different Masses and get a feel for the parish, to see if it would fit our needs.

On the way home, we stopped at IHOP for a pancake breakfast. As the kids were busy coloring their activity pages and waiting for their special pancakes, Piet and I talked about our morning. What a difference there was between the archconservative Wisconsin diocese and this liberating Minnesota diocese. If the rest of the liturgies were like the one we had just experienced, then we might have just found an oasis in our religious desert.

I was excited to meet other ex-priests and nuns with their families. Don Mielke had even married an ex-nun. He shared how special Guardian Angels was, and how pleased he and his wife were with the congregation and all it offered. Maybe we would find peace and happiness in the Catholic Church after all.

After several weeks, we decided to join Guardian Angels and learned that a small group of active parishioners wanted to create a Family Group. Before we knew it, we were on the planning committee for this new group. Jane, the family parish coordinator, just happened to have been an ex-nun married to an ex-priest. They, too, were excited to be involved with the start-up of this new Family Group. Six other couples joined us as we shared visions of what our group could become. That first meeting cemented our willingness to continue our involvement with the Catholic Church.

The idea was to have a small community of like-minded people within the larger community. This group would have monthly adult meetings to discuss theological topics, as well as monthly social get-togethers for entire families. We would plan a yearly family retreat, prepare monthly liturgies for a weekend Mass, and help with needed social issues within the larger parish community. Our new Family Group wanted to be able to teach religion at home to their children. This sounded just great. It would mean that we wouldn't have to be driving Bret and Pyra several times a week for catechism classes.

Soon after our first meeting, Piet and I invited four of the couples to our home for an evening meal. As we sat around the table sharing food, drink, and conversation, we started sharing our life stories. We were engrossed in each story and realized we had a common thread: Each couple had been a priest and a nun, and now all had children.

Then it was time for Chuck and Donna to share. They looked at each other and started to laugh. "Maybe we don't belong here," they said. "We don't seem to have the pre-requisites. In fact, we never even thought of being a priest or a nun!" We all broke up in laughter. To this day, when the couples get together, that story brings lots of laughs.

All the couples agreed that it would be invigorating to become a small community within the larger parish community, because Guardian Angels parish had several thousand members. As part of this smaller group, we would be able to communicate easier and have a feeling of real community. Among the families who had joined the group, Bret and Pyra discovered new friends their own ages.

One of the greatest benefits was to have rich, deep discussions with people of like backgrounds and principles. Since spirituality was key to our group, we decided to plan the first family weekend retreat. We discovered that Onamia, MN, had a Lutheran retreat center called Camp Onamia that fit our needs. How ironic that Piet would be returning to his first U.S.A. place of residence, but this time as a father of two children. We decided that the Crosier Seminary needed to be a field trip, at least for our kids, during retreat weekend.

Because our group contained so many talented people, planning and volunteering for different activities during the weekend retreat was not difficult. Musicians, liturgists, counselors, social workers, teachers—each person used his or her individual talents and became responsible for an activity.

The fall family retreat became a highlight of each year. Camaraderie and close friendships began to form as families became more acquainted. This led to camping weekends, adult suppers that were rotated at the different homes, as well as preparing amazing interactive Sunday liturgies for the whole parish. Our Family Group became enticing for more families. Each year we gained new members. Ah, it was great to be back in the fold again!

Aarden Family Fashions! Hand-crafted by yours truly!

The Aarden Family, 1976.

CHAPTER NINE
Busy Lives: 1976-1980

Despite the good fortune of finding a parish as vibrant as Guardian Angels, I often harbored negative thoughts when I recalled the suffering and injustices we had experienced in our hometown parish. Our kids had to go to another state to attend catechism and other religious activities, instead of attending a parish with their schoolmates. It seemed so unfair. On the other hand, it gave them, and us, wonderful opportunities to be with families who were vibrant and shared the same beliefs as we did.

We lived in Wisconsin, but Piet's job and our church regularly took us across the river into Minnesota. We never once thought of moving back to Minnesota; Piet had poured his heart and soul into creating our home.

We LOVED our location and seclusion in the wilderness. Our home and the woods were a haven for Piet after a stressful day at the prison. Working on our home was his "therapy." The peaceful enclosure of the wooded acreage had a retreat-like feel to us. The woods took on a different personality with the changing of each season, each one more beautiful and breathtaking in its natural beauty than the next.

From early on, Bret loved anything that dealt with musical sounds. So when he turned three, I decided to drive him to a Suzuki studio in St. Paul, on Saturdays, to learn the keyboard. As I watched their teaching techniques, an idea began to germinate. Here I was driving a half hour every Saturday and paying for expensive lessons to have someone else teach keyboard to my son. Why couldn't I do it? I had many years of piano lessons under my belt.

That same fall in 1976, some neighbors wondered if I would teach piano lessons to their kids. I really did miss teaching. Maybe this would be a way for me to earn some money and keep my fingers in the teaching field. I, myself, had started learning piano with the Robert Schaum piano method, but what else was available now?

I researched the Robert Pace group piano method and learned that I could take classes in the Twin Cities to become a Pace teacher. I signed up for their piano pedagogy classes. The Robert Pace certificate gave me the credentials, and within several months, I was busy planning my own studio. Piet and I found a cheap, used upright piano. Because the Robert Pace method was founded on the concept of teaching two or more students at a time, I needed another piano. A neighbor had a piano she was willing to donate so that group piano lessons could become a reality.

The room that was intended to be our seasonal porch now became my piano studio. Piet discovered a huge piece of slate at Goodwill and attached that to one wall in my studio. I painted the treble and bass clef on it, and now had a "musical" blackboard for lessons. Using household items, I created many homemade devices to teach music theory, a key component of the Robert Pace method.

Piet helped me make "musical" magnetic fishing poles using dowel sticks, string, and a magnet tied at the end. My canning lids became the "fish" as students fished for musical notations and notes that had been written on the lids with permanent black marker. After the students caught a "fish," they had to play the notation on the piano, as well as add it to the blackboard clefs.

I knew Bret was too young for keyboard lessons. Those few Suzuki lessons made me aware of that. Why not create a non-keyboard music class? Using my new knowledge from the Pace method, I decided to create a class called, Treble Tots, which would be a class for preschoolers and kindergarten children to learn musical rhythms while developing coordination skills with musical instruments.

Since Piet was handy and creative, we worked together to design homemade instruments out of wood. Finding other inexpensive ways to make musical learning more fun kept both of us thinking creatively. How fortunate that Piet was so willing to be part of this venture! Between the two of us, we rigged up drums, maracas, rhythm sticks, and anything in his workshop that could be used to create musical sounds.

We had a phonograph, and I bought Hap Palmer records as another outlet for fun musical experiences. My fabric stash became a gold mine for my music teaching. I sewed colorful scarves that the children could wave in graceful movements. The scarves also served as color recognition in the fun children's songs that directed the children to have the "blues" stand up and the "reds" sit down, etc.

Winkie Coyne, one of my friends in town, offered her basement for our Treble Tots class so people would not have to drive to the country for lessons. She and I teamed up to teach a dozen pre-school and kindergarten children weekly, including my kids and Winkie's girls.

During our second year of teaching Treble Tots, Karen Enerson asked if we would let her blind daughter join our group. Sheila was five and LOVED music. Winkie and I soon discovered that Sheila did not have the visual distractions that the other youngsters had. She responded beautifully to every musical direction. Soon, the others were motivated to listen as well as she did. They, in turn, helped Sheila with movement activities; they took turns being her "guide on the side" as they moved to specified locations in the room as directed by the music commands.

When Bret was five, I created a class called KinderKeys for students just learning to play the piano. It was a stepping-stone to the Robert Pace group piano lessons, using the Pace keyboard books. This class used creative ways to acquaint students with the keyboard. I used games, manipulatives, and visuals to make this a fun intro class.

Sheila told her mom she wanted play the piano, too. Couldn't I be her teacher? I had no idea how to teach piano to a blind student, but she was so eager to learn. How could I refuse? Thus began an amazing, yet challenging, teaching opportunity as I attempted to be her piano teacher.

After a few years of trying different ways to teach piano to Sheila, I learned about a blind piano teacher and musician in the Twin Cities. After contacting him and telling him about my precocious blind student, he invited us to visit him and to give me pointers on how to be more effective in my teaching.

I will never forget the day Karen and I took Sheila on this adventure. When we knocked on the door, the musician introduced himself in a hearty melodic voice: "Welcome to my home, Sheila. I have been awaiting your arrival and am so happy to meet you."

He invited us in and proceeded to walk forward with his white cane. As he walked, he explained to Sheila how to find one of his pianos, and asked her to play for him. With no hesitation, Sheila played several pieces and then shyly asked if she could share one of her own creations. The two bonded beautifully, and the hour went by too quickly. He praised her amazing ability and then shared techniques that I could use to facilitate her learning. Reluctantly, Sheila said goodbye and thanked him for the opportunity to meet and learn from him.

We stopped for lunch to celebrate our day's adventure. It was then I learned how Sheila knew where everything was positioned on her plate. Her mother told Sheila her hamburger was at 3:00 pm, her French fries at 9:00 pm and her drink at 1:00 pm. It was my first meal with Sheila, and I added to my learning curve in yet another manner. Sheila and I bonded on many levels that day. Our friendship has lasted all these years.

I taught four afternoons each week. The lessons were after school, with groups of eight students. Like Noah's animals, the students came two-by-two. Two students would arrive for a half-hour keyboard lesson, and then play outside while I taught the next two students. After their half-hour lesson, I had four more students join us, and these eight students were in one big group to learn music theory for a half-hour.

After that the first four students left, and I had two students on the keyboards while the other two went outside to play. After another half hour, those two left and the last two came in for their lesson. This rotation approach allowed every student a half hour on the keyboard, plus a half hour of music theory.

Our living room became the sitting room for moms to wait for their children. Piet became the babysitter for our two, as well as other children waiting for their parents to pick them up.

Group piano lessons created companionship and built-in competition for the students. It was also a way for me to continue to develop my teaching skills and strategies while I was a stay-at-home mom. I kept taking classes and workshops to learn more, and passed these new techniques on to my students.

Over the years, Bret and Pyra developed very close ties with our neighbor girls, Amy and Cathy Hallstrom. They seemed more like a brother and three sisters. Bret and Amy were only three months apart and played together with no friction or disagreements. The two were a match made in heaven! Pyra and Kathy added colorful fireworks to the arena at times, but they quickly made up and were friends again before we knew it. Being a year and a half younger than their siblings, they needed to show their independence. Playing in the woods and using Piet's trails kept them busy for hours. Having peanut butter and jelly picnics was grand enough for them.

Bret and Pyra tried selling rocks and popsicle-stick creations at the end of our driveway, but so few cars passed. They became discouraged with the lack of sales and income. Piet and I ended up being their best customers. Ironically, we were buying back our own stones!

Since Becky and Dave's house was on a more-traveled road, the four kids decided to create a lemonade and cookie stand during the summer. This meant using expensive real lemons and baking several kinds of cookies. Somewhere, they had learned about Boston cream pies and thought that would be a great item to sell. At least, it kept them occupied. Thankfully, passing neighbors recognized the need to support these local entrepreneurs. One day a construction crew passed by and bought up all their goodies. That day raised their hope of future sales—alas, it was the only bonus business day.

Becky and I had worked out a great babysitting plan during the kids' preschool years. Each week, one of us would have a "day off" while the other babysat all four. On Saturdays, the two of us would alternate driving to local garage sales. That week's driver was responsible for mapping out the places we would check out for great sales. We became queens of garage sales and never came home without a carload of great bargains, whether it was clothing or household "must-haves."

Meanwhile, Piet continued finishing the inside of our home. The basement level housed the canning and winery room, recreation room, and the third room was my sewing area. It also was a second kitchen, used for canning, and a laundry room. The basement became a late-night haunt for Piet and myself as we worked on building up our food and wine supply. It was also a time for the two of us to talk while I sewed clothes for the entire family: from tricot underwear to polyester suits for Piet, tops for Mom and Dad, outfits for the kids, as well as my own wardrobe.

Bret and Pyra were often mistaken for twins. Their "frugal" mother didn't want to waste fabric, so I sewed matching outfits for both of them. When the children were very young, they knew no difference, except when they appeared in public together. They showed off their identical bowl haircuts from their dad, and their twin outfits from the same bolt of cloth, sewed by their mom. It was at these times that Pyra became very upset when people would say, "Aren't those the cutest twin boys?" Needless to say, it became necessary to become more creative with the fabric. The haircuts, sad to say, stayed the same.

The real wake up call to dress them differently came Christmas of 1978, when Pyra was four years old. We went to the local truck stop for a free Santa supper. Bret decided he needed to sing *Jingle Bells,* not only for Santa, but for all the audience, including many truck drivers. Pyra, not to be outdone, decided to share her vocal talents with her version of *We Wish You a Merry Christmas.*

Comments were heard from the audience: "Aren't those twin boys the cutest ever?"

"My, those boys certainly can sing!"

Right after Pyra seized the microphone for her solo, the owner of the restaurant appeared. He announced that he would pick the name of the huge Christmas stocking winner. It was a custom for all the kids to put their names in a

"Twin outfits." Pyra and Bret.

box and one lucky child would go home with this six-foot stocking filled with prizes of all kinds. He drew one of the names and said, "The lucky winner this year is Pyra Aarden." Pyra screamed and ran up to get her huge stocking. The owner said, "Let's all give a big applause to this cute little boy." With that, Pyra grabbed the microphone and quickly informed everyone in the truck stop that she was not a boy! She was a girl! Blushing, the owner apologized. She gave him a big hug of forgiveness when he handed over the stocking prize that was almost as tall as her own dad.

After that Christmas scene, I decided it was time to let Pyra have longer hair and definitely change the twin outfits. After all, she was our little girl. I needed to get some cute, girlish patterns and definitely not use the same bolt of fabric for both kids!

The fall of 1979, Pyra started kindergarten and Bret was a big first-grader. Piet and I had discussed that maybe I should go back to school to get my Master's Degree, once both children were in school. We had been living on one salary for so long, why not a bit longer? Thinking it would be easier to get a teaching job with a Master's Degree, I started classes at River Falls University. I was able to take both day and evening classes. Several of my teacher friends decided to also get their Master's. We organized an evening carpool, since we were all working toward a Reading Specialist degree.

Also in 1979, the prison warden realized how efficient and organized Piet was in his work with the inmates. He asked Piet to take on the new job of Activities Coordinator, which organized all the ways people from the outside entered the prison—attorneys, social and religious groups, all visitors, etc. Piet's height, his pastoral experiences, and the way he was able to deal with people, as well as his ability to say, "No," made him an excellent candidate for this new position.

Since this involved creating a new department, Piet would have the challenge of its inception, as well as the manner in which it would be organized. Piet said he would take on the challenge on one condition: He wanted the option of returning to his job as a social worker with the inmates, after he accomplished this new task. The warden assured Piet that would happen, once he had this new department organized and running successfully.

During our years at Guardian Angels, Piet and I became lectors and Communion distributors. Bret decided he wanted to join the choir. Piet also joined, so the two could have a musical evening together. Pyra went out on a limb and chose to be an "altar girl," though there were only altar boys at that time. Thanks to her insistence and determination, she became the first altar girl at Guardian Angels. She created a new opportunity for other girls who had secretly wanted to, but had not dared to ask.

I graduated the summer of 1981, only to find the field of Reading Specialists and Learning Disability Teachers flooded with applicants. My years of teaching became a detriment rather than an asset. It was much cheaper to hire inexperienced teachers.

Since I had taken so many English courses in undergrad, I discovered that I needed only a few more to complete a Master's degree in English. So that fall of 1981, I landed a part-time high school English position, on the condition that I take the classes needed to complete my English degree. Asked if I had ever taught Debate, I laughed and said the only thing I knew about it was that there was a Negative and Positive side. The principal smiled and told me not to worry. The students were great and would help me in this after-school activity.

One of the classes I was to teach was called Futuristics. The only thing I knew about the future was that I needed a full-time job in my qualified fields of teaching. The senior high students were expecting a knowledgeable teacher, and here I was trying to figure out what Futuristics meant. Finding some interesting projects for the class to pursue, we began the year building a time capsule. We took a short field trip to a farmer's field next to the school. The farmer's son was in my class and was willing to use some of the farm machinery to create a huge hole. We buried the futuristic "capsule," which was a sealed garbage can containing memorabilia for a future generation to find. We created a sealed letter to be opened fifty years later. The principal put the envelope in the school safe. I assume it is still there!

My debate group was also extremely challenging to teach because I knew nothing about how to teach it. Thank heavens they were self-motivated learners and literally ended up teaching me.

My next challenge was being told that I would have to obtain a chauffeur's license to drive the students to their debates in the big school bus. That's all I needed to add to my stress—a driving test with a school bus! Time was of the essence, as our first debate was the following month. The PE teacher said he'd give me a few on-the-road lessons. He handed me a manual to study for the written part of the test.

One tip the PE teacher shared: On the day of the road test, I should take out the crowbar and pound each of the tires to make sure they were inflated enough. This was supposed to impress the officer giving the test. On the day of the road test, I boldly performed the crowbar feat, and then entered the bus, giving the officer a huge, knowing smile.

His first directive was, "Show me where the first aid safety box is stored." I tried to quickly think of a logical place and opened the glove compartment with NO success. He pointed to a container underneath the driver's seat. I sheepishly pulled it out and opened it to see what it contained.

Next, he said, "Show me how to unlock the back door, in case of an emergency."

Once again, I had no idea. Why hadn't the PE teacher shared this vital info instead, of how to hit the tires with a crowbar? By the time I started the actual road test, I was a bundle of nerves. I tried to remember how far from the railroad tracks to stop, and how to even reach the handle for the retractable stop sign on the bus.

When the officer asked how I would handle dropping students off and picking them up, I rattled off every single scenario I could think of. The officer just kept shaking his head. He told me that if I talked that much when students were actually on the bus, it would take all day to do a bus run, and that wasn't counting the return trip!

At the end of the harrowing road test, the officer sat tabulating my plus/minus points. He turned to look at my ashen face that had taken on the resemblance of one big question mark. "Mrs. Aarden, I hate to say this, but you actually passed, by one point." Shaking his head, he continued to say, "Please take it easy on the students. Don't forget where that first aid kit is, much less how to unlock the back door." With that said and done, he told me to sign the papers.

I stood up and gave him a huge hug. I had passed this hurdle and now needed to go home and prepare for the next day's class.

The following day at school, the principal called me into his office. At a meeting the night before, the school board had decided to buy a van that would be large enough to fit all the members of my debate group. There would not be a need for me to get a bus driver's license!

That same fall, Piet decided to erect a huge pole shed (32x48) at the foot of our hill. It was to become his woodworking shop, a garage for the pickup, and a place to harbor the rows and rows of neatly chopped wood. Dad, once again, volunteered to assist Piet with this building project.

At Thanksgiving, I received an offer from the Stillwater School District for a position of teaching students with Learning Disabilities. It was a job I was definitely qualified for, and a full-time position, much closer to home.

I was struggling daily with my high school teaching and decided to accept the offer. This was easier said than done. The New Richmond school board and my principal were not happy, and decided to penalize me for breaking my part-time contract. They slapped on a huge monetary penalty for doing such a thing and thought that would deter me. The rewards of the Learning Disability teaching outweighed the negatives of leaving my high school teaching. I chose to leave my part-time job.

Teaching students at two different elementary schools meant working with two very different faculties. It also meant not really being able to fully participate in either school. BUT, on the positive side, I loved working with the students and trying so many of the techniques I had learned in my university classes.

The Stillwater Prison was on the way to my two schools. Being able to drive to work with Piet every day was an added benefit of my new job. It gave us one extra hour each day together. Not having the stress of teaching high school classes, trying to learn debate strategies, and not having to take more university classes, all made life so much easier.

That winter, Piet was busy splitting logs with a pneumatic log splitter. He had a high school wrestler, Dan, helping him. The strong, young man couldn't handle one of the unusually sized logs, so Piet came to his rescue. I had just driven the pickup, loaded with split logs, up to the house and was unloading it when I heard Dan scream.

Trying to get the gnarled, gigantic log onto the splitter, Piet's hand got between the log and the sharp blade. I looked down the hill and saw Piet walking up the hill. In a calm voice, he told me to get a clean rag. He was holding onto his glove. I rushed in and grabbed the first rag I saw. Piet looked at it and said, "I said a CLEAN rag!" I ran in and found one. "Now call the hospital. Tell them we are coming in. It's an emergency."

Fumbling with the phone, I told the hospital receptionist my husband had cut his finger on the log splitter, and we would be coming in immediately. I asked Dan to stay with the kids, then raced to get the car keys.

When we got to the Hudson ER ten minutes later, they looked at the finger and said they needed a special surgeon. With no painkillers and no one wanting to do anything with his hand, we waited for three hours.

It was the weekend, and no local surgeons could be found. Eventually, our neighbor, Dr. Fermin, came in. He analyzed the situation and said surgery had to be done immediately to try to save the pointer finger of Piet's right hand. But, he explained, Hudson Hospital did not have the latest equipment.

Since Dr. Fermin had performed ER surgery in the Philippines during the war, he was capable of using makeshift supplies. He would do his best to try to reattach the finger. Doctor Fermin was not happy with the staff who had not cleaned the wound when Piet had arrived. Bacteria had had a chance to grow in the open wound, but he would do his best. On Monday, Piet would have to see an orthopedic surgeon in the next town.

Infection set in, and after weeks of trying to save the finger, Piet chose to have it amputated. The finger was totally cut off, right down to the knuckle at the base. He spent six weeks out of work, and never once complained about the pain

Piet's work as Activity Coordinator required lots of typing, so he now needed a secretary for that work. There was a time for humor, especially within the prison walls, when Piet would be using his middle finger as his "pointer" finger. Because Piet had such large hands, the loss of that finger was not too noticeable, and he was determined to make the best of the situation, as he always did with everything.

The following winter, Piet managed to clip the tip of the middle finger of that same hand when he was trying to remove some packed snow from our ancient snow blower. This proved to be a painful ordeal during the cold, winter months. He would have phantom pain from the amputated finger and freezing pain from the area that had exposed nerves on the middle finger. The only positive result of this accident was the purchase of a new snow blower that had much better safety guards.

Life was certainly filled with interesting events that led to unknown detours!

Our home in the Hudson woods.

CHAPTER TEN
Tangled Alcohol Roots: 1982

It was the spring of 1982. Life in the Aarden household had settled into satisfying routines with our jobs and the children's school hours. We were happily enjoying the fruits of our labors.

My entire family came one Sunday in April, to help Pyra celebrate her First Communion. As she walked down the church aisle, Pyra proudly carried the banner our family had helped her create. Since she loved hearts, hearts were placed on the corners and scattered around the banner to accentuate her name and the date. There were representations of the chalice and host placed in the center. After Mass, everyone drove to our home for a celebratory meal and the opening of gifts. Food and drinks flowed freely.

Dad!

My dad ended up celebrating more than he should have with the drinks. It was time for everyone to leave. My sister, Flo, drove my parents to their Twin Cities apartment. When she dropped them off, my mother assured her that all would be fine. Dad just needed to go to bed and sleep it off. After my sister left, my dad became belligerent with his speech and was very unsteady on his feet. He fell and hit his head. My mom was unable to help him up. She immediately called my sister to come help. Flo lived about fifteen minutes away, and came right over with her husband to take care of Dad. Being a nurse, she was able to bandage the cut on Dad's head, and got him settled in for the night.

After forty-seven years of living with my dad's drinking problems, my mom told him that this had been the last straw. Either he would give up his drinking, or she would leave him, and that was final. Dad was not happy with this ultimatum, but Flo found a treatment center in the Twin Cities, and Dad went reluctantly.

My sisters and I were expected to take part in a week of family therapy. We each were able to take time off from our jobs to be there for Mom and Dad.

That week was horribly difficult—a week of being forced to think back and remember things about Dad's drinking, and how his drinking had affected us in our growing up years. We also had to share and give an accounting of dealing with Dad's drinking in our adult years. We were told to be brutally honest and look each other in the eyes as we shared our painful memories. The caseworker bluntly said that we were not to sugarcoat anything and should dig deeply into our emotions and hurts.

I remember looking at my seventy-five-year-old dad and seeing him for the first time as a hurt, helpless man. He was being bombarded with painful sharing of how his drinking had affected us as children, and still did as adults. My mind took me back to funny stories I had heard about Dad, my itinerant father, who had the amazing ability to always make people laugh at his jokes or antics.

Dad was a talented "jack-of-all-trades" person who could do anything he set his mind to. As a young man, he had run away from home during his senior high school year. He rode the rails for adventure, after a heated argument with his father. My dad worked on farms and at many different odd jobs before he got married in 1935, at the age of 28. Mom had been a schoolteacher for seven years and had to quit teaching when she married Dad. No teachers in the rural schools could be married at that time.

In their first years of marriage, Dad set up his own business as a tavern owner. Mom and Dad lived in rented homes, and then in rooms behind the tavern. With Dad's alcoholic tendency, this was not a good environment for them.

Flo was four and I was two years old when they made the decision to change their lives. In 1942, my great aunt, Clara, offered Mom the opportunity to become the next Postmistress in Naytahwaush. My mom jumped at the chance and passed the Civil Service exam with no problem. Aunt Clara even purchased a four-room home for my parents, with an additional two rooms for the Post Office and lobby.

Mom could be at home with her children, and work at the same time. She assured my dad over and over that it was a relief to get away from the tavern atmosphere and have a real home of their own. At the same time, Uncle Howard became the owner of Aunt Clara's general store, located just down the hill from the Post Office. We were surrounded by extended family all living within a block of one other.

Since my dad was always looking for adventure, a buddy easily convinced him to go to Alaska for a good-paying job building roads for the new pipelines. After a year of that, Dad decided to enlist in the Navy, during World War II. He was stationed in New Guinea for two years, working in the postal office, since he had previous experience in this work. This meant he did not have to be in the combat zones and was able to return safely home at the end of WW2 in 1945.

(Years later, I snuck into my parent's bedroom to open Mom's trunk to see what treasures lay there. The photos of the New Guinea women with bare breasts were shocking to my young eyes. After my dad had shown the photos to Mom, they were quickly hidden from view so we children would not see them. Modesty was a virtue of great importance during those young years, so to see a photograph displaying bare breasts was not for children to gaze upon. In fact, outward affection to each other was frowned upon in those days. Intimacy was definitely something shared behind closed bedroom doors. There are very few times that I can recall my mom and dad kissing in front of us.)

During my elementary years, Dad worked with a local company that contracted out-of-state construction jobs in the summers, so Dad spent those months away from home. In the winter, he returned home and got a job plowing roads to remove snow, or other odd jobs in the area. When those jobs were not available, he set off for Duluth, MN, to learn welding. He later found work in the Twin Cities to put his newly-acquired skills into practice, but that also meant being away from home.

Dad built a two-room addition to our home, and added electricity and running water. In the late 1950s he built a screen porch addition that was enjoyed immensely during the summertime and for years to come. To keep himself occupied when he wasn't working on the road, Dad even started a small wood carving business with my Uncle Howard. They created spoon and fork sets for sale.

Whatever my dad decided to do, he did it well.

I had many fond memories, but that week of family therapy, I had to think of the negatives connected to Dad's use of alcohol. The work ethic and wonderful characteristics my dad possessed were tainted by his love of booze. He loved to spend time in the Mahnomen "library" (local slang for the liquor store) with his cronies. All during my childhood, I believed he was in the library reading books. The buildings *were* side-by-side. Instead, he was bellying up to the bar.

As my sisters and I recalled our growing up years, we realized that, no matter what time our dad might come home at night, our mom always kept his supper warm on the back of the stove. Having warm food to eat every night must have kept him nourished; he always remained healthy. Some nights he would come home late from drinking. Since my mom was an avid reader, she would sometimes be in their bedroom reading late into the night. My dad was an alcoholic who used his words as weapons when he was drunk, not his fists. I would cover my ears and cry, not wanting to hear the loud arguing. I realized early on that the shouting matches were always about his drinking. Why did he drink? Why did he make my mother so sad? Why?

It hurt so much to tell Dad how his drinking had affected us. Going through the week of therapy—sharing our painful, heart-wrenching stories with Dad—left all of us raw. Emotions overtook us, intermingled with uncontrollable sobs. We were overflowing with grief. It was the first time in our lives that we, as a family, were addressing the elephant in the room. Every night, we tearfully left Dad behind, and returned to Mom and Dad's apartment, weary and spent with grief.

Dad came out of the treatment center after a month and never drank alcohol again. What a change that was! He lost some of that humor, spontaneous joking, and dancing that always prevailed when he got "tanked up." Life was much more mellow, and definitely easier for Mom. She rarely touched an alcoholic drink because she was so thankful my dad had made the sacrifice of giving up his alcoholic drinks.

That pain-filled week was a double whammy for me. I realized how many years of my own marriage had been swallowed up with Piet's daily drinking. In the years that followed that intensive, emotionally draining week with Dad, I realized how I was internalizing so much of the information we were given, and applying it to my own home situation. I became so aware of the pitfalls of alcohol, and how it was an addiction that destroyed family ties and communication.

Six years earlier, in February of 1976, Piet and I had made a Marriage Encounter for a weekend in St. Paul after I had seen an advertisement:

> Marriage Encounter Weekends offers couples new discoveries for practical and meaningful communication. Our weekends are not about more theory. Marriage Encounter Weekends unpack the real stuff of married life that has been tried and tested. Come discover something more about communication that is proven to strengthen a relationship and deepen intimacy.

I got excited and thought that this would be a great way for us to deepen our ability to communicate. And, it would be a safe place and way for me to address my concern about Piet's drinking.

Piet was not a man who went to bars to drink. He was a home drinker. I cringed as I heard the ice cubes clinking in his glass every day after work. Then there were more drinks after supper. He was a quiet drinker, and seemed to go inward as he drank. Because of this, I seemed to only know the surface of who Piet really was. It was difficult to communicate on any deep, emotional level with him.

I hoped the Marriage Encounter weekend would help change that. We listened to married couples share experiences and strategies for deeper communication. After each lecture, we went to separate places and wrote our reactions in journals. Later, we returned to our room and presented our written responses to each other. We silently read our spouse's journal entry thoroughly, before discussing each other's responses.

I loved the Encounter weekend and, as always, went overboard with my ideas of how we needed to continue this type of dialogue. I wanted to do this on a daily basis, using the same format we had learned in Marriage Encounter. I typed marriage-themed topics onto multiple slips of paper and put them in a container on top of the refrigerator. Piet reluctantly went along with this for a few weeks, then said it was too much, too often. I had over-reacted and a good thing had lost its luster.

To replace that idea, I learned about creating groups with other couples that had made a Marriage Encounter weekend. Soon, six couples were meeting on a monthly basis at each other's homes. The couple sponsoring the evening furnished the topic to be shared, as well as refreshments. This went on for several years, but the topic of alcohol remained our Achilles' heel. It was too painful, and one topic Piet chose to ignore. It drove a wedge in our attempts to communicate.

Piet was certainly not an extrovert, but it would have been so nice to have intense conversations between us. This was not possible with the alcohol taking over every evening. Guilty thoughts kept gnawing away at my inner soul. Piet had been such a successful priest; he had been given the hardest assignments and always made the best of them. All his parishioners had loved him and gone to him for guidance and support. Why couldn't we manage that same sharing in our marriage? Was I so overbearing that he had lost his desire to express himself?

Often, when he had been drinking, he would not realize his strength while playing with the kids. His "tickle-monster" would go to extremes, and I would be forced into the role of the constant nag. I was constantly saying, "Don't be so rough, Piet." After the kids were put to bed, another drink or two and he would be nodding his head while sitting in his chair. That left no time to communicate.

Yet, no matter how much he drank, he was an amazingly hard worker who, like my dad, could do anything he set his mind to. Never once did he lose a day of work because of his drinking. Piet was an intellectual giant who never wanted to show off his many talents.

Despite his drink, he had managed to complete our home and then set out to create walking trails in our five acres of woods. The hill behind our home was steeper than we had originally realized. Piet designed a triple-tier wall of stone to stop the dirt from eroding. He decided not to use cement. We had lots of limestone from the excavation of the hillside behind our home. Piet chose just the right rock to butt up against its neighbor to create a strong defense—a wall of creative ingenuity. When he ran out of stone from our place, Piet set out to the neighboring hillsides, dug up stones with his crowbar, piled them in his old pickup, and brought them home to continue his wall. Many Saturday mornings, he would be out at daybreak and worked on the wall until sunset.

When the wall was finished, he dug up an area on the far side of our home so I could have my much-desired garden. Hidden under the topsoil were huge pieces of limestone that were backbreaking to excavate. I smiled sheepishly and asked if he needed any more stones for his wall!

I had not thought ahead. When the trees were in full leaf, they cast a never-ending shade over my new garden patch. Thus my first garden had spindly plants that never matured. Where could I find a garden space?

One day, while we were walking through the woods on top of the hill, we found an area that was not totally wooded. Piet began to dig, again, for a garden spot for his persistent wife. He never complained and was always ready for any new challenge when asked. I never once thought of how we would water the new hilltop garden if no rains came. That first summer was very dry. The hose we dragged up the hill had very little water pressure due to the length and height of the hill. We did manage to grow things, but Piet then had to build a fence around the garden to keep out all the animals. Throughout all of this, silent Piet never complained.

How could I still be so disgruntled with his drinking?

Piet didn't want Bret and Pyra to be exposed to the elements of the cold Wisconsin winters while waiting at the end of our road for the school bus, so Piet decided they needed a shelter. It wasn't just a simple shelter, but a one-room, multi-purpose playhouse: A place to play, as well as a place to keep warm in the winter wait.

Did I mention the fact that Piet played Paul Bunyan in his cutting down of trees? Every weekend, we all jumped in the old red pickup to gather our wood harvest. Working in the woods became the Aarden weekend pastime and trademark, much to the kids' chagrin. Bret, Pyra, and I developed muscles as we carried log chunks back to the truck. When asked by their classmates what they had done over the weekend, the kids had a repetitive answer. After splitting all those gigantic log sections, Piet would meticulously pile them in rows that never collapsed.

After he built the huge shed at the bottom of our hill, Piet decided we needed to have a circle drive in order to make it easier to get in and out of our uphill driveway. When that was completed, he created a beautiful water fountain and birdbath within the circle. Piet also designed a wrought-iron sculpture, with seven doves in flight, in memory of his parents' seven children. He placed the sculpture in the center of the fountain with a memorial plaque, inscribed with his parent's names.

Not only did Piet create a lovely landscape for our home, he was also concerned about the animals that graced our woods. He built multiple bird feeders to keep the birds well fed. Squirrels defied his plans, and ate much of the bird feed. Undaunted, Piet built the squirrels their own feeding station complete with two rooms and a ladder. They used the ladder to race up to get corn Piet had stuck on a nail protruding from the floor. Deer appeared and wanted the squirrel's corn. This caused Piet to design a feeding trough to supply corn for the deer. (The corn supply came from a local farmer's surplus.)

All Bret, Pyra, and I had to do was sit in our living and dining room area, gaze out the floor-to-ceiling windows, and enjoy the fruits of Piet's labors. We often had a dozen or more deer to watch, squirrels constantly chattering and wanting their turn at the feeding station, and birds of every color and hue that kept the feeders occupied.

Piet stayed at home, was an amazing father to our children, and worked constantly on our home and surroundings. Why was I STILL so occupied with his drink?

The week at Dad's treatment center sent me over the edge and kept me constantly thinking and worrying about Piet's daily drinking.

Now that Dad no longer drank, I became even more obsessed with Piet's drinking. All the information about the harmful effects of alcohol abuse were constantly on my mind. I did not want to wait until Piet was in his seventies to do what my mom had done.

The summer of 1984, I decided I needed to go for counseling. After several sessions, I was led to the painful conclusion that Piet needed to come with me if any changes were to be made. After many refusals, he finally caved into my nagging. The long, silent drive into the Twin Cities for that session still remains a pain-filled memory.

The counselor asked Piet to hold his hands in front of him. Seeing the tremors, the counselor shared that tremors were an indicator of alcoholism. After hearing our story and asking more questions, he told Piet that he needed to go for treatment. It was necessary, if he valued his family and wanted them to remain a vital part of his life.

There was an intensive one-week program starting the next day, and the counselor felt that would be the best plan for Piet. The counselor called the facility and learned there was space for another person to join. He told us it would be best for Piet to go there, immediately, and get enrolled. I could bring his clothes and toiletries later.

Everything happened so quickly, and Piet was not a happy camper. He kept saying that he did not need this and that I was forcing him to do it. I begged him to try it and give it a chance. His drinking was destroying our relationship and was affecting our children. Didn't that mean anything to him?

Amidst my tears and terrifying thoughts and wondering if I had done the right thing, I left an angry Piet at the facility. I don't know how I managed to drive home that day, sobbing uncontrollably. My brain was swimming in conflicting thoughts of guilt. My heart was breaking with painful memories. How did we go from idyllic, passionate love, to this angry, silent void? How had our lives disintegrated to this level of pain?

That next week was filled with sessions trying to figure out who we were in this drinking relationship, and where we were headed. Bret and Pyra had to be there for some of the sessions. They were nine and ten years old, and were expected to share with their dad how his drinking was affecting them. Much of the week remains a blur. It was so much easier to try to quarantine this hurtful, emotional week into the dark recesses of my mind. I kept trying to rid myself of the guilt.

We did not accomplish much during that week of rehab, except to drive the wedge deeper between us. Piet claimed I was going overboard with this drinking fetish because of my dad's problem with alcohol. I began to think that maybe that was the truth, and if Dad had not been through treatment, I would not have insisted that Piet needed to be treated for alcohol addiction.

That week of treatment became a conflict that never quite got resolved. When I re-read my infrequent journaling over the years, I saw that I often referred to Piet's drinking and its negative effects on me, as well as the children. I tried going to Alanon meetings, but never found the right fit. They only led to a further wall between Piet and myself. We could talk about so many other things, but not his drinking.

Life was filled with so many twists and turns that forever remain a mystery. Which twist was next on the horizon?

CHAPTER ELEVEN
Family Fun: 1982-1986

The summer of 1982, I found myself unemployed. My teaching job in Stillwater had been a one-year position. Back to the job hunting! Nothing was open in the educational field. I needed a job badly, to help pay off my school debt and contribute to our income. The house still needed some finishing touches, bills were piling up, and I was getting desperate.

One evening that winter, Piet and I shared our current dilemma with some St. Paul friends. Dick told me that they needed a secretary-receptionist at St. Paul Seminary, where he was working. He pulled some strings and arranged an interview. Even though I had almost failed my typing class in high school and knew no shorthand, I could certainly answer a phone. My gift of gab might just prove to be an asset.

The Seminary was definitely desperate. I got the job. On my first day, I nervously tried to type and answer the constantly ringing phone. I found myself saying, "Hello, St. Paul Cemetery. How may I help you?" Giggling, I then corrected myself to say, "St. Paul Seminary." With that bit of mistaken humor, I made it through the first week—barely!

No one had clued me in that the previous secretary often typed papers for the professors. During that first week, Fr. Paul brought his grades for me to type, as well as another page of statistics. I looked at that paper swimming with row upon row of numbers and very reluctantly took it. The least I could do was to attempt to type this new assignment. My fingers knew where to find the letters on the keyboard, but numbers were a different can of worms.

In between ringing phones, using a jar of white-out, and trying to learn where everything was located, I left crying and wondering why I ever thought I could do that job. When Fr. Paul came by my desk the next day, I had an Excedrin Headache from all those numbers. I looked him straight in the eyes: "I don't care what the previous secretary did for you, I am NOT following in her footsteps. You can pass the message on to the other professors." I also added that if any other professors ever brought me typing jobs again, the seminary would be looking for a new secretary.

He looked at my name on the desk. "Yes, my name is Yvonne Aarden," I explained. "You probably were in the seminary with my husband, Piet Aarden." Then I hastily told him that if he asked Piet, he would agree that he had married a very independent, bossy woman.

I still laugh when I recall that startled look on his face. He took his report and never graced my desk again! During those six months of trial and error, I actually had some fun times acting as secretary, but could never see myself playing that role for very long.

My final day at the Seminary that May was memorable. I decided to wear my Native American jingle dress and have soft drum music in the background as my swan song. The office staff had often kidded me about my Native background after they discovered my Indian ancestry. Catching wind of my plan, my friends in the office decided to "teepee" (T.P.) the entire room the morning of my last day. When I arrived, the office was overflowing with toilet paper banners, like spider webs penetrating every nook and corner. We had lots of laughs. I played the drum music louder than planned. I am sure the St. Paul seminary priests clapped their hands as I bid my fond farewells that day! Hopefully, the next secretary was more qualified and saner than I.

Final day as receptionist/secretary at St. Paul Seminary.

At this point, with no great teaching prospects, Piet and I looked at the possibility of moving somewhere South, where more teaching positions were being offered. I found a plethora of teaching jobs in Houston, Texas, and decided to go for some interviews that spring of 1983. I had friends I could stay with in Houston, so it would only cost us the flight and rental car expenses.

When I returned home after a week of interviews—and several job offers—I received an offer for a teaching position at Oltman Jr. High, east of St. Paul, about a half hour from our home. This would involve teaching reading classes for both struggling readers, as well as a gifted class. After discussing the pros and cons of the Texas offers and the Minnesota offer,

Piet and I decided it was better to choose the Minnesota job. After all, Piet had been working in the prison for over twelve years and was hoping he could return to being a social worker. He felt he had organized and set up the Activities Coordinator position so that he could be replaced. He really wanted to return to being a social worker where he felt he was serving humankind in a more meaningful way.

That summer Piet, the kids, and I were driving around the area of my future school and discovered a used motorhome for sale in someone's yard. We had previously discussed how fun it would be to take trips in an RV with our kids. It would be a great way to combine easy camping and not pay for hotel rooms, while becoming acquainted with areas of the United States. The prices of new motorhomes were nowhere in our budget, and the used ones we had looked at were too expensive. It wouldn't hurt to just stop and ask what price they wanted for this one.

We knocked on the door of the home that was advertising the RV. It turned out that the owner had broken his back and could no longer drive his motorhome. He would be happy to have a young family become the new owners. His wife showed the kids and me the inside, while the owner showed Piet the mechanics of the vehicle. When we asked what price he was asking, he wanted $5,000.00. We realized what a bargain this was. The kids were excited about the layout of the RV. They told us how we could keep the back sofa open as a big bed and they'd have room to stretch out and read their books while we were driving. Since there was a second generator, they could even pop popcorn while we were moving and we could make coffee at the same time! "Please, oh, please, couldn't we buy it?" was their plea.

Once again, we made a call to Fr. Reynolds and asked if he would be willing to loan us money like he had done on prior occasions. As before, we promised to send monthly payments with interest. The following week we were the proud owners of an RV with two generators, plus a wooden box in the back to hold firewood or whatever. Since Piet and I said we would be sleeping on the back sofa that made into a queen size bed, Bret said he would take the dining room table that made into a bed. Pyra wanted the overhead bed above the driver's area. Sleeping quarters were claimed and all were happy with their choices.

Soon after buying the RV, we decided to make a maiden voyage to visit Mary and Dan and family at their lake home in northern Minnesota. It would give us the chance to see how our new purchase worked. How exciting to travel and not have to stop for food or bathroom breaks! After proudly showing off our RV to my sister and her family, we stayed the weekend. At dusk on Sunday, we set off for home. Coming over a steep hill, Piet saw the car in front of us signal for a right turn. As Piet swerved into the left lane to pass it, the car instead made a left turn.

Thankfully, we were not going at full speed; the damage to the vehicles was not severe, and no one was hurt. We were in the middle of nowhere, so we exchanged names and phone numbers. Our insurances would have to handle everything. Our maiden voyage ended up being scary and a bit expensive! That RV served us well after that first mishap. We took month-long trips in the summers to Florida, California, and Canada, as well as shorter trips within Minnesota and Wisconsin.

One summer weekend in 1984, we camped at Jellystone Park near the Wisconsin Dells. An influential salesperson conned us into purchasing a small lot. This limited the variety of camping places to travel to, but with all of the amenities of the park, we had many enjoyable weekends. Pyra will never forget Yogi Bear and his friends always delivering her a birthday cake in August. They even sang "Happy Birthday" in their "bear-tones!" It didn't take us long to buy the property, but in later years, it took a long time and was very difficult to sell it. This purchase promised as a "money-maker" became a money loser, but we were enriched with lots of good memories.

In 1984 we purchased guitars for Bret, Pyra, and myself. Our family volunteered to provide music for my parent's fiftieth wedding anniversary the following year. Bret and Pyra took to the guitar like bees to honey, but I was another story. They did not need the practice like their mother, but I needed them to practice with me. Bret played bass guitar for the rhythm, Pyra played the melody on her acoustic guitar, and I was to add the chord strumming on mine. In my attempt to make us the *Aarden Family Singers*, I was no Julie Andrews! But the show needed to go on, despite the mother's primitive chording.

In June of 1985, my sisters (Mary and Flo) and their families joined us to celebrate our parent's fiftieth anniversary. Mary and Dan prepared a slide presentation to show Mom and Dad's history together as a couple. During Mass at their parish church in Richfield, Minnesota, Mom and Dad renewed their vows. Piet prepared an amazing presentation of prayers to celebrate their

Mom and Dad at their 50th Anniversary.

lives. The eleven grandchildren processed one by one (from the youngest to the oldest) to place the symbol on the altar as Piet read each prayer.

Prayers of Petition and Gift Bearing:

1. GREG: Carries a banner with two interwoven rings as symbols of the intertwined lives that Bo and Phil have lived in married life for the past fifty years.

"That God's blessing may be sufficient to give all married couples the determination to make sincere efforts to iron out wrinkles in the fabric of married life, and give each other support rather than retaliation. We pray to the Lord:"

2. MELISSA: Carries in the crocheted tablecloth mindful of the many hours of handiwork on the part of Phil to brighten the homes of loved ones or promote financial gain for the Church

"Let people understand that handicraft and recreation are essential ingredients of every-day living. We pray to the Lord."

3. PYRA: Carries in a letter suggestive of the many years Bo and Phil spent in the home Post Office of Naytahwaush.

Lord, let us never forget that there are many lonely people and that we may bring a ray of light and joy into their lives through correspondence. Let us pray to the Lord."

4. CAMI: Carries in a peace pipe representing Phil's heritage and Bo and Phil's many years spent on the White Earth Indian Reservation.

"May we and our present generation come to a full realization that God created all—men, women, and minorities of all colors—to be equal to one another. We pray to the Lord."

5. BRET: Carries in a hammer representing the hours of labor on the part of Bo to help others in the attainment of the necessities of life.

That all people may become concerned about the needs of others—not only in regard to food and shelter of the impoverished in foreign lands—but also of those living in our own home. We pray to the Lord:"

6. SCOTT: Carries in a welding helmet reminiscent of the many years Bo worked in the welding trade.

"May our economy be developed to the point where every person may find honor in gainful employment. We pray to the Lord."

7. NANCY: Carries a cap and grade book as symbols of the years Phil spent as a teacher in Northern Minnesota schools.

"Grant people the stamina to direct their goals to the furtherance of the education of our young people despite the fact that material rewards may be greater in other professions. We pray to the Lord."

8. KAREN: Carries in a BINGO card representing the many evenings Bo and Phil have enjoyed together with this entertainment.

"May all married people understand that happiness is not something available in the supermarket but is stimulated through cooperative and recreational efforts. We pray to the Lord:"

9. DOUG: Carries in a Navy jacket representing the times of separation from one another during Bo and Phil's communal life for purposes of defense, training and employment.

"May God inspire heads of state to meet at a summit table rather than direct their military forces into the battlefield. We pray to the Lord."

10. BARB: Carries in a doll symbolizing the three children that entered into Bo and Phil's married life.

"Lord, bring enlightenment and understanding to humankind that the unborn child is also a creature made in the image and likeness of God. We pray to the Lord."

11. SUE: Carries the CROSS to remind us of Bo and Phil's undaunted service to their Church through labor, CCD, and making their home an extension of their local church.

"May the message of Calvary — submission to God's will and giving of oneself for others — be perpetuated in people of all states and walks of life. We pray to the Lord."

Flo, Vonnie, Mary, Mom, and Dad.

Piet and I created a liturgical booklet for each person attending the celebration. During the Mass, Piet led the singing as Bret, Pyra, and I accompanied him on our guitars. Afterwards, the kids begged me to not plan any more musical events that would require the three of us to perform together! The *Aarden Family Singers* was short lived.

After the church service, everyone gathered at Flo and Rome's home for a grand day of food and celebration. We created a book of memories for our parents for which everyone in the family, and many other friends and relatives, sent photos and stories they remembered about our parents.

That summer, Pyra again begged us to get her a horse. We told her it was not possible, but we would arrange for her to attend a horse-riding camp for a week. We thought she would come to realize all the work and time needed to care for a horse, and would cause her to change her mind.

While Pyra was away at horse camp, I happened to find a beautiful, small accordion at a garage sale for only $50.00. I was sure that she had said, at one time, that she would like to learn how to play the accordion. My dad had played the accordion, so maybe she wanted to be like her Grandpa! The price was right. I proudly purchased the shiny, black accordion with gold keys. When I returned home, I showed Piet my purchase that I just knew was the perfect gift for Pyra's birthday. I found a big box and wrapped it so it would be a surprise for her special day.

When we picked up Pyra from her horse camp, she was more determined than ever to get a horse of her own. The camp had backfired on our hopes: It only fueled her desire to own a horse. The following week was her birthday. At the party, I proudly brought out the box containing her gift from us. Her eyes lit up! The box was the same size that a horse saddle would fit into. Pyra excitedly tore the wrappings from the box. She was sure her parents had changed their minds and had secretly bought her a horse. Inside was going to be the saddle for it.

How does one describe the tears of disappointment streaming down your daughter's face when she opens her birthday box and discovers it contains an accordion, not a saddle. She cried out, "Why are you giving me an accordion? I thought this was a saddle! Mom, I NEVER said I wanted to learn how to play the accordion!"

Even though I tried to tell her that I was sure she had told me that, nothing could take away her bitter disappointment. Her hopes of having a horse of her own were never to be realized. Turning eleven, was not what she dreamed it would be.

1986 marked the year that Bret became a teenager. He plagued his parents with *Styx* music, a constant reading of science fiction, as well as constant reminders of his need for the latest in computers to write his own sci-fi book. His love of *Dungeons and Dragons* found us driving him to friends' homes to play, when the friends were not at our home. Pyra and Bret were both involved in competitive swimming. Many weekends were spent sitting on hard benches watching them compete with backstrokes, butterfly, and long distance competitions. With weekly piano and guitar lessons, voice lessons, choir, and lots of homework, there was not much free time for other things—except weekend wood gathering!

That summer of 1986, we flew to Holland to visit Piet's family for two weeks, and then spent two weeks in Germany and Austria. I was so excited to think we could trace the Von Trapp Family's adventures from *The Sound of Music*. Ever since I had seen that movie as a young nun, I dreamed of visiting Salzburg and seeing where Maria Von Trapp had been a Benedictine nun, and the various locations that marked her life with Captain von Trapp.

When we arrived in Salzburg, we learned about *The Sound of Music* tours, but they were too expensive. I found a brochure that outlined all the places the tour went; we could do our own Aarden-Von Trapp tour! After renting a chalet on the outskirts of Salzburg, we began our *The Sound of Music* tour. We reached the Abbey and found it locked, but there was a notice that there would be a Mozart concert that evening at the Abbey church. The rest of that day we toured all the Von Trapp locations described in the brochure. By the end of the day, Bret and Pyra stated very emphatically that they were NOT going to one more *The Sound of Music* place, but would stay in the chalet.

Piet very reluctantly said he would go with me to the concert at the Abbey. I was ecstatic and couldn't wait to see where Maria had lived in the convent. Before the concert started, I looked up to the church rafters and saw the nuns, sitting primly waiting for the concert to begin. All except one nun. She was busily bustling about downstairs, turning on and off the lights surrounding the vestibule and altar. I nudged Piet.

"I just know that is the Mother Superior," I whispered with confidence. "I need to meet her and tell her that I personally saw Maria Von Trapp in Stowe, Vermont. I'm sure she will be excited about that."

Piet looked at me with questioning eyes and raised eyebrows. During the concert, I kept trying to figure out how I would be able to talk with the Mother Superior. The perfect time came at the end when she was again bustling about with the lights and the organist was about to leave.

I rushed up to the organist and asked, "Excuse me, but what kind of organ is this? You played so beautifully."

He looked at me as if I had come from outer space. "It's a portable organ!" he gruffly answered and huffed off.

No matter. I looked and saw that the Reverend Mother was just a few steps away from me. I tapped her on the shoulder. "Excuse me, Rev. Mother, but I just wanted you to know that I have seen your Maria Von Trapp in Vermont. It is so wonderful to be here in her convent." The nun gave me a puzzled look and started to respond in German. Oh, no, I needed Piet to translate. I gave her a sign to wait. I rushed back over to Piet who had been watching his wife make a fool of herself.

"Piet, she doesn't speak English. Please help!" I pulled on his arm and he reluctantly followed me up the altar steps to the bewildered Mother Superior. "Tell her I was a Benedictine, just like Maria and herself. And tell her how I met Maria at her home in Stowe, Vermont," I begged Piet.

Piet hesitated and then translated for me. The nun nodded and Piet told me that this had gone on long enough. We needed to leave. "Oh, no!" I told him. "I need to have my photo taken with her. Please ask her."

After he took the photo, Piet gently but firmly took my arm and said, "This is it. We have had enough of the Von Trapps for a day!"

I turned and thanked the Mother Superior and waved my fond farewell. Mission accomplished!

When we returned to the chalet, Bret and Pyra were still up, waiting to share the story of their evening. They had gone down to the chalet's lobby after we had left for the concert. The planned entertainment for the guests was to watch the movie, *The Sound of Music*. We burst out laughing as they shared how the people watching it had fun participating in the songs during the movie. Bret and Pyra enjoyed making fun of several scenes they had witnessed earlier in the day.

Piet then entertained the kids by sharing their Mother's efforts to talk with the Mother Superior at the Abbey. A pact was made that night among the three of them that the video of *The Sound of Music* would never be allowed in our home!

After Austria, we returned to Piet's family in Holland. Since I did not have to teach in the summertime, Piet and I had decided that the kids were at a good age to become more acquainted with his family. We would farm the kids out for one week at a time with his brother's families. During that month, I would travel to Europe to visit friends and spend a week in London for the International Reading Conference.

Piet returned to the U.S.A. to work, the kids set off to be with a different Aarden family each week for the month, and I set off to visit our friends, Ruth and Joe Campion, former neighbors in Hudson, who were living in Brussels, Belgium. From there I went by hovercraft to the white cliffs of Dover to meet up with a teacher friend, Nancy Hof. We explored southern England for a week of adventures before the conference.

After the conference, I went by train to northern England to meet Joe and Ruth McCarthy (my friends that were from Mahtomedi and who had helped me find the Marzolf home the year I left the convent). Joe had relatives in England and Ireland. They invited me to travel with them as they explored these countries and renewed acquaintances with family members.

When we arrived in Dublin, Joe told Ruth and me to find a bed and breakfast rental while he went to rent a car. Ruth said, "When we travel with my cousin, we share a bedroom. Are you OK with that? It would be a lot cheaper for you." I readily agreed.

When we arrived at the bed and breakfast, the elderly Irish lady looked at the three of us. With a twinkle in her eye, she winked and said she hoped the room would meet our needs. Then she quickly added, "You know what I mean?" Joe looked bewildered, but said he was sure it would, since the ladies had chosen it.

When we got to the room, Joe looked at me and asked where my room was going to be. Ruth laughed nervously and told him I would be sharing the room with them, just like her cousin did.

"But Yvonne was a nun, not our cousin," Joe sputtered. "We've known her as Sister Mona. How can she share our room?"

"Oh, Joe!" Ruth retorted. "She's not a nun anymore, and she's practically like my cousin."

I chimed in that I had no problem sharing the room either. Two of us against one. We then left the room to find a great pub to enjoy food, drink, and entertainment. After our night on the town, we returned to our room. Joe quickly disappeared to find the bathroom down the hall to change into his pajamas. Ruth and I changed in the room. We laughed at Joe's embarrassment of sleeping in the same room as "Sister Mona."

I slipped into the small cot gracing the one wall and Joe and Ruth got into their small double bed with squeaky springs. Ruth giggled hysterically as they both met each other in the middle of the sagging mattress. Every time one turned, there were squeaks and both would end up in the middle butting up to one another. The multiple times this happened, Ruth and I would bust out in hysterical giggles amidst Joe's "harrumphs." The next morning, Joe told me that from then on, I was going to get my own room. Two giggling women were not his cup of tea!

At breakfast the next morning, our hostess, with her quick Irish wit, interjected the phrase, "You know what I mean," between almost every new sentence. Her wink accompanied the phrase. Ruth and I were in stitches trying to hide our amusement. We had found the perfect phrase to use the rest of the trip, "You know what I mean?"

Visiting Joe's Irish family was another adventure. One cousin owned a pub, so the entire clan was there to celebrate the U.S.A. family visitors. A fiddler and piano player offered the entertainment. Amidst the hubbub of laughter, jokes, and several beers on the house, Joe told me to stop talking and listen.

One of his cousins then told everyone in the pub that it was my birthday (it really wasn't). Everyone sang *Happy Irish Birthday* to me. After that, the beers never stopped flowing to our table and I had a new dance partner for every song. Now I celebrate two birthdays a year, hoping that the leprechauns I chased that night will keep me forever young!

After our Ireland visit, we flew to Dusseldorf, Germany, where Joe was working for 3M (Minnesota Manufacturing and Mining company). At the end of the month, my friends drove me to Aarle-Rixtel to reunite with Bret and Pyra. We were scheduled to leave the following day for the U.S.A. During their stay, the kids had been to several carnivals with their Dutch relatives. Each had managed to win a huge stuffed animal. Since the Dutch cars were small, I explained that they would not have room to bring these monstrous souvenirs, as well as our luggage, back to the U.S.A. Besides that, I told them that each animal would take up a seat on the airplane and we could not do that. Bret and Pyra would not accept this. The Dutch relatives gave in, and we took up every inch of crowded space in the compact car for the uncomfortable three-hour ride to the Amsterdam airport.

I tried again to persuade Bret and Pyra to leave the animals with our Dutch relatives. They would end up having to leave the animals at the airport when we checked in, so it would be better to have the Dutch family take them back home. Absolutely not! Rather than create more of a scene, I gave in. We hugged our Dutch family, said our farewells, and headed inside the airport.

How was I to know that the people checking us in at the airport would be so excited about the huge stuffed animals? They assured Bret and Pyra that there would be extra seats on our flight. Each animal could have its own seat! To this day, I can still visualize the, "I told you so, Mom!" look in their eyes. To add insult to injury, the animals became the big hit on the plane. People stopped to look at them, ask questions, and then petted them on their way to and from the bathrooms. Bret and Pyra could not wait to show their new acquisitions to their dad and tell him how I had tried to make them leave the animals behind in Holland.

Piet was extremely happy to have his family return home. We kept him busy sharing our travel adventures of the prior month. His peace and quiet in the woods no longer existed!

That fall, when Pyra walked into the Junior High building on her first day of school, the basketball coach took one look at the six-foot girl and rushed up to her. "You do play basketball, don't you?" he queried.

"No." answered Pyra.

"Well, you do now," he laughed. "We need height on our team. Come to practice and we will definitely show you the ropes." Thus started the future career for Pyra in the sport called basketball.

CHAPTER TWELVE
Memorable School and Family Events: 1987-88

The fall of 1987, I made a professional change. Instead of teaching K-6 Learning Disability students in a pullout program (which I had been doing since 1984), I decided to teach third grade at Bayport School in the Stillwater School District. This would give me a chance to employ new classroom strategies I was learning in the Whole Language classes I had been taking.

I told Dave Graham, our principal, that I would take all the third-graders with learning difficulties into my classroom. He agreed. It was wonderful to have the same students all day long as I taught thematically, connecting all subject areas. That first year our theme for the year was: THE WORLD OF COLOR. I decided to write frequent letters to the parents to keep them abreast of what was happening in our classroom. Here is an example from September 1987:

> Dear Parents:
>
> This year we will have "CELEBRATING A COLORFUL YEAR" as our theme in third grade. We will begin the year learning about color and how it affects our lives in so many colorful ways. It is a great way to begin the bicentennial of our constitution with the red, white, and blue patriotic colors. We will be searching for colors across the curriculum, as well as the world around us. "Color us Curious" as we begin the year!
>
> Our year is off to a colorful start and the excitement of reading fills the air. The students are in the midst of reading over 60 books written by our three authors for Sept. and Oct: Tomie de Paola, Peggy Parish, and Brian Wildsmith. Please ask your child to tell you about these authors and their books, as well as the activities they are working on.
>
> On Friday afternoons from 1:20 - 2:20, we are celebrating "Parents-Poetry and Punch". Please sign up for one Friday during the year. That entire week your child will be the special "Student of the Week" and will be privileged in many ways. A bulletin board display will show the life-size figure your child created for Open House. Your child will decorate the bulletin board in any manner to celebrate their life. Every student is to memorize one poem and will share that on Friday afternoon. I'm asking you to share one of your favorite poems

(doesn't have to be memorized). Please bring a treat for twenty-six and I'm asking each student to bring a drink each Friday for our poetry and punch celebration. If you can't attend then please choose someone to take your place (or smile lots at your employer and tell him/her how important it is for you to share this hour with your child at school!) A grandparent, neighbor, aunt, uncle, etc. may take your place if you can't possibly get time off. It is very important for each child to feel special and important for this week of individual recognition. Enclosed is a sign-up sheet. Please write in your first and second choice for a date not already spoken for.

We are using a "Whole Language Approach" this year in our classroom that has a heavy emphasis on the reading-writing connection using quality children's literature instead of the basal reading text and workbooks. This approach enables me to use themes and correlate all subject areas into one meaningful unit.

The theme of "Color" is expanded into art as we learn about the spectrum of colors as well as the science of colors. Volunteer picture persons will be giving special art lessons on color. Our social studies unit on the Constitution ties in with our study of patriotic colors and as we study the three colorful authors, we will compare and contrast their illustrations and use of colorful words.

If any of you were unable to attend either the parent meeting on Sept. 17 or Open House on Sept. 24th, please realize that I am very open for Parent Volunteers either during the day in the classroom or work time you can offer at home.

On Wednesday, Sept. 30, we will be taking our first field trip to Bayport Printing Co. to learn how printing is done. Mr. Mike Swisher has been very eager to help us. He will be supplying paper for the books the students will be publishing during the year as well as offering to be a resource person in any beneficial manner he can. How fortunate to have such generous, interested people within our own community.

Included with this letter is a copy of our PASSPORT TO READING. Each month we will study a different country and so please take time to help your child learn about that country. We will have resource people, films, slides, etc. to increase our understanding and will culminate each month with the preparation of a food from that country. If you have anything you can personally share about that country, let me know. In order to partake of the culminating activity, I'm asking each parent to read 15 minutes a day to your child and that your child read 15 minutes each to himself/herself. This will be the daily homework.

Please record in the passport book the following:

Parent's Page: Date/Book Read/Time involved

The students will do the same on their page for that month. I will require this to be done five days out of each week. At the end of the month, the passport book is to be returned for an official stamp of that country and we will then launch off to our next country. Please take the time for fifteen minutes of reading each day to your child. It is vital to our program.

Countries being studied are England, Zaire, Scotland, Greenland, Netherlands, Australia, Korea and Brazil. These will correlate with the regions of the world to be studied in third-grade social studies.

Please fill in the 1st and 2nd choice dates you want for your child's week and also state when you can volunteer time in or out of the classroom.

Thanks for your cooperation and I will keep you posted regularly on our classroom activities. Feel free to come and visit anytime.

Books Forever!

Yvonne Aarden

The success of the Whole Language approach I adopted for my students became beneficial in a way I had never conceived. Kelly Carmody was one of my third-grade students who had been diagnosed with brain cancer two years earlier. After trying every treatment possible and realizing his tumors had returned, Kelly still wanted to come back to school to be with his classmates. He came in the mornings with his mother and did as many of our classroom activities as he could. He fell in love with the books of Tomie de Paola. Kelly loved the artwork and messages of de Paola's books. When he went for radiation treatments in the afternoon, his mom tucked three de Paola books under her arm to read to him after therapy.

Tomie de Paola was appearing at the Children's Theatre for a production of his book, *Strega Nona*. Our class had tickets to attend. Kelly was so excited and couldn't wait to see Tomie, as well as the play. The morning we were scheduled to go, Kelly's mom called to say that he had another setback and would not be able to attend. While we were watching the play that afternoon, Kelly died. She called me that evening to share the sad news.

The next morning, Kelly's mom came to our classroom with photo albums. She had the class sit around her on the floor as she talked about Kelly and dying. Barb shared that it was their close friendships, and the books by Tomie de Paola, that had made Kelly's last months more bearable. Mrs. Carmody asked for questions. The conversations between my students and Kelly's mom went full circle from death to life. Barb Carmody was such a brave, caring person who wanted my students to hear first-hand about Kelly's life and death.

When Barb left, I asked the school psychologist to come in to help my students, as well as myself, in our grief and loss. We brainstormed how we might help the family in their grieving. We decided to raise money to buy more of Tomie de Paola's books for our library. We composed a letter to Tomie de Paola to share what had happened to Kelly, and our plan to buy more of his books. Tomie wrote back to us and said he would give us a discount and personally sign each of the books and ship them to our school.

The letter we sent to all parents in our school was the following:

A TRIBUTE TO KELLY CARMODY

There is no frigate like a book
To take us lands away.
Nor any coursers like a page
Of prancing poetry
This traverse may the poorest take
Without oppress of toll.
How frugal is the chariot
That bears a human soul!"
Emily Dickinson

Kelly Carmody was a special Bayport student who loved books. He became acquainted with Tomie de Paola's books during the last months of his life and loved the beauty of Tomie's art and messages. Barb Carmody said, "We gobbled up all de Paola's books at the library and shared his wonderful works together."

Tomie de Paola's latest book, "Merry Christmas, Strega Nona", had its message: "Christmas has a magic of its own."

Kelly Carmody had a "magic of his own" for all of us at Bayport School and as a tribute to him, we at Bayport School would like to set up a special book fund to remember Kelly in a meaningful, personal way. Anyone who wishes to contribute to this memory of Kelly, please bring or send contributions to Bayport School. Make checks to Kelly Carmody Memorial Book Fund. Thank you!

At the end of that school year, my third graders presented a special "Kelly Carmody and Tomie de Paola Celebration" for the school and community. On display were all the autographed Tomie de Paola books purchased with the monies people had donated. The students presented skits they had created and shared special memories of Kelly, as well as information about Tomie. Mitch Carmody, Kelly's father, shared a poem he had written about Kelly. (See Appendix 3)

The memory of Kelly still lives on in the books displayed on the library shelves in the Bayport School—as well in the hearts of all those of us who knew and loved him.

The annual Aarden Christmas letters originated the year Bret was born (1973) and became a family tradition that continues to this day. Our Aarden yearly adventures became summed up in the wrappings of a Christmas epistle, another Aarden trademark.

In our annual Christmas letter of 1987, the family news of the year was summed up in the following missive:

Bret's Bytes

Hello again! This is the second year I have been granted the privilege of writing my own Christmas greeting—what exuberant joyfulness. And now for the traditional recounting of the past year. Age: 14. Height: 185cm. Weight: 75kg. First, as always, I am involved in music. Over the past year, I arranged a four-part accompaniment to the song Desert Moon, which went over rather well at the spring concert. During the summer, I spent my second year at the Summer Science Institute (SSI) learning about electronics and generally enjoying myself. Then, in a massive effort that spanned the entire month of August, I succeeded in completing my first novel: Time's Eyes. (Don't expect to see it in bookstores anytime soon, if ever.) Sometime during the summer I also learned of the existence of the Apple IIGS, and our computer has never quite seemed such a wonderful thing since. School has started now (obviously), and I begin my first year at the Senior High as a sophomore. (Wow!) I was accepted into the University of Minnesota college-level calculus course sometime after the school year had begun, and much of my time has been occupied with homework from it. This year is really beginning to look up, however, especially because our Senior High Wind Ensemble has been granted a special honor: We have been invited to perform at Carnegie Hall in New York! The band hopes to leave during Easter vacation if enough money can be raised. By now the swimming season has started, and Hudson is once more in the running for the first place at sectionals. Well! Breathe a sigh of relief, and have a Frohliche Weihnachten!

Pyra's Perks

Presently I'm in 8th grade. 6' tall and 134#. I love to P-A-R-T-Y and shopping is right up there on the top of the list. I also love talking on the telephone to friends and watching TV (the few times I get to). I'm really into sports, art, reading eating junk food, collecting stuffed animals and babysitting and I AM NOT into work. I'm presently playing the clarinet in Band I and am also taking chorus. I still have my loveable calico kitty! I'm thoroughly interested in going to SSI (a science camp) this summer. I LOVE the Holiday Season so I wish you a Merry Christmas and a Happy New Year!

Piet's Projects

Early SPRING kept Piet busy in the basement finishing off the rec room—a place the kids enjoy. With the arrival of more clement weather, he moved outside to finish the landscaping around the fountain. Animals LOVE the newly created water source. Heavy rains of the SUMMER pushed a section out of the rock retaining wall and provided Piet some wall construction exercise. The FALL took him out in the woods to replenish the WINTER wood supply—only had to go across the street this year. He makes almost daily taxi runs to get the kids back and forth to extra-curricular activities.

Yvonne's "Yeses"

Being president of the St. Croix Valley Reading Council this year requires HOURS of my time and adds that grey and the extra wrinkles I see in the mirror. The IRA reading conference I attended in May in Anaheim caused me to find those many hours of needed sewing time but this was made easier by a serger and computerized sewing machine I happily acquired in January—I'd still rather sew than clean! A week of learning about the latest in reading and children's books plus a Whole Language Workshop was all that it took to create a new learning environment for my 3rd-grade room with library books as the rich foundation from which all thoughts bloom. Currently planning a reading trip to Winnipeg during February break: WHOLE LANGUAGE AND CHILDREN'S AUTHORS are my latest causes at stake.

Family Fun:

3 ½ week RV trip to California and back (white water rafting, Tijuana shopping, ocean and desert wanderings, Ojai visit with cousins Leo and Mary from Holland). Leo fixed our RV as we traveled in his Volvo – THANKS! Three-week visit by Hein and Riek (Piet's brother and his wife from Holland) but aided by a two-week visit from Mary to help translate Dutch and English – THANKS! Jellystone Park camping with family and friends many weekends plus 3 fun-filled days with Mom, Sue, Mary, and kids. LOTS OF LAUGHS! Seventh family retreat in October to Onamia!

The next year I continued teaching third grade at Bayport School. Parents shared with me how much they had appreciated the parent letters and wanted me to continue them. They wanted to be informed and involved in our classroom activities. The following October 1988 letter gives an idea of our third-grade classroom learning for that school year:

October 28, 1988

Dear Parents,

STATE REPORTS;

What a creative hard-working group of students we share! The state reports were fantastic and so original. Thanks for all the family involvement and encouragement given to each student. We will offer the video to Channel 10 and will also have a videotape available for sign-out at school. Due to the enthusiastic response for different types of state reports, we ended up having to tape two days so you are in for a real treat! Thanks to Jean Larson who did all of the camera work and to all the parents who came to support and help our production.

HANDS AROUND THE WORLD:

November will mark the start of our cruise around the world following the countries of the Antarctica ski explorers led by Will Steger. Our first stop will be Great Britain, the home of explorer/skier Geoff Somers. Anyone who has materials or information about this country can bring it to our class. The students will be bringing home a new PASSPORT TO READING book with Great Britain on the cover. Please record your daily reading of 15 minutes to your child and have your child read 15 minutes to him or herself. Check out books from the library on Great Britain and write facts learned in the booklet and draw pictures of interesting British objects. These books will be due November 31. HAPPY READING!

MATH:

Our kitchen math classes with our cook, Barb Johnson, have been highlights for the students. This month the students cooked Fry Bread of the Ojibwe Indians. The recipe is as follows:

4 cups flour

3 Tbsp. baking powder

2 cups warm milk

2 tsp. salt

1 Tbsp. shortening (oil is better)

Mix baking powder, milk, salt, oil, and then mix in flour. Turn out on floured board and knead until yeast bread consistency. After mixing, let rise for 20 minutes. Shape into balls the size of an egg and flatten out, making a hole in the middle of each. Proceed to fry in heated oil. Serve with butter, syrup, or anything else your heart desires. Good old Chippewa recipe!

PARTIES FOR THE YEAR:

To make parties fair and easy to work on, the students themselves will plan the food and activities for each party. Each student has a number in our room and the following students will be responsible for the following parties:

Halloween: Monday, Oct. 31: Students 1-5

Christmas: Wednesday, Dec. 21: Students 6-11

Valentine's Day: Feb. 14: Students 12-17

Belated April Fool's Day: April 6: Students 18-21

End of the year party: June 7: Students 23-27

This system worked well last year so I hope you will find it satisfactory. Any moms or dads who wish to help out are surely welcome!

FIELD TRIPS:

On Monday morning, Oct. 31, at 9:30 we have been asked to go to the Croixdale Nursing Home in our Halloween costumes. We will walk over and each student will recite one of their memorized poems for the residents. Each student will also make a card for two senior citizens at the home and so we will be giving our time and love to make the day special and fun for the Croixdale residents.

On Thursday, Nov. 3, we will be walking over to Bayport Printing Company to tour their facility. We will learn how they use both lithography and type-setting presses to produce the print. Mr. Mike Swisher has been so kind as to allow us to visit and I could use two parent volunteers at 10:30 for the first group touring the facility and two volunteers for the 11:00 shift. Thanks.

On Friday, Nov. 4, we will be taking the bus to the Lee-Warner Nature Center to learn about "Mammal Life". We will leave shortly after 9:00 and will take a bag lunch (no lunch boxes) and drink (no glass containers, please) as our session will be from 10:00 to 12:00. Mr. Gehring's third graders will be joining us for this trip.

WILL STEGER TO SPEAK ON: "ANTARCTICA: THE LAST FRONTIER": Tonight, Friday, October 28, from 7:00 – 9:00, Will Steger will present a slide lecture about his trip to the Antarctica. It will be held at the Student Center Ballroom on the Hamline campus and the fee will be $2.00. Call 641-2900 for further info. Sorry, this is such a late notice, but I hope some of you will be able to attend. I am assuming that children would be free but call to be sure.

PARENTS – POETRY – N' PUNCH:

Our November star of the week people are:

Oct 31-Nov. 4: Talia Olding

Nov. 7 – Nov. 11 Maria Battaglia

Nov. 14 – Nov. 18 Laura Bliss

Parents, please bring any poem(s) to share that are special to you or were your childhood favorites. Please also bring a treat to share! Your child has a bulletin board to decorate as he or she pleases and will be the STAR OF THE WEEK —get to be first for everything!

I invite you to come and visit us at any time. Would any parent be willing to be responsible for organizing information on a country as we "visit" it on our tour around the world visiting the countries of all the Antarctica explorers? The countries are: Great Britain, France, Russia, Antarctica, China, Japan, and Australia. Please let me know and I will explain my idea further.

Continue your great support and we are certainly having a fun learning year in Room 106!

BOOKS FOREVER!

Yvonne Aarden

That year teaching third-graders changed my life forever. It was an amazing year of bringing the outside world into our classroom in many diverse ways. One student brought in gerbils which ended up becoming a first-hand science study that became even more interesting as the gerbils procreated to help us with math concepts as well. Honey, our guinea pig, started gaining weight and gave us two babies. A hermit crab became another scientific study in our classroom, as did fertile chicken eggs. When the guinea pigs became too fertile and increased their numbers to ten, the students and I took eight of them to Pets Unlimited. We kept a male offspring of Spike and Honey as well as a female offspring of Spike and Minnie. When Andrew researched the state of Utah, he came to the conclusion that Spike was Mormon, since he had so many "wives."

In our study of the U.S.S.R., students wrote actual letters to Mikhail Gorbachev and President Bush asking them to work toward peace. They each suggested at least one way they could think of to make the two world powers live more peacefully.

Each student made a Matryoshka Doll bank with their parents and collected money until March. The money was given to people in Armenia, victims of two earthquakes that had killed over 60,000 people. One of our local teachers traveled there in March, and took the money, letters, and artwork my students had created for the children of that country.

During this school year, I had wonderful parent and community volunteers. Marilyn Selb, Jean Larson, and Jean Kantke were invaluable mother volunteers in our classroom every week. In late January, Marilyn saw the following notice in the St. Paul paper:

> U.S. WEST SEARCHES FOR OUTSTANDING TEACHER
>
> U.S. West is searching for outstanding teachers in each of the 14 states served by the company's subsidiaries. Teachers must be nominated by someone familiar with their classroom work, such as students, parents or associates. Nominees must be currently teaching full time in grades K-12 and have a minimum of two years teaching experience.
>
> Each state's outstanding teacher will receive a $5,000 award to be used for professional development. Also, three of the 14 state finalists will be provided year-long sabbaticals to pursue activities relating to future plans as teachers in their communities. Nomination packets are available from Marilyn Leonard, U.S. West. 200 S. Fifth St., Room 395, Minneapolis, Minn. 55402

(U.S. West, Inc. was one of seven Regional Bell Operating Companies known for its telecommunications. The company wanted to recognize and honor teachers who, "Reached beyond classroom walls.")

Early in February of 1989, the three moms rushed into my classroom to say they had the application forms. They had filled out their form and all I needed to do was to fill out a one-page form that asked what I would do if I were to receive the year's sabbatical. They would not take "No" for an answer. I felt I owed them, and I filled in the form. At the end of March, I received a letter from U.S. West congratulating me on being selected as one of six Minnesota finalists. My half-hour interview was scheduled for 1:30 pm on Monday, April 10.

Dave Graham, my principal, said I could only take the afternoon off but would have to teach that morning. I sewed a beige skirt and dark green blouse for the interview. Since I wanted it fresh and clean for the interview, I brought it to school and changed in the teacher's bathroom at noontime. Just as I was walking out the door to meet Piet, who was taking time off from work to drive me to the interview, one of my third-graders rushed up to me. "You have to come and see the new gerbil babies before you go, Mrs. Aarden. There are ten of them!" he yelled as his unwashed, greasy fingers grabbed my beige skirt and pulled me back into the classroom. How could I resist?

After sharing their excitement, another student dashed up with a yen coin from our Japan study and said, "I know this will bring you good luck with your interview!"

Armed with my lucky yen and the new handprint design on my skirt, I dashed from the building, hoping we wouldn't be late for the interview.

Upon arrival at U.S. West's building in Minneapolis, I was taken for an official, professional photo shoot. Wow, this really was a formal interview, with photos and all. I asked the photographer if he could avoid showing my fingerprinted skirt. He grinned and said, "I promise to take only an above the waist shot!" We laughed and I felt more at ease.

When I was ushered to the scheduled interview room, a prim and proper young woman—dressed in a business suit and carrying a leather briefcase—was just coming out of the conference room. I felt like I wasn't properly dressed—the country bumpkin coming to the big city.

"Oh, well, teachers work with children and learning can get messy," I told myself, as my name was called. I walked into the conference room that contained a huge, elongated, wooden table. Around this table sat fifteen serious-faced adults, all in business attire, staring at me.

"Mrs. Aarden, you have one half hour in which we will ask you six questions. You will have five minutes for each answer," stated the man to my right. Immediately the questions began. Their difficult questions varied from, "What did I see education looking like in ten years?" to "What was my basic philosophy of education and how did it match the current standards of education?" to "Why should I be considered for a year's sabbatical?"

By the end of the half hour, my green blouse had telltale perspiration rings under my armpits, and my soiled beige skirt was more wrinkled than ever. I was as close to hyperventilating as I had ever been in my life, but I needed to show my thankfulness for this unique opportunity.

"Ladies and gentlemen, I'd like to thank you for this amazingly difficult interview, and I can't wait to tell my third-graders about it. I just have to add that I was teaching my students this morning before I left for this interview," I blurted out. "Just as I was leaving the school, one of my students came rushing out of our classroom and grabbed my skirt with his unwashed, lunchroom hands. He said I couldn't leave until I returned to our room to see our ten new, baby gerbils. Another student raced up to give me this lucky yen, since we're studying Japan. He was sure it would help me in answering your questions." I then told the interviewers I had never experienced a more difficult half-hour of questioning, but wanted to thank each of them for the privilege of being there.

I left feeling that I had failed miserably. Piet took one look at me when I met him at the front of the building, hugged me, and said we needed to definitely find a quiet place to eat and relax. He wanted to know what had happened to make me look so exhausted. After dissecting the thirty-minute disaster, I told Piet that the panel said they would make their decision in the following three days. Well, I didn't have to worry—I certainly would not be the chosen one.

That night while I was sharing my day's adventures with Bret and Pyra, the phone rang. Piet said it was for me. I listened in total astonishment and disbelief: I was the Minnesota U.S. West teacher winner! They would be honoring me and the other five teachers with a special banquet, "Reaching Beyond Classroom Walls" at the Whitney Hotel on April 19th. More details would be forthcoming, they assured me. On May 3rd, I would be flown to Denver, Colorado to compete with the other thirteen state winners. If I were to be one of the three winners in Colorado, I would receive a year's paid sabbatical.

I hung up the phone and screamed hysterically: "I won! I won! I won! Oh, my, God, I won!!"

When I arrived at school the next morning, the Stillwater newspaper reporters were there to greet me, ask questions, and take my photo. Our school district had made the news, what an honor! Bayport School decided to have an assembly to celebrate my victory, with all the district dignitaries present. My "speech" of excitement and disbelief overcame me. I ended up in tears as the superintendent presented me with a beautiful bouquet of flowers and congratulatory words. All the students stood and cheered. My third-graders ran up to give me their hugs. My principal wished me luck on the next step of the journey to compete for the National Teacher of the Year in Colorado.

Because my dad had been sick with lung cancer, I so wanted him and Mom to be present for the recognition dinner. Piet and Pyra and Bret were automatically invited. No problem to include my parents, was the answer from U.S. West's manager. One more favor. I had heard that the Superintendent, and Assistant Superintendent, and our Principal, had been invited. Would it be possible for the three moms who nominated me, as well as our school cook—who was a vital part of my classroom—to attend? I thought it appropriate that the moms, who had initiated my entry for the award, should be a part of the celebration. Once again, U.S. West said they would be delighted to include these important people. I was thrilled and thanked the manager over and over again. How exciting!

That dinner will live on in my memory forever. It was first-class in every sense of the word. I felt like a queen. After all the awards had been given to the runner-up teachers, my name was called. I was presented not only with a check of $5,000.00, but also a crystal obelisk with my name and honor engraved on it. I gave a tearful speech of thanks as I honored my parents (my dad stood and gave his smiling victory "thumbs up" sign), Piet and the kids, the special moms, and Barb, our cook. Photographers were all over the room taking pictures. It was a fairytale evening that I didn't want to end.

Little did I know that when we dropped Mom and Dad off at their apartment, that that would be the last time I would see my dad alive. He hugged me so hard and with tears in his eyes, he said, "I'm so proud of you, Vonnie." The last words he ever spoke to me!

Dad died four days later.

To demonstrate what an amazing, caring company that U.S. West was, the manager, Marilyn Leonard, came to my dad's wake. She brought a beautiful bouquet of flowers, as well as a photo album of pictures taken the evening of the banquet. Everyone saw the photos of Dad in all his glory, making everyone laugh as he shared a joke or two.

Having been in education my entire career, I had never experienced the world of business with its treatment of clients and those they honored. Piet and I flew to Denver the morning of May 3rd. After an individual, taped conference with Sam Burns from Fort Lewis College on my philosophy of education, Piet and I attended a recognition supper for all fourteen state finalists.

The next afternoon I had my interview with the president of U.S. West, a New York City University Dean, a Harvard University Dean, and Senator Byrd of Wyoming. The room was small and intimate, and the panel of interviewers sat at a roundtable. Smiling, they welcomed me. The Harvard Dean of Education, Vito Perrone, looked at me and said, "Why don't you share with us your philosophy of Whole Language and how you implement it in your classroom?" I could not have been given an easier question. I "ran at the mouth" for a half hour, sharing how much fun we were having in my third-grade classroom, learning with an integrated, child-centered approach that encouraged bringing the world inside our classroom walls. The half-hour flew by, and I felt that I had just started with my response to the question. What a world of difference between this and my Minnesota interview!

The following morning, we had a recognition breakfast, followed by the U.S. West Annual meeting and announcement of the three sabbatical winners. The first name was the high school math teacher from Iowa. Next, they announced a high school social studies teacher from New Mexico. The third winner—Yvonne Aarden—a third-grade teacher from Minnesota! I jumped up and down screaming and hugged everybody in sight. How could this be? I was going to have a paid, one-year sabbatical to pursue my dreams of visiting child-centered classrooms all around the U.S. and Canada, maybe try for a Ph.D. or write a book about Whole Language! I had won the National U.S. West award. Could life get any better?

Minnesota Teacher Awards Banquet, with Piet and my folks.
This was the last time I saw my father alive.

CHAPTER THIRTEEN
Changes for the Aarden Family: 1989-91

The fall of 1989, Bret became a senior, at the age of sixteen, with a dogged determination to attend Massachusetts Institute of Technology. This became a reality the day he received a letter of early admittance to become a member of the graduating class of 1994. His dream, since sixth grade, had come true. Bret was one happy camper. We were happy for him.

During his senior year, he continued with guitar, bassoon, and voice lessons. He even composed a piece on his Macintosh MIDI system for the spring Pop Concert. At graduation, he was voted the Most Musical Senior and ranked 4th in a class of 215. (Bret claims he had too many other projects going, and couldn't spend all his time hitting the books). He was a National Merit PSAT finalist and had the second best score in the entire state of Wisconsin.

Pyra was a sophomore and again a member of the Hudson Varsity Girls' Basketball Team. At 6'4", she already had colleges interested in her. Pyra was also reaching great heights in her academic world. She was active in choir, the school newspaper, and Student Council. She worked with children at a nursery school and dabbled in photography, theatre, and modeling. She even managed to squeeze in homework!

While I was on the road visiting schools for my sabbatical, Piet began getting first-hand experience as a single parent. His work as Activities Coordinator remained the same; the new prison warden said Piet would have to get a Master's Degree in Social Work if he were to return to his former job as a social worker. New guidelines had been enforced, so Piet was stuck with his current position. His hopes of returning to work one-on-one with inmates were dashed to the ground. Once again, he put his desires and needs on the back burner and thought only of his family and their happiness and needs.

Bret finally received his driver's license, which lessened the burden of Piet making several daily trips to and from Hudson. Becoming chief cook and bottle washer, as well as laundry person, kept Piet busy. Add to that the chores of keeping the road plowed, the wild animals fed, and an 8:00 – 4:00 job, he never seemed to have enough hours in the day.

As for me, I was "foot-loose and fancy-free" with a year's travel planned for school visits, researcher interviews, and literacy conferences in both the U.S. and Canada. I modified my plans after I attended a class presented by Pat Shannon, a University of Minnesota literacy professor. Pat asked me to co-author a Whole Language book with him. Since he had published so many books for Heinemann, he was able to procure a contract before we even wrote the book. I would use the $10,000.00 that U.S. West had awarded me for my travel expenses; Pat would help me with contacting the people employing child-centered Whole Language philosophies in each area. The plan was, after I had visited each geographical area, I would write a chapter about the strategies and methods I'd observed, from a teacher's point of view. Pat would read my perspective and then add his view as a literacy professor and researcher.

Pat put me in contact with Whole Language professors across the U.S.A., as well as child-centered schools to visit. The year's sabbatical schedule for 1989-90 looked like this:

July: New Hampshire: Attend a three-week writing conference

August: Minnesota: Present workshops

September: Iowa/Missouri: Attend conferences and visit schools

Oct.-Nov: Arizona, New Mexico, California: Visit schools and researchers

December: New York City: Attend conferences and work with researchers

January: Ohio, Michigan, Canada: Visit schools and attend conferences

February: Minnesota, Canada: Visit schools and attend conferences

March: Hawaii – Visit schools

April: Massachusetts, New Hampshire, Nova Scotia: Visit schools

May: Georgia: Attend conferences and Visit schools

August: Missouri and Minnesota: Presenting and Teaching classes

Beginning the sabbatical year with a three-week writing conference at the university in Durham, New Hampshire, was a total literary "frosting on the cake" experience. To rub shoulders with writing researchers Donald Graves, Jane Hansen, and Donald Murray was a dream come true. I had read their books to learn more about writing, but never dreamed I would be on campus with them.

One of my instructors, Kathy Andrasick, was from Hawaii. She expected us to complete one piece of publishable writing each week. (The favorite piece was a play I wrote which can be found in Appendix 1 of this book. It was a spoof pitting the traditional Basalized Reading system and the old way of teaching vs. Yvonne Aarden and her Progressive/Child-Centered Approaches.)

Missing out on Bret's senior year activities and Pyra's sophomore year activities were the downsides of my exciting sabbatical year. In between school visits and conferences, I would return home, but I had to spend many hours trying to complete the next chapter of the Whole Language book.

When I finished a draft chapter, I was to send my writing solely to Pat, and no one else. At the time, I did not question this setup. I was simply ecstatic to think I would have a book published, and I was having amazing learning adventures!

In September of my sabbatical year, another teacher friend (Peg Schwob) and I traveled to Iowa and Missouri to observe classrooms that were using Whole Language strategies. As I viewed the excitement of students taking charge of their own learning, and the intensity of their commitments and responsibilities, I became more convinced than ever that the old "sage on the stage" type of teaching needed to change as quickly as possible. Teachers of all ages had embraced the Whole Language approach, and schools were revolutionizing their views of how children learned best and most effectively.

Peg and I spent hours on the road discussing the need for these changes. We had the opportunity to attend a Missouri Whole Language conference where we spent valuable time with researchers who shared their visions and ideas. We traced the beginnings of this amazing movement to New Zealand and Australia, where it had been implemented for years with great success.

Mom turned eighty in 1989, was alone, and ready for an adventure. She accompanied me to Arizona and California in November. We visited schools, talked with researchers, enjoyed the scenery of the West coast, and loved our special time together. We were encouraged to visit Debra Manning's classroom of second graders in Fresno, CA. Here we saw child-centered learning in action. Debra was confined to a wheelchair, and her students were the most responsible, receptive, caring young people we ever met. Mom and I were greeted at the door of the classroom by two of the students. They introduced themselves, shook our hands, and proceeded to tell us that they would be our guides during our stay.

Since it was quiet reading time, they invited us to find at least three books and read quietly with the rest of the students and their teacher. Then, when the quiet reading time was over, they asked us to choose the favorite of our three books and read it aloud to the rest of the class. What an honor! (I still have the beautiful photo of my mom reading to those students.)

After we read to the class, our little guides proceeded to show us all around the crowded room and explain all the different things they were learning. They proudly showed us all their projects and work. They had created their own radio station and broadcasted weekly. These second graders were even using the daily newspaper to check the stock market prices for math problems!

Our little guides took us outside to see their tiny, productive garden, squeezed between the sidewalk and fence, where they grew their own vegetables. Near the front door, they showed us the fruit trees that they had pruned and were trying an experiment to have several different fruits on the same tree. During a short recess, Debra came over and shared her story of how she had become excited with Whole Language and how it had changed her teaching. Mom and I had a difficult time saying goodbye, but the memories live on of that special teacher and her amazing students.

Since I was halfway through my sabbatical in January, I thought it would be a good idea to give a progress report to my school district. I wanted to share some of the amazing educational research and travel I had experienced. At my meeting with the Superintendent and Assistant Superintendent, I offered multiple ways to help my district when I would return the following year.

 As I shared, they looked at me, hesitated, and then said that just maybe I had outgrown my school district. What did I want to be?? An author? A consultant? A Whole Language professor? Did I expect to return and change the schools in our district, just because I had won the U.S. West awards??

I could not believe my ears! Instead of getting excited about my new learning, the district was setting up blockades for my re-entry after my sabbatical. When I won the award, the district had promised U.S. West that I would not be punished in any way, shape, or form. I was entitled to my former teaching position when I returned. After all, U.S. West was paying for my year's wages, as well as all my benefits. Instead of leaving the district office with exhilarated feelings, I felt dejected and unwanted. I would NOT, could NOT, let them spoil the rest of my sabbatical year.

During my writing course at the University of New Hampshire in Durham, I had been invited by my Hawaiian instructor to fly to Hawaii to visit and work with teachers both in Oahu and the Big Island. Kathy invited Piet to come along, but he felt he needed to stay home. Pyra jumped right in and asked if she could accompany me. So in March, she and I spent two weeks in Hawaii. While I visited schools and worked with teachers, she took in the sights and activities offered on the islands. That included snorkeling, swimming, sea sailing, and time to hang out with Kathy Andrasick's two sons. She also accompanied me when she wanted to go to the schools I was visiting.

Since I was going to be in Boston in April, I had Bret fly out with me so we could check out MIT and the surroundings he would be enjoying the next fall. It was an exciting time to visit the university and explore the city. What an honor to have early entrance! His dreams of studying Artificial Intelligence were about to come true!

So, there were a few benefits my kids shared on my whirlwind year of travel. That sabbatical year changed the direction of my teaching career and there was no going back...

The year 1990 was a BUSY time for the Aarden family.

Bret graduated from high school, set off for MIT, and quickly added many musical activities to an already busy schedule. He joined a frat house, despite his pledge to never do that. A basement filled with available computers in the fraternity house definitely created that mind change. One of his busy weeks included a chemistry test, physics test, Chamber Chorus concert, plus dress rehearsals. He was thrilled that the first year at MIT had a pass/fail grading system. This enabled him to pursue his musical interests, along with the stringent academic curriculum. He became part of the MIT Logarhythms, which was an all male acapella singing group. Bret also became involved in several musicals including *H.M.S. Pinafore* and *Sweeney Todd*.

Pyra was "up to her neck" with basketball practices, games, voice lessons, volleyball, three choirs, forensics, theater arts class, and working as both advertising editor for the school newspaper and taking care of children at church during Mass. Her junior year involved lots of driving to and from school; having her own car was a blessing for everyone.

Piet claimed he had become "disgustingly domesticated" with all the meal planning, laundry, and housecleaning while I was on the road. He constantly tried to remain positive in the negative prison setting. Piet never worried about losing his job. The crime rate kept his employment more secure all the time!

In the spring of 1990, my assistant superintendent and principal called to arrange a meeting with me. They informed me that some of the teachers at my Bayport School had petitioned that I not return there. They did not want to be forced to become a Whole Language School. Since Dave, my principal, did not want any agitation, the district decided I should teach at Marine-on-the-St. Croix School. This school was located in the northern part of the district, isolated from the rest of the schools. The teachers there were trying to become more child-centered. This would be a better fit for me, so I was told. I looked at them in shock.

U.S. West had definitely told them I was not to be penalized in any way when I returned from my sabbatical. I had every right to return to my same job. How would the parents in Bayport feel about this? What about the three moms that had nominated me? Dave and the assistant superintendent told me not to rock the boat, and do what was best for everyone. To this day, I don't know why I allowed myself to be swayed by the administration's stance on this. I loved teaching the students at Bayport School and the parents were the most supportive people I ever had. They would think that I had abandoned them after all they had done for me! How could I not return to Bayport? The administration insisted.

I chose not to tell any of the Bayport parents the REAL reason I did not return to their school. Reluctantly, that fall of 1990, I set off for my new assignment. It meant not being able to drive to work with Piet, and that I had to drive a half-hour longer to and from home. It also meant that I would be faced with third-grade parents who wondered if their children were becoming my "guinea pigs" for trying out new strategies. It became one of the hardest years of my teaching. Trying to build trust with the parents and students took so much time and effort. Was it worth it?

During my sabbatical, I learned about the Student Ocean Challenge that would connect schools to the BOC Challenge, a single-handed yacht race around the world. The race was scheduled from September to May 1990-91, with sailors competing from all over the world. The 27,000-mile race would run in stages from Newport, Rhode Island to Cape Town, South Africa to Sydney, Australia, to Punta de Este, Uruguay, and back to Newport. The race was run every four years with three categories: Class 1: 50-60 foot boat; Class 2: 40-50 foot boats; Corinthian Class.

I got so excited when I researched different ways that schools could connect with the skippers during their race. This would work perfectly for our year's theme, and be an amazing opportunity for my "Classroom going Beyond the Walls" project. Many of the students in my newly assigned school were acquainted with sailing, since they lived by the river. Nautical terminology would be a known language to them. I knew nothing about sailing, but I could learn. It was a great example of the teacher being a learner and the students being the teachers!

I had twenty-five students and there were twenty-five sailors competing. Each student adopted a skipper to communicate with during the year, while the entire class studied the countries they were from. The math of navigation and sailing techniques fit so well, as did the geography of the world since the sailors were from so many different countries. Once again, I was able to connect all the academic areas into one theme that had relevance in the world outside our classroom walls.

Despite all of this, the parents were dissatisfied: This was not the way other teachers had taught their children! In October, after struggling with multiple school issues, I wrote the following letter to the parents of my third-graders:

> October 15, 1990
>
> Dear Parents,
>
> This is a difficult letter to write but a necessary one. In all my thirty years of teaching, I have never had such negative reactions to my teaching. I felt that by taking an evening to share my philosophy and manner of teaching, you would understand why there are no worksheets coming home and why I feel so strongly about your child learning how to become an independent learner in a very child-centered environment. I asked that you please come into my classroom three different times before you criticize me or my classroom.
>
> The number of hours that apparently are spent on the telephone and within the home discussing my teaching ability could certainly be better spent visiting my classroom and seeing first hand how I believe learning should happen!
>
> It is not fair to me or your child to be treated in such a manner. Your criticism of a teacher in the presence of a child can only harm the bonding relationship between teacher and child. It will have a negative effect on your child's learning development. From now on I will not grant a conference of complaints until you have spent three different hours on different days in my classroom.
>
> I have won several Outstanding Teacher Awards on local, state, and national levels and have been recognized as an excellent teacher in many other ways. Apparently, this holds no water with this community. No parent from Marine will come and tell me how to run my classroom as I am a PROFESSIONAL who has been developing her craft for over thirty years and has never stopped taking classes or believed that she has reached her potential.
>
> I am and will always be a LEARNER and I try to model this philosophy within my classroom. I do not believe that learning is done from 8:30 -2:30 and that parents have no responsibility in helping their children after school hours.
>
> Learning MUST be continuous and be modeled by parents as well as teachers. My learning philosophy is not a worksheet philosophy. Your child did not learn to walk or talk using worksheets and I do not

believe that they learn to read and write using worksheets. All are natural learning PROCESSES and can only be learned by DOING. Eg: I learn how to walk by walking. I learn how to write by writing.

For those of you who have given me support, I thank you and appreciate it. Each teacher has different gifts and talents to give your child and because of the diversity of gifts and talents, your child becomes enriched in a different way under the guidance and love of each teacher. Please allow us to each teach in our own unique and personal manner. My goal is to create the best learning environment that I can for your child. Your acceptance of this is the key to allowing your child to grow in learning not only how to learn but enjoying it in the process.

BOOKS FOREVER! Yvonne Aarden

In January, I struggled with the report cards that our district had adopted. This meant I had to inform the parents why their students would be bringing home two different report cards:

Dear Parents:

It is with great reluctance that I place a "+, S+, S, S-, or U" on pieces of paper and then expect that these "marks" can begin to tell the story of what your child is or is not learning. To really see the growth, the "highs and the lows", that we experience each day would be to have a constant videotaping of each individual child every minute he or she is in the classroom each day. Please accept the "marks" I gave your child as I share with you the agonies of this type of report system. Believe me when I say that I did my best to be as fair as I could be and to share with you in my honest perception of where I see your child according to his or her capabilities at this moment in time.

To get a better idea of your child's progress, you need to be in the classroom frequently and see your child interacting with his or her peers and "elders." I urge you to seriously talk with your child and explain that being a student is their "occupation" that needs to be taken seriously and responsibly. Your child's behavior can be a deterrent or a catalyst for the entire group's learning, Failing to complete work, your child affects our entire group because learning is SOCIAL and we are a community of learners who help each other within the learning process...

Included in this report card is the report card your child wrote for himself or herself. As you can see, your child and I don't always agree but I thought it would be revealing to both you and me as to what "marks" they would give themselves. Also enclosed is a line graph to show you the data on the 60-word spelling test I gave them in September and in January. Please return this as they will take the same test again in May so you can see the growth in the four-month intervals. This is just a bit of "research" for you and me to visually see how spelling improves because your child reads good children's literature and reads more. Increased reading and being exposed to much print increases spelling ability—not weekly spelling lists which take words out of context and are memorized for the week and forgotten the next week.

We have much to celebrate within our third grade learning community at Marine School because they have developed their capabilities in so many areas:

-their reading stretching to many genres of literature

-their oral presentations improving each report or project

-their ability to memorize poetry as a pleasurable and satisfying feat

-their knowledge of geography and world cultures spanning the entire globe

-their ability to read and write silently for greater lengths of time

-their understanding that math is more than digits on paper

-their increase of deductive thinking through the mind-benders

-their acquiring of scientific observations and data-collecting

-but the greatest of all is their LOVE of reading and writing that is manifested by these third graders. All this in four months? Give your child a huge hug and tell them they are wonderful...

The months that followed were filled with ups and downs. In March, I received a notice that all third-graders in the district would be taking the California Achievement Test (CAT) the week of April 8-12. My research during my sabbatical had involved assessment and evaluation. How could I just sit back and not try to create a change within our district and its mode of testing and using these results to judge students? So I sat down and wrote the following letter to our school administrators:

> March 19, 1991
>
> Dear Dr. Wettergren and Dr. Weingarten,
>
> The state and district's policy to give standardized tests to elementary students has disturbed me for many years. As I research this issue of testing, I become even more disturbed. Why are we giving so much time, money, and validity to tests that "deprive students of equal educational opportunities, trivialize learning, demoralize teachers and increase public skepticism?" (Marlene Corbett in The Delta Kappa Gamma Bulletin, Winter 1990)
>
> My educational philosophy demands that I only allow my students to participate in activities that will be for their educational benefit and growth as learners. The standardized tests fail to meet

these criteria as I have failed to see any positive educational benefit derived from the taking of these tests.

The students lose sleep, become anxious, worry about how "smart" they are in comparison to others, become "uptight" with the timed elements as well as the format and UNNATURALNESS of the whole testing situation. Parents, in turn, become uptight, concerned about how well their child will perform, and then judge their child's academic worth on a set of numbers that does not give a true picture of their child's potential or current capabilities. The test results are not understood by them (or by few educators). These test results are based on a few questions of isolated skills that can NEVER give a true composite of a child's ability or capabilities. The teacher is also affected by the amount of time needed to take these tests, the time spent in "assuring" the child that this is only one test and not to worry etc., and the teacher then feels accountable to the tests even though the tests do not reflect what the curriculum needs are, much less the needs of the child.

Testing is a multi-billion dollar industry that we have nurtured for too long. I would like to know how many of our district's educational dollars are placed into test and testing. I would then challenge us to look at these dollars and use them for REAL education of our children and in-service of teachers on learning how to evaluate (VALUE what is being done by the student rather than label by a deficiency of test results.)

Since I have discovered no positive, educational benefits for giving these tests, I will refrain from administering these CAT tests to my third-grade students unless I am ordered to do so. I have seen these tests used only as a numbers game to compare students, schools, and districts. These tests are then used to LABEL students and place them in programs that "pull out" the students who have either done well or poorly. These numbers are used for state and district dollars for programs that reinforce the differences of children rather than allowing these students to be one in heterogeneous groups of all abilities learning from each other's strengths.

I am including several articles that reaffirm my thinking and position I am taking on this issue. Why are we not in the forefront of the real educational needs of our students rather than allowing ourselves to be entangled in the numbers game called testing? Let's look at some the most LITERATE countries and learn from them as they do not allow elementary students to be driven by test scores. If we want to know about the students in our schools, then we need to be in the classrooms observing the learning that is happening. Teachers need to be given time and in-services on effective EVALUATION (done by the teacher as she observes the students on a continuous, ongoing, cumulative basis) rather than being told they must test their students on a given, isolated date with invalid, unreliable tools called standardized tests.

Sincerely

Yvonne Aarden

Cc: School board members of District #834

Principals of District #834

State and Assistant Commissioner of Education in Minnesota

On March 26 I received this letter from the District Office:

> Dear Yvonne:
>
> The concern you expressed in your March 19, 1991 letter about the value and effects of standardized testing of young students is not new. The pros and cons of group-normed standardized assessment have long been a topic for educational debate.
>
> Nevertheless, to comply with M.S. 126.666, Districts 834's testing program includes standardized assessment (California Achievement Test) at grades 3,6,8,11 in addition to the required Minnesota assessment of state essential learner outcomes at grades 6,8,12 in the core content areas.
>
> All third-grade teachers in District 834 will administer the California Achievement Test during April 8-12, 1991, yourself included.
>
> Yours truly, Mary Jo Weingarten, Asst. Superintendent

On April 5, 1991, the following letter came from the Minnesota Department of Education:

> Dear Yvonne,
>
> Thanks for sending me a copy of your letter on testing. I had not seen any of the articles that you sent and I appreciate having those too. I will be interested in knowing what happens in response to your letter.
>
> As teaching approaches change, the need to change the manner of assessment will need to change too. Every school system needs some form of accountability. Many districts find that the current tests are in conformity with their present instructional approaches. You and I might think that both should change—and soon—but I think we are getting some encouraging changes in the least expected places. If a district has done the wrong thing well enough, they come to notice that it is just not working.
>
> There are many reasons not to test young children. I am sending you two articles from Young Children that discuss this. I am also sending you information about the folks from Fair Test. If you haven't heard of them, you may be interested. I have their book called Fallout...
>
> Thanks, too, for your work with Zhining on the observation instrument.
>
> Sincerely,
>
> Corinna Moncada, Specialist, K-4 Education

After months of letters and invitations during the year, many parents made it a point to visit our classroom to find out first hand what was actually happening. Gradually, I began to see progress. Complaints became fewer and fewer.

My students were totally involved on so many different levels with their "adopted" yacht sailors. We followed them with computers, newspapers, TV broadcasts, and personal letters to each skipper. Learning longitude and latitude became fun when students used them to locate their sailor's position in the ocean. Graphs became necessary to record their data and compare their sailor's position in the race with another classmate's. The skippers became the first topic of conversation every morning in our classroom.

Josh, one of my third graders, adopted Yukoh Tada, a sailor from Japan. Since Josh did not have a father in his home, Yukoh became a sort of surrogate father for him. The Japanese skipper took on great importance in Josh's life. Josh suddenly developed a zest for learning all about sailing and following the latitude and longitude of his skipper's journey. Our study of Japan became Josh's specialty because his skipper was from that country.

In March, this article appeared in the newspaper:

YACHTING: Japanese Sailor Is Dead

Yukoh Tada, the Japanese sailor who won his class in the first BOC Challenge race, apparently committed suicide Friday in Sydney, Australia, said an official for one of the teams in this year's race. He was 61 years old.

Tada had been staying with relatives in Sydney, said the official, who insisted on anonymity. The BOC office in Newport, R.I., said yesterday that it could not comment on Tada's death until relatives were notified.

Tada withdrew from the current BOC round-the-world race after a grueling voyage to Sydney from Cape Town. The passage took him 50 days when others in the fleet finished in as few as 26. Tada told race officials that his new boat, the 50-foot racing yacht Koden VIII, was faster than his previous BOC boat, and "easier to capsize." Tada said his boat had been knocked over by wind and waves five times in that passage. He designed and built the craft himself.

In the 1982-83 race, Tada made up valuable time by taking his boat through a shortcut that helped him to win first place for the 50-foot boats.

Tada, who was not married, was a taxi driver in Tokyo. He was also a painter, poet, author, and musician. At every race port, he would entertain his friends with solo concerts on his saxophone, or gather fellow sailors for homemade dinners of Japanese delicacies.

I agonized over how to share this horrific news with Josh and the rest of the students. I had read an article about Japan's cultural traditions which stated that taking one's life was seen as an honorable way of atoning for public disgrace, and expression of one's deep sense of shame. Yet, how difficult to present this sailor's suicide to a nine-year-old who had very little interest in school and learning until he bonded with this skipper's challenge of sailing around the world in a boat he had built himself. After sharing the sad news with Josh, we cried together and tried to think what he could do.

In the end, we decided he could create a book for the skipper's family living in Japan. Josh used his artistic talents for the illustrations in his book. He began to research more about Japan to make his book more authentic. Josh also included his own story about what an important figure the skipper had become in his life and why.

Through the BOC, we were able to obtain the family's address in Japan so that Josh could send the amazing sailing book he had created. Just before the school year ended, he received a beautiful thank you letter from the skipper's family. As Josh shared his letter with all of us, he gained new respect from his classmates. They expressed how proud they were of him for what he had done to ease the grief of his skipper's family.

I had the privilege of being invited to Newport, Rhode Island, for the celebration that honored the eighteen skippers who completed the course. I shared Josh's story, as I presented a workshop to teachers. I explained how we had revolved our year's learning around the amazing race. Piet had purchased a small video camera for me, so I was able to bring "live" action back to my students of the skipper celebration. My students were so excited to not only see the skippers, but to actually hear them talk about their adventures.

During the school year, I received many offers to give workshops in different school districts. I was already busy on different weekends, teaching classes I had created for Hamline University ("Creating a Whole Language Classroom", "Integrating the Curriculum", and "Teacher as Reader/Writer/Researcher"). Whenever I had some spare moments, I spent time writing my book on Whole Language. My schedule was way too busy. I needed to rethink what I wanted from my teaching career.

The spring of that year, I learned about the possibility taking a three- to five-year mobility leave from my district. Piet and I talked about that and—as he always did—he told me to do whatever I wanted; he would support me in whatever decision I made. I applied for the leave. The district decided I could have three years, not five. I took it! In June, I said goodbye to my students as well as my school district. I was about to start a new life as an Independent Literacy Consultant!

As I wrote my last letter to the parents of my students, I shared my decision to leave the school district:

> ...As some of you already know, I will be taking a three year leave from the district to spend time completing my book, "Impressions of the Whole: Whole Language Classrooms Across North America." I will also be a literacy consultant to school districts setting up Whole Language classrooms and will teach graduate classes for Hamline University and Stout University. I feel that after thirty years of working in different capacities as a teacher of "children" of all ages, the time is ripe for me to spread the good news of child-centered education to as many people as possible. I believe so firmly in this philosophy of education and have seen how children of every race, culture, economy, and ability can thrive and really become LOVERS of literature as well as INDEPENDENT learners. I need to do this now while I have the energy and the time to devote to such a wonderful cause—making learning fun and exciting as well as worth while and relevant for our leaders of the future...

Many parents came to wish me well and many wrote letters to me at the end of the year, after they received my letter. Two of those letters were:

> Dear Mrs. Aarden,
>
> We want to thank you for all the time and energy you've put into teaching our third-grade class. We're so glad you stayed, especially after that shaky start! The kids have learned more in the last nine months than in the first three years of school. Hopefully, this class can inspire other teachers to adopt your method of teaching because it really works.
>
> Helping in your class gave us the chance to see first hand how the kids have improved. It was amazing to see some kids who never even liked school just blossom! Everyone seemed to find their own little "nitch." Good luck on the lecture circuit! Our school system sure could use a boost, and you're one who can do it! We really do appreciate you, Mrs. Aarden.
>
> Let me end with a short quote from a famous book: "Teach a child in the way he should go, and when he is older, he will not depart from it."
>
> BOOKS FOREVER! Scott, MaryAnn, and Arthur Andersen

> Dear Mrs. Aarden.
>
> Of poems memorized and recited, of poems written with such imagery, I would never have imagined.

Of the "Grinch Who Stole Christmas" so well learned and expressively presented.

Of the poise and confidence to stand up and present the most impressive Country-of-the-Month reports and to videotape them so we all could see.

These are the things that I will always remember.

Of the monthly newsletters, the Ocean Challenge, and the many, many projects too numerous to list, Thank You.

And most of all for the respect, appreciation, and love of books and reading, Thank You.

Chris has always been an enthusiastic boy, but, oh, how you have channeled and fueled his quest to learn.

You have richly endowed Chris' lifetime journey of learning.

With heartfelt thanks and appreciation,

Ken Thompson, Sue Thompson

My school district did not change any of their traditional teaching methods, much less do anything to change their testing procedures. Districts all around them asked for my services. Not my district! My administrators had bluntly expressed their thoughts: "I think you have outgrown your own school district." Maybe someday they would change!

That summer Pyra played in Basketball Olympics with her AAU team from June to August. This paid off when she was offered full-ride scholarships from several Division I schools. She narrowed her choices to five. This meant home visits from the coaches of each university, all using their best methods of trying to persuade her to play at their school. They arranged for her, as well as for Piet and me, to visit their campuses during the following school year. After a whirlwind of campus visits, Pyra chose Nebraska. She felt Nebraska had great basketball offerings and the best pre-med opportunities. Her senior year of high school was taken up with basketball, volleyball, women's choir, school choir, student council, National Honor Society, forensics, editor of school newspaper as well as taking her academic classes. Her reading, artwork, modeling, and her own personal time became very limited!

During the summer, I met with Pat Shannon several times at the University of Minnesota to work on the book Heinemann had agreed to publish. Pat gave me feedback on my work each time we met. During all our writing sessions, I never saw or read his contributions to the text. I guess I was just too busy trying to revise my own writing—and too caught up in the unbelievable opportunity of actually becoming a published author—to ask to read his contributions to our book.

Bret remained in Boston that summer, working in the MIT library while being involved in several music groups and musicals. He left the fraternity and began his sophomore year needing to keep a "B" average. Taking two computer courses and linear algebra, he realized he could not participate in all the musical groups. MIT did not offer the combination of both music and computers as an alternative. He returned home in October to work at temp jobs and to figure out which college would meet his future music career intentions.

In November of the previous year, Piet had pushed a wheelbarrow full of chopped wood up our steep hill and lost his footing on the snow-covered driveway. He personally diagnosed it as a sprained shoulder and lived in pain for a year. He finally conceded to go to a doctor, only to find out he needed his rotator cuff repaired. The shredded shoulder tendons had atrophied from lack of use. (Not that the bum shoulder kept him from his usual Paul Bunyan activities, or any other task he needed to do.)

I began working as an independent consultant that fall, which was exciting! I had become known around the state of Minnesota, thanks to the U.S. West awards. Schools all around the state were clamoring for workshops. I taught classes I had created for Hamline University on weekends, and some districts hired me to do long-term consulting throughout the school year. Wisconsin Universities also hired me as an adjunct professor. My already-overbooked calendar was filled through May of the following year.

With everyone back home, Piet said he felt like he was the maintenance employee of the Department of Transportation: He constantly repaired all four of the vehicles now parked in our driveway. We each needed our own transportation. Having a new car was never an option; Piet always found us good deals at the Minnesota State auction held every year at the prison.

Life for all the Aardens in 1991 was a'changing, and headed in new directions.

CHAPTER FOURTEEN
Life Changes for Everyone: 1992 – 97

On October 8, 1992, Piet officially retired. He had put in his time of twenty-three years at the Minnesota State Prison in Stillwater, Minnesota. That was the year he turned sixty-five, and was definitely ready for a change of scenery. We celebrated with a gala retirement and birthday party with family and friends.

Pyra was enjoying her first year of college in her role as a Lady Nebraska Cornhusker and as a Pre-Med student. She managed to carry a 4.0 GPA while juggling basketball and academics.

Bret chose the University of Illinois at Urbana-Champaign for his schooling, and switched his major to Vocal Performance. He was finding the intellectual rigors of music theory much more fascinating than physics or differential equations!

Since child-centered learning was my priority, I constantly searched for classes in that realm. One of my teacher friends, from our Reading Council, told me about a Rigby course called ELIC (Early Literacy In-service Course) for K-3 teachers being offered in Eau Claire, Wisconsin. The Wisconsin class was an experiment to promote the class nationwide. Tony Brady, a businessman in Chicago, worked out a partnership with Rigby, an Australian book company. He then invited an Australian administrator to the U.S.A. to teach the course.

ELIC was a twelve-week teacher in-

Pyra and Mom.

service program that included professional readings and weekly discussions on chosen topics of seminal importance. It advocated teaching students in small groups, with Rigby leveled readers that matched each student's reading ability. The course embodied the philosophy of Whole Language. I signed up for the course, even though it meant driving seventy miles each way.

After attending several sessions, I knew this was another appropriate topic for the literacy workshops I offered to districts in Minnesota. I met with Minneapolis school districts to offer them this model, as well as my Hamline University Classes. The administrators were excited and wanted to know when I could begin staff development for their teachers.

At one of our ELIC sessions, the director of ELIC flew from Chicago to meet with me. The facilitator of our weekly sessions had shared my background and my neophyte attempts at being a literacy consultant. After I talked with the director, she offered me the job of becoming a consultant with their Rigby company. The company was just starting their focus on employing independent consultants.

The long-term goal of Mr. Brady was to offer the ELIC course to school districts across the nation. This would involve hiring qualified consultants and training them to teach the course. Rigby would furnish each consultant with a rental car, travel expenses, meals, lodging, as well as $500.00 a day. This job would involve being away from one's home for twelve weeks at a time. Would I be interested? If so, they would train me during a two-week Facilitator Training session in Idaho.

At the same time, Hamline University offered me the opportunity to become their first Whole Language Director. I would create more classes, develop ways to work with school districts, and teach several child-centered courses at the university.

Piet and I weighed the pros and cons of changing my current direction. I was teaching workshops in Minnesota and Wisconsin, but Rigby offered an opportunity to travel all over the United States. I would have a four-day week demonstrating strategies in classrooms during the day and presenting a two-hour workshop each day after school for twelve teachers. I would work with forty-eight teachers during the twelve weeks, and arrange at least three demos for each of them in their classrooms.

The pros were that I would no longer have to locate districts to work with, and I would have materials already prepared for my teaching. Rigby would furnish everything I needed. The cons were that I would be away from home for long periods of time.

The university offer would mean I would be traveling around the state of Minnesota, developing new courses and creating the new department. That held interesting challenges for me, but the prospect of working nationwide held greater allurement and meant more income.

Piet, once again, stepped up to the plate and said he could manage things at home. Since he was retired, he could even join me on many of my travels. I had two years before I had to make a decision about returning to classroom teaching. Why not give it a try? I decided to accept Rigby's offer.

The following fall, while I was in Facilitator Training in Idaho, I received Pat Shannon's section of our book. It was NOT what I had expected. My 250 pages of writing were to be complemented with only thirty or so pages of his writing! His forward described me in what I believed to be belittling terms: He was the professor and I was the mere teacher.

I was so angry; I called Heinemann instead of Pat. I told the publisher that I did not accept what Pat had written, and would not want the book published. Learning that I had done the majority of the writing, they said I was the main author, and could do as I wished. In hindsight, I should have talked with Pat first. I was a neophyte, unaware of the protocol for the publishing arena. Later that year, I tried to revise and re-write the book, but I had lost my voice, and my passion for spending more time on it. My book was not to be published. Chalk that up as a difficult learning experience.

In September, I started my first Rigby assignment in Sunnyvale, California. I soon learned what traffic congestion really was. Because of the distances between my assigned schools, I needed to add another day to my work. That meant I was working a five-day week instead of four. This was necessary in order to give the teachers the number of classroom demos we had promised. It was totally exciting, but very demanding.

That fall, both Pyra and Bret were in college, so Piet planned to spend his days basking in the California sun while I taught. That was not to become a reality. We had signed up to have natural gas lines piped into our property. The gas company told us the lines would be brought in during the summer. Believing them, Piet removed our old oil-heating furnace and replaced it with a natural gas furnace. The lines were delayed and the furnace could not be hooked up until the lines were in place.

Wisconsin winters come early and know no mercy. Piet had to stay home until the gas lines were laid. He used our fireplace to keep the house warm to prevent the water pipes from freezing! With the lines finally in place, Piet joined me for several weeks in November. But, Piet had house improvement projects to complete, so he returned to Wisconsin to work on them. He wanted to have everything completed before the kids and I returned home to celebrate Christmas together.

Life at Nebraska kept Pyra extremely busy juggling basketball schedules and Pre-Med classes during her second year of college in 1993. She told her coach that the latter came first, but that she would certainly work hard at improving her basketball skills as Center for their team. During Christmas vacation, the team traveled to Puerto Rico for a tournament. Naturally, Piet and I joined them to give our support. It was oddly different to spend Christmas relaxing by a swimming pool surrounded by palm trees—a slight change from the snow banks of Wisconsin!

After a year at the University of Illinois, Bret decided the music classes offered were not what he wanted for his career. He informed us he wanted to become an "autodidact." After consulting the dictionary for different definitions of that term, we asked him what that would look like for him. He wanted to teach himself, using many different formats of study to expand his musical understandings: online classes, reading, taking some lessons, experimenting with different musical forms. Bret asked if he could live at home while exploring his new avenues of music. He would get a part-time job for his monetary needs. We agreed and Bret came back to live downstairs in our Hudson home.

Piet joined me for different stretches of time at my next Rigby assignment in warm Florida, near Orlando. In between, he worked on several home improvements in Wisconsin. One of the projects, scheduled for Christmas vacation, was to install new carpeting throughout our home. The kids and I helped to pull up the twenty-year, orange-brown, 70s shag. We replaced it with a beige Berber carpet—a Christmas gift to all of us! The new carpet "required" new living room furniture. So within one week, our home took on a totally refreshing, new, modern look and feel. The kids told us that the orange countertops and burnt-orange refrigerator in the kitchen needed to go next.

In May and June, Piet and I went to Europe, as a belated retirement gift for Piet. We had not seen his family for seven years. We stayed with Piet's brother and wife and helped raise the per capita beer consumption statistics. In our Netherland's sightseeing, Piet and I even rode the canals in a small motorboat maneuvered by the native himself!

We also did some sightseeing in various countries nearby, including a trip to Norway. We visited a former classmate of mine, Bonnie, who had also been a parishioner of Piet's in Kelliher, MN. Bonnie was in the convent with me, left and married Magne, a man from Norway. As Bonnie and I spent hours reminiscing about our convent days, Magne and Piet shared their ancestral roots. We Minnesota convent girls never imagined we would be sharing stories in Norway with European husbands!

In the fall of 1994, I had to make my decision to either return to teaching in Stillwater, or continue with my literacy-consulting career. Piet and I discussed how difficult it was to have time together, because of my travel schedule. He was retired and now had time for us to be together, but I was always gone. It was necessary for him to keep the house and property well maintained, but that meant he had to stay home much of the time. Piet did not want this kind of life. What should we do?

We talked and wrote down all the pros and cons of our future. I decided to resign from the Stillwater school system, and continue my career as a literacy consultant working for Rigby. This required a nomadic way of life. It meant that we needed to sell the house if we wanted to be together. Pulling up our deep Wisconsin roots after twenty-three years was a HUGE, difficult decision.

Selling our house meant leaving our home and five acres of woods into which we had poured every fiber of our being. For Piet, it had to have been the hardest decision since leaving the priesthood. His heart and soul were in that home and land. If I chose to remain in the Stillwater school system, we would not have to move. As always, Piet was willing to sacrifice for the needs of those he loved.

As we talked about selling our Hudson home, my mind wandered back to those first days in 1971 when we started to prepare the land for our home, as well as all those years of toil and backbreaking work to accomplish our dreams. Then there were all the people we had become acquainted with over the years, and the amazing life-long friendships we were still enjoying. If we sold, there would be:

...no more neighborhood Christmas caroling in the freezing cold, warmed by laughter, hot toddies in our thermos bottles, and the blanket of friendship that wrapped us closer together, no matter how out-of-tune our voices were.

...no more family get-togethers over the holidays having Dad's famous brandy and rum Tom and Jerry drinks, Mom's special green Jello salads, Flo's delicious, flaky-crusted pies made with that secret ingredient called lard, or Mary's savory wild rice dishes that she claimed were "so forgiving" of the ingredients.

...no more exploring our five acres of woods, admiring the gorgeous trilliums that covered our hillside when they popped their heads up in May and disappeared a few weeks later.

...no more sitting in the living and dining room areas to watch the woodland animals feast on the corn and seeds from the multiple feeders that Piet had built.

...no more nights relaxing by the crackling fireplace, sprawled out on our home-made bean bag chairs, enjoying the expertly chopped wood of Piet's hard labors.

I needed to change gears in my mind, be thankful for all those memories, and believe that there were many new adventures around the corner. Now we must put our best energies into making this move become positive and believe it was best for us at this time of our lives.

We put the house up for sale in June and sold it the first week of August. Pyra could live off campus her last two years at the university, so we decided to rent an apartment in Lincoln, Nebraska. She would live in the apartment and we would join her in between my consulting assignments. Living in Lincoln would give us opportunities to attend her basketball games the times we were there.

Because we would have limited room in an apartment, we sold our extra belongings to an auction company. In August, we filled a U-Haul trailer, and our pickup, with our belongings and moved into our new dwelling in Lincoln.

Proud parents of #44.

Celebrating mom's 85th. (L to R) Dan, Mary, Flo, Mom, Rome, Vonnie, and Piet.

Pyra told us she "needed" the master bedroom suite so that she could have her privacy and study room when we would be living with her. Piet and I agreed to her wishes because she would be the main tenant. Nebraska Furniture was happy to see the Aardens, as we had sold most of our belongings and needed new furnishings for the apartment.

Bret returned to the world of books and academia in 1995. After searching for a university that offered courses he wanted for his future music degree, he chose New College in Sarasota, Florida. The university offered a non-graded system in which all academic reports were subjective essays from each professor. A drawback of moving to Florida for Bret was the heat. If Florida and Alaska could have exchanged places, he would have been in total euphoria. Bret's classes of epistemology, music analysis, piano and guitar lessons, electronic music lab, drama lit courses, and computer work, kept this nocturnal, young man busy. He continued his vegan diet and swam for daily exercise.

Pyra traveled to Europe for a month that summer with her basketball cohort, Karen Jennings. Pyra (with her 6'4" frame and blond hair) and Karen (with her 6'2" frame and red hair) must have been quite a sight hitchhiking in Ireland when the drenching rain made biking impossible. Stories abound of their fun adventures—quite a change from grueling basketball practices and schedules! Pyra ended up being the highest scorer and rebounder on her team that year and was designated as the tallest and strongest female team member in Nebraska history. Piet assured her that this was because she had all those years of hauling wood for our Wisconsin home! During her senior year at the university, she spent hours filling out applications for different medical schools.

Piet and I continued our nomadic life as I traveled to various locations, training teachers for Rigby. My assignments were in California, Washington state, Oregon, Florida, and Nebraska. Several of us consultants were trained to become facilitators. This involved training teachers all over the U.S.A. in an intensive, two-week seminar during the summers. These seminars became my favorite work as a consultant, because it was like experiencing a two-week literacy retreat spent in in-depth research, discovering literacy strategies.

As Piet traveled with me on my many assignments, he became extremely knowledgeable of my child-centered approach and philosophy. Of course, I was constantly sharing my new learning with him, and he witnessed classrooms that espoused these practices. So, he became a spokesman to defend this method of teaching whenever he had a chance. Piet was my advocate, and he often shared with others the power of having students take responsibility for their own learning. Piet even spent time working in classrooms with students. This gave more credence to his advocacy. It was so affirming to have my spouse support my every attempt to make changes in the world of education.

For our twenty-fifth wedding anniversary gift to each other, Piet and I flew to New Zealand and Australia for two months in the summer of 1995. *The Los Angeles Times* offered an airline deal too good to pass up. I told Piet it was meant to be—perfect timing and a great way to celebrate a quarter of a century together. During our travels, I included some school visits and working with researchers. We stayed in B&B's and loved getting to know the local people.

My favorite story of the New Zealand trip was our visit with Margaret Mooney. Margaret was a famous literacy researcher I met at a conference. She invited Piet and me to stay with her in Aukland for our first week of vacation there. Not taking "no" for an answer, she met us at the airport 5:30 a.m., drove us to her newly-built home, and made us feel entirely at ease. That first evening, she served a delicious meal of lamb and its trimmings, as well as the New Zealand dessert specialty, pavlova.

During the week Margaret took us sightseeing around the northern areas of the island. She took us to visit schools, museums, beaches, and visits with the locals. One morning, she had to attend a district meeting. While she was gone, Piet suggested that we wash all the windows of her new home, inside and out, as they still had the stickers from the window company on them. What a grand idea! By the time Margaret returned, we were just finishing our work. She could not believe our gift to her. Years later, she kept saying how she would love to have her "window washers" return for another visit. Piet admired this amazing woman as much as I did. It was a great introduction to the country that we fell in love with.

In 1996, Pyra finished her basketball career and graduated with a Sociology degree, with minors in biology and chemistry. She was accepted at Omaha for her medical school.

Since Pyra graduated and no longer needed the apartment, we decided to do for Bret what we had done for Pyra. The Aardens moved again! This time we headed south, to Florida. Bret had two more years before he would graduate from New College.

Piet and I found a new, three-bedroom rental house in Sarasota, near the college. Bret laid claim to one bedroom for his music-computer studio. That left the other two for sleeping, so the arrangement worked fine. Bret shared with us how happy he was with his choice of schools. The culture of New College fit his academic personality very well.

Piet claimed our lifestyle reminded him of the gypsies in Holland that traveled all over, and a home was wherever they stopped for the evening, week, or whatever time. That year we spent time in the Los Angeles and Sacramento areas. At this point, I had been trained to teach ELIC (Grades

K-3); LLIFE (Grades 4-8); Facilitator Training and Administrator Seminars. The variety of training I facilitated for teachers and administrators was challenging. It kept me constantly researching and learning, as well as being extremely happy with my career choice. While I taught, Piet explored each new geographical area and planned weekend travels for us. (Of course, he also did the cooking, cleaning, and laundry!)

Bret and Piet in Florida.

1997 became the year Piet and I decided to make Florida our permanent home. Because we did not want to put our life's savings back into an expensive home, we looked at several affordable manufactured homes in the area. One of the times when Piet and I were with a realtor, we decided to call it quits for the day. The realtor hesitated and said there was a home that recently came on the market. It might be just what we were looking for.

After Piet and I walked into this particular home and had a tour of the premises, we both agreed that this was THE one. It had been built with extra additions on both sides of the doublewide—even a small workshop for Piet and a sewing area for me. We could even find space for the thousands of professional and children's books that I had accumulated and needed for my work on the road. Even though it was a 55+ community, we learned that Bret would be able to live with us for his final year at New College.

We made an offer much lower than the owners were asking. To our surprise, they accepted; they were desperate to move north to be near their children and grandchildren. Our new home was the total opposite of our Wisconsin home, which had been nestled in five acres of beautiful woods with no neighboring homes visible. In Florida, we were "nestled" in acres of other homes with only a few feet of openness between them.

Bret and Piet moved our belongings in August while I was teaching elsewhere. It was wonderful to come back and enjoy our new home with everything totally clean and furnished. Piet and Bret had done an amazing job, for which I was truly grateful. Because I was still busy year-round with my consulting work, I had little time to become acquainted with our new neighborhood. When I did return home, I was content to just enjoy time with Piet and develop materials for my next assignment.

On October 8, Piet spied a 650 custom Honda motorcycle for sale in our neighbor's yard. It had been over forty years since he

Back on the bike...

had owned such a method of transportation, and his yearning for repeating the experience had never left. The next day the motorcycle was parked in our driveway with a smiling, new owner. Happy 70th, Piet! The freedom of the road was his again, and the flat, Florida scenery and warm weather warranted the purchase of just such a machine for Piet Aarden.

On November 18, 1997, my mom moved on to her eternal life, after suffering a heart attack. I was teaching in West Palm Beach, but able to fly home to be with her the day she died. How do you say goodbye to the most amazing woman you have ever known in your life? At her wake, I shared an essay I had written to my mom when I had made my final profession as a nun on July 3, 1962:

A Valiant Woman

"Who shall find a valiant woman? Far and from the uttermost coasts is the price of her...The woman that feareth the Lord, she shall be praised. Give her of the fruit of her hands, and let her works praise her in the gates." Proverbs 31:10-31

"...with the fruit of her hands, she has planted a vineyard..." Philomene was but eight years old when she suffered the loss of her mother. It took courage to attend the Indian boarding school at White Earth, Minnesota, but her father thought the nuns would help replace her mother. She would see her family only two times during each school year because of that great distance of fifteen miles. Many other heartaches crept into her early life but there were always her three brothers to keep her in good spirits. Could she ever forget their chiding when she baked her first chicken? She made the sad mistake of leaving the insides in the chicken!

"...she hath opened her mouth to wisdom..." Philomene LaVoy finished grade school, high school, two years of college, and began teaching in a rural school. These were years when her beau came to court her in his battered Model T, which could be heard two miles away! Her next job was in her hometown where she taught some pupils her own age. She punished one by hitting him with a ruler and the harder she hit, the more playfully he yelled, "Mosquitoes, mosquitoes."

"...she hath opened her hand to the needy..." As postmistress in Naytahwaush, she was loved by the villagers immediately. Whether they needed assistance in writing letters, signing checks, filing income tax returns, or just licking stamps, they all came to Philomene then, as they do now. At Christmas time she secretly keeps the Santa Claus letters until the parents come for the mail. When that sled or pair of skis came through the mail, she gladly stored them away for the owners until the eve of Christmas.

"...she hath put out her hands to strong things..." Phil, the name by which everyone knows her, is seen cleaning the church each week as well as washing and ironing the priest's vestments. As secretary of the Community Council, a job she has had for years, she is very active in helping to develop the Indian village. The sick, the dying, the ones down and out—all these and many others come to Phil. She is one they can trust.

"...strength and beauty are her clothing..." But most of all, this woman is a mother. This valiant woman is a mother to all in her community and best of all she is a mother I can claim as mine - my own mother!

We buried my mom next to my dad in Fort Snelling Cemetery in Minneapolis, Minnesota. Bret shared his last goodbye to her by singing in his deep, rich baritone voice (the voice that his grandmother always loved to listen to) in Latin, "In Pardisum":

In paradisum deducant te Angeli; in tuo adventu suscipiant te martyres, et perducant te in civitatem sanctam Jerusalem.

Chorus angelorum te suscipiat, et cum Lazaro quondam paupere æternam habeas requiem.

May the angels lead you into paradise; may the martyrs receive you at your arrival and lead you to the holy city, Jerusalem. May choirs of angels receive you and with Lazarus, who once was poor, may you have eternal rest.

Another chapter in our lives had come to a close.

CHAPTER FIFTEEN
Travels and Tribulations: 1998-2002

The year of 1998 can best be summed up by sharing what we wrote in our annual Christmas missive to friends and family:

PYRA

Happy Holidays to all of you from the University of Nebraska Med Center! My hours have been filled again with endless hours of reiterating anatomy, embryology, genetics, histology, biochemistry, etc. in order to be able to repeat them to someone else on a specific day.

A very brief rundown on my year since December of 1997: I left you in Seattle, uncertain yet as to where my year away from medical school would take me. What happened turned out to be one of the best experiences of my life. I left Seattle in February making a straight drive to Omaha in the LONGEST non-stop road trip I've ever taken. I visited old classmates and friends for a few days and then flew to Florida to finalize plans for a trip around the world. After long, frustrating hours of dealing with airline brokers, exciting hours in researching our likely countries of sojourning, the trip crystallized.

So off we (Yvonne, Piet and myself) went on our whirlwind nine-country tour-de-force. I can't even begin to tell you of the impression it leaves on your soul when you actually see and do things that you never really thought you would. The Great Wall of China, The Taj Mahal, the Pyramids—the list could go on and on. But the experience was wonderful, eye-opening, challenging, stressful, relaxing and amazing. Anyone, whoever wants to hear a good story or see two albums worth of pictures, has an open door to my apartment any day—except during test weeks!!

One noteworthy story worth sharing was in Egypt where my mother "married" me off. We met an American man, Taylor, who ended up traveling with us throughout Egypt. After viewing the Pyramids of Giza, our driver took us to Memphis where we were invited for a home cooked meal at a stranger's house. My hands had been recently Henna-painted in India—a ceremony typically done before weddings so I was asked if I was just married. I replied jokingly, "Oh, he's the one," as I patted Taylor's leg. But no, Yvonne had to take it further by saying, "They are on their honeymoon." Everything escalated to the point from which we couldn't turn back so... I was "married" in Egypt!!!

After the trip, I was in a best friend's wedding (Jill Maresh, now Garfield) and then found an apartment in Omaha, moving in (fortunately) with my brother's and Erin's help. The weekend before July 4th, I packed up to head for Vermont where I met a fabulous group of old friends who took me in and we celebrated the fourth of July in grand style by singing, hiking, canoeing and eating fabulous food.

Then I set off what was to be a one-month hiking trek on the Appalachian Trail. Well, I saw one day of sunshine and that was my first day. Hiking long days, and camping in the isolated mountain lean-to's is refreshing and a daily challenge. However, after summiting three or four 3,000-4,000 foot mountains and never seeing anything but gray mist, along with two close calls of falling on slippery rocks, I made it to Killington, VT, with the aid of a lovely woman who picked me up on the road in the mist. I decided that without medical coverage and with the miserable conditions, I would end early and try again another year.

Slowly traveling back towards Omaha, I visited friends along the way and spent a week with Bret and Erin in Ohio. Right before I started school, I added two members to the household –two little kittens who have finally been named Lucy and Linus. They are an adorable addition to my life. They entertain me and luckily have each other to entertain one another on the days when I am tucked away in the library. Well, that wraps things up. I hope you've enjoyed my jaunt down memory lane and hope the beauty of the seasons and holidays fill you and loved ones with joy.

BRET

I'm writing this year from a dark, windowless, concrete room lit only by a single small lamp, alone except for the guards who patrol the halls every couple of hours and stop to check on me. Yes, it's what it sounds like—I'm in graduate school! With me in the room are two sound-insulated booths, four high-end workstations—only one of which carries the Microsoft contagion (the others run Linux.) I have some small amenities and the occasional decoration (the dry-board is especially fetching.) This is the Cognitive and Systematic Musicology laboratory in the School of Music of the Ohio State University in Columbus, my home for the next five years, should I decide to go all the way in music theory to a Ph.D. I'll be 30 by then, and unless a new G.I. Bill gets passed in the meantime, I'll be facing a job market in which every opening has over 100 qualified applicants. But that's five years from now. Ha.Ha! Until then, they're waiving my tuition and paying me money. And after all, what's five years when at the end of it you can be a leading expert in music cognition theory—especially when you like blank looks as much as I do!

Here's the low-down on the rest of my year: I spent January completing and rehearsing my musical, which we performed in mid-February to fairly good reviews but small crowds. I spent the rest of the term scrambling to finish my thesis in which I discussed relationships between vocal intonation and vocal melody. I really flubbed up the Music GRE last fall, but that didn't seem to have an effect on my graduate applications, which is a reassuring sign that standardized scores aren't everything. Especially since there was no GPA to fall back on. (New College doesn't have grades.)

I had an opportunity to go to school in places like Manhattan and Chicago, and given my interest in musical theater, you might get an inkling of how impressed I was with the program here at OSU. All the while I was dealing with graduate schools, my advisor did a credible job of keeping me in fear of not graduating, and of course, everything came down to the last minute.

After graduation, my girlfriend, Erin, and I relaxed by driving around most of the U.S.A. for a month, finally settling in Columbus until she had to leave for Florida again.

Since autumn quarter started, I've been busy with classes and the various research projects my new advisors and I have devised. I'm wrapping up the analysis of a 5,000 song database of European folk songs to find musical features that show any geographical distribution. Next on our list: Does classical music tend, ever so slightly, to cycle downward on the musical scale over the course of a piece? After that... well, there's lots to do. I hope you're finding pleasure in this year, and best wishes for the next.

(Note from mother: Bret had been warned if he attended a college that did not give academic grades, he would lose out on opportunities for any graduate school scholarships. He proved them all wrong. In his senior year, he received five different fellowship offerings for grad school. In the end, he chose Ohio State University with its five-year offer of free schooling all the way to a Ph.D.!! Would that there were more academic institutions like New College that realize that number-letter grades are farcical.)

PIET AND YVONNE

Last Christmas Pyra approached Piet with the idea of traveling around the world with her. Later in January, she asked again and he agreed. When Yvonne heard about these intentions, she wanted to know whether this was a father-daughter affair—or could she join? Of course, who would dare to exclude her?!!

March 19th saw the three of us with our backpacks, setting off for Fiji to trek the table-lands. We were even accepted into a tribal village with a kava ceremony. After touring Sydney, Australia, by foot, we flew to the Great Barrier Reef for scuba diving, snorkeling, and even early morning searches for tree kangaroos!

Bali saw us climbing an 1800-meter mountain to see the morning sunrise and enjoying a $3.00 one-hour massage in a secluded resort. Trying to read Chinese characters, not knowing what food would be brought to you, called for frustration and laughter. Touring the Forbidden City and recalling the scenes on Tiananmen Square made history come alive in Beijing.

In Thailand, our trio took a twelve-hour train ride from Bangkok to Chiang Mi so we could take a two-day trek into jungle villages. The congestion on roads in India made the Los Angeles traffic jams a piece of cake. Trying to outmaneuver camels, bikes, tractors, buses, donkeys, taxis, and people, one learned the virtue of patience while praying for one's life.

Floating down the Nile on a felucca, being escorted by armed police, plus an offer of 600 camels for Yvonne were a few highlights of Egypt. (Piet now wonders if they meant Camel cigarettes!) In Greece the Parthenon made history come alive for us while the monasteries perched on huge monoliths in northern Greece brought gifts of serenity and peaceful meditation.

We finished our five-continent, nine-country trip around the world by visiting Piet's family in the Netherlands—a great relaxing week before returning to Florida on May 19th. Arriving home two days before Bret's graduation, we were extremely thankful for a safe and once in a lifetime experience.

This summer Yvonne taught four facilitator training sessions and Piet kept the home cool and clean. Piet and Yvonne have spent the fall in Worcester, MA, traveling the New England area during the long weekends. For a busy, eventful, wonderful year we give thanks!

May this holiday season be filled with happiness and love for each and every one of you.

After our travels of the previous year, you would think the Aardens would have been ready to stay at home and just bask in the Florida sunshine, reminiscing. But in 1999, Bret managed to tour the U.S.A the summer before graduate school. Pyra returned to medical school and had the unique opportunity to accompany Patch Adams and a small group to bring laughter and hope to the Kosovo refugees in Macedonia.

Pyra had attended an Alternative Medicine conference in Washington, D.C. where Patch Adams was one of the speakers. She had lunch with him, learned more about his philosophy and dreams for the future. He must have been verily impressed with this young medical student, because he called her a few weeks later to ask if she would accompany him to help the Kosovo refugees.

Piet and I received that famous phone call from our "I can't believe this is happening to me" daughter, who excitedly shared what had just happened. Of course, we would furnish her airfare and expenses for this once-in-a-lifetime opportunity. Later, another phone call from Pyra gave us more details. She needed to find a clown suit (though she had never "clowned" before), and try to get medical, personal hygiene, and educational supplies to give to the refugees. The next phone call was filled with disappointment—her conservative Omaha Medical School was not going to give her supplies, and no businesses would donate on such a short notice. She was devastated and leaving in a week.

Piet and I decided that if no one else were willing, we would send her money for supplies. I encouraged her to go to a store like the Dollar Tree and buy as many supplies as possible, so she would be able to bring more articles to those in need. A local theatre company found a clown suit, complete with plastic shoes and a multi-crowned juggler hat, that fit her six-foot-four frame. With that, and a bulbous nose, her clown costume was complete.

Unbeknownst to her, her fellow med student friends contacted the local TV station to inform them of this amazing trip that Pyra was about to set off on. The TV crew appeared at her small apartment the night before, as she was packing all the supplies. She made TV coverage, but too late for further donations.

Pyra was to join the rest of Patch Adams' group at the JFK airport in New York City. She had tucked her clown suit in her carry-on luggage, and upon arrival at JFK, she noticed this group of clowns. Rushing to the bathroom, she changed into her clown suit. She had thought Patch was kidding when he said to come dressed in her clown attire! He then explained that even people in the airport needed laughter and cheer!

The time with Patch and the refugees was a life-changing experience for Pyra, and one she has never forgotten. She learned first-hand the need for compassion and laughter in her everyday life now as an Emergency Medicine Doctor. Who could ever forget some of Patch Adams' quotes that have made a difference in Pyra's life and those she serves?

> See what no one else sees. See what everyone else chooses not to see out of fear, conformity, or laziness. See the whole world anew each day.
>
> The most radical act ANYONE could ever commit is to be happy.
>
> You treat a disease: You win, you lose. You treat a person, I guarantee you win—no matter the outcome.

My consulting assignment for that fall was in Dallas, Texas, teaching junior high and senior high teachers. Since Asherton and Carrizo Springs were within driving distance, I wanted Piet to experience first-hand that part of my nun's life. Seeing the convent and school again flooded my mind with memories of the 60s.

I absolutely needed a photo of me standing by the now "half-hanging" broken vestige of the clothesline in our convent backyard. That clothesline and I had been daily friends when I had to wash out the salt rings of perspiration that gathered on my long, black habit. Since we had only two habits to wear, (a polyester one for weekdays and a serge one for Sundays), I had no choice but to carry out my nightly routine of washing my habit. Each night, without interruption, I washed it first in the bathtub we all shared. I would wring it out to the best of my ability, then rush to hang it on the outside clothesline. I used a garden hose to douse my habit to remove any other telltale salt stains. (No such thing as automatic clothes washers or dryers at that time.)

Each morning, at the crack of dawn, (hoping no one would see me), I would run out in my long, white nightgown and night veil and pluck my dry habit from the line. I would then don the habit that soon became drenched, yet again, in perspiration. It was such a hot outfit! We wore white pleated coifs around our face, as well as silk "sleevelets" to prevent our arms from showing. Black stockings and black shoes were also part of the attire. The tall, white plastic band around our head was the base for our long, black veil. This habit was our regulation Minnesota garb and was definitely not made for the blazing hot temperatures of the Texas desert area, but no one thought to let us wear different clothing in the blistering heat. Having no air conditioning in the convent or school, added to our discomfort. When we received word in the late 60s that we could modify our habit, (thanks to John Paul XXIII, who was making changes within the church), we were in seventh heaven. BUT there were still restrictions: The veil could not be shortened, the main part of the habit could be no more than thirteen inches from the floor.

Piet shook his head in disbelief at my Texas stories. I wanted to visit with some of the people who had been so good to us nuns while we taught there. It was a memorable time visiting with Lucia Chapa, one of the cornerstones of the Asherton parish. She had been the pillar of the small community in every aspect of its life. Lucia had a beautiful singing voice and helped to drown out my mistakes on the organ, when I was first learning to play Spanish hymns for Masses. The rhythm of the choir moved differently than the written notation, but she was my guiding light with her constant smiles and encouragement.

When Piet and I stopped to visit her, she wanted to know about all the other nuns that she had known over those many years. In her 90s, she was still vibrant, with that smile which made everyone feel comfortable and welcomed. We also visited the churches of both parishes where I had worked. The school in Carrizo Springs was now a catechetical center, no longer an elementary school. The beautiful, stone church had not changed and still had the enormous, poinsettia plants adorning the outside walls. Nuns from Mexico had replaced our Benedictine nuns.

Visiting many old friends and having them call me Sister Mona, made me nostalgic; I realized how deeply-rooted and special my memories were of that time and place. I had been SO young and impressionable, thinking I could do anything, no matter the circumstances. I would never have left Texas, if I had been given a choice. Part of my heart is still there.

That summer of 1999, Mary and Dan invited Piet and me to travel to Montana and Canada with them. What a treat to spend a few weeks with my sister and brother-in-law, as well as tour scenic areas. Mary and I sat in the back seat so we could direct the "boys" in the front. Attempting horseback riding in the Glacier Waterton Park was quite a Kodak moment for the two sisters.

After our Canada trip, we all attended the yearly LaVoy reunion in Naytahwaush at Pinehurst Lodge. My sister, Flo, had the fun idea of having everyone don white t-shirts on which we were to autograph and write "clever" sayings. As the drinks flowed, the joking and signing of shirts caused raucous laughter. We accumulated all the indelible words of wisdom from each other and for all to read.

During our Minnesota tour of friends, we even included the nuns at Mount St. Benedict. Of course, I had to share details of my Texas visit with them. When Piet and I were in Hudson, WI, we decided to drive by our former home. We were startled to still see our name on the mailbox; it had been five years since we had sold our home! Driving into the winding driveway, we were shocked to find Piet's beautiful fountain overrun with weeds. The same thing was true with his manicured trails of yore. We decided we should not have come back. It was too painful to see what had happened to all the work Piet had lovingly and painstakingly done all those years!

That fall, Piet had his annual physical exam and after a series of tests, it was determined that he had prostate cancer. After consulting several doctors and looking at different treatments, Piet decided to go with a newer procedure called Brachytherapy, an implanting of radiation seeds directly into the tumor. The treatments could be done at a facility about sixty miles from our Ellenton home. They were scheduled to begin the following February. Piet said he had great faith in the procedure and was sure he would conquer this disease.

In 2000, Piet had the radiation treatments for his prostate cancer and by the end of April, his PSA blood count had receded from 6.8 to 0.3. He had to return every six months for checkups. In June, he began to have lower back pains that were diagnosed with lumbar spine degeneration or spinal stenosis. After trying different steroid injections and getting no relief, he chose neuro-surgery on his lower spine in December. Could all that back-breaking work of building our home and digging up various places for his wife's much-wanted garden spaces have taken a toll, and now he was suffering the consequences?

I decided in October of that year to inform Rigby that I would no longer contract with them. The two original CEO's had retired, and their new CEO and his policies and philosophy did not match mine. The child-centered and teacher-empowered philosophy of Rigby was no longer of key importance in their decision-making. It was time for me to leave. Even though it was a difficult decision, I knew I had to make it. I could never teach what I did not believe in.

With Piet's health issues, it seemed like great timing for me to end my Rigby consulting. I decided to set up my own business. When districts heard of my branching out on my own, they started calling me for my services! I could work when and where and for how long, and create my own schedule from now on. I turned sixty that June and it was exhilarating to begin anew on my own terms in the workplace.

With his health issues, Piet decided it would be time to search for a more sedentary hobby at the age of seventy-three. Colony Cove had an Art Club that offered painting classes. Piet joined the club and decided that watercolors were the media he would like to use when he painted. After learning the basics, he took more advanced classes. One Valentine's Day, he proudly presented me with a special valentine from him. It was a beautifully painted rose of various pink hues in a golden frame. He told me that this rose would never die and would be an expression of his eternal love for me! Could any woman ask for more?

Also, being on my own work schedule meant I now had time to take over the house chores that Piet had done all those years. My questions at our home took on a new flavor such as: "Where do we keep the floor wax? Did we ever have a strainer? How does the dryer really work? What settings do you usually use for the dishwasher? What day do they pick up the garbage?" These essential questions were sprinkled into our more philosophical questions of "What do pregnant chads really look like? Why does Florida have such antiquated electoral machines and voters?"

In November we celebrated our 30th wedding anniversary with a seven-day Caribbean cruise. Pampered is the word for that week, and Piet spoiled me even more by purchasing a diamond and opal, reversible ring to begin our next thirty years!

The year 2000 saw both Bret and Pyra "over-their-heads" in the world of academia. Having both of them come home for the Christmas holidays was a gift. Piet enjoyed the attention of all three of his family members while he was recuperating from back surgery.

I was kept busy working in Oregon, California, Massachusetts, and Florida with my consulting work. I flew Delta airlines and managed to reach Gold Medallion status with them. This meant I was able to get free flights for our family trip to Europe with all the miles I had accumulated!

2001 will be remembered as the last time we vistied Holland with Piet. Piet and I invited Bret and Pyra to take time from their busy schedules and travel to Spain and Portugal with us, then we would end the trip by spending several days in Holland with Piet's family. It had been fifteen years since the four of us had been there together.

Unbeknownst to us, the Aarden family planned a huge family reunion for that special occasion. They rented a tavern for the evening to celebrate our visit, so the entire Aarden clan could spend the evening getting re-acquainted. The family presented us with a three-ringed booklet in which every single person had contributed their photo, as well as personal information to help us remember them forever. This was presented to us along with a monetary gift and a pair of wooden shoes with the words: Aarden Family Reunion, 2001. We were told to buy something we wanted as a memento from Holland. After much thought and shopping, we decided that a sturdy, beautiful set of silverware would be a constant reminder of our Holland family.

Pyra's big news and an amazing accomplishment for 2001 was that she passed her medical boards, and was now officially called an M4. This was the year that she would spend most of her time working with patients, and also the year to determine which branch of medicine she wanted to pursue for her medical career.

Bret's surprising news occurred on December 22, when he announced his engagement to Althea, a violist whom he had been dating for about a year. He completed his Master's degree in Music at Ohio State, having completed his thesis document called, *An Empirical Study of Chord-tone Doubling in Common Era Music*. Needless to say, Piet and I just nodded and smiled; we had no idea what the title meant, and did not ask to read his complex music thesis.

Piet had periodic check-ups for his cancer and repaired back. He was thrilled that he was recuperating well and had to have fewer checkups. He had heard about a non-profit group called Project Light that taught English to Hispanic and Haitian immigrants. Piet volunteered to teach English several hours each week. He remembered how grateful he had been, many years earlier, when fellow students helped him learn English.

Since we had visited Piet's family in June, Piet and I decided to drive to Minnesota and Wisconsin to be with my family in July and August. We packed in a tight schedule so we could include as many family members and friends as possible. Our time was constantly filled with food, fun, and incessant talk. How we missed all of them and longed for our Hudson home and connections.

Once again, I feel that sharing our Christmas missive of 2002 tells the story of the Aardens' activities, as it reflects each of our personalities via the writing process. Our mailing list reached about two hundred recipients, including people Piet and I had known over the years. Then we added people our kids became acquainted with during their lives. As friends responded, they always told us not to stop sending our yearly updates, so the Aarden Holiday letters have become a history of our lives together. I created albums containing each of the annual Aarden letters for Bret and Pyra, as well as for Piet and myself. Each album contained all the holiday letters that we had written since 1973, when Bret was born.

PIET

May the BLESSINGS of the season accompany you not only through the holy season but also throughout the coming year!

On December 4th, I received my first Christmas present of the year! On that day I had my quarterly visit to my oncologist and he informed me that my bladder was free of cancer and my blood test indicated the same for the rest of my body and ultrasound in June reflected the same message.

Around the middle of April Yvonne and I ventured on a three-week trip to Ireland with a cousin of Yvonne's and her husband. It was an enjoyable journey, to say the least.

On a weekly basis, I am still involved in a tutoring program for non-English speaking adults and young people. However, my involvement has deepened since I have become one of its board of directors.

Let me wish all of you a happy and healthful New Year.

With love, Piet

YVONNE

Dear Family and Friends,

May this holiday season bring both peace and joy to your hearts and hearths. It is a time of togetherness and we will celebrate the gift of our family being together again this year. God is good!

Peering back into this past year's events, they could be summed up in travel and work but who would want to be that brief? For those who want the details, read on.

Jan: Piet and I enjoyed my sister Mary and her husband Dan for their first visit to our Florida home. We gorged ourselves on Bohemian kolaches and rolikes (crescent rolls) as well as laughter and talk. Sharon and Mike Stevens arrived later that month to plan our Ireland trip. Irish intensity and the luck of the Irish was with us as we set dates, arranged airlines, read books about Ireland and enjoyed each other's company. Get ready, Ireland, here we come!

Feb: Sunnyvale School District renewed another year's contract so it was wonderful to return to teachers excited about literacy learning. Alicia Mathews, Jan Ferraro, and Cricket Guyer arrived for a visit to plan our July trip to England, Scotland, and Wales. Of course, our PRIMARY reason was for education—the World Reading Congress in Edinburgh. Piet was "blissfully" happy having all the giggling gals gracing his abode for five days. Sister Marguerite Streifel arrived later that month for a renewal of friendship. We were in the novitiate together and have not had time to really spend together since 1960. What a treat to have five days to get "caught up" on events of the last forty-plus years.

Mar: I returned to Reading, MA, to work with teachers for the third year in literacy strategies. A great group to spend time with even in blizzards!

Apr/May: Returning to Sunnyvale, CA, for a few weeks of work with teachers is always a treat as I work with Allene Flanders. Upon my return, I had a few days to pack the bags for Ireland. We met Sharon and Mike in Shannon and had a WONDERFUL three-week self-guided tour via rental car throughout the entire island. Come and visit and I will share the memory book of all our adventures. Driving on the left, visiting pubs, churches, castles and staying in B&B's added to the delights of this trip. Talk and laughter abounded plus some great one-lane rides. Ready to go again!

June: We drove to Nebraska to visit Pyra and had Bret and Althea fly in for the weekend for a family reunion. Managed to bake bread despite the heat and no air-conditioning. Great fun in Omaha! From there we drove to the Twin Cities to visit my sisters and their families. We stayed up at Mary and Dan's lake home and enjoyed reuniting with family. Minnesota is truly a beautiful state. No time to visit friends as I had to get back for my European trip—next time!!!

July: Four women traveling for three weeks in Europe—watch out! We did London in four days/nights non-stop with theatre every night. I rented a car and we took off for Stratford-on-Avon, the famous pudding club area and on to southern Wales. While the three went to Ireland, I took off by myself in the rental car to explore Wales and the Lake District. Those days would take a book to tell about so come and visit so I can share them with you! I met up with Jan, Cricket, and Alicia in Edinburgh and enjoyed a week of the reading conference——a new extension to my literacy learning. Spent our last day back in London taking in two more plays. Have suitcase –will travel!

Aug: Back in the USA in time to prepare for my next Sunnyvale in-service training.

Sept: There must be a goof-up. I stayed home all month!

Oct: Can you believe my spouse of thirty-two years turned three-quarters of a century young? For this gala event, I bought an air-conditioner for his work shed as well as a workbench and chair along with new shelving. Then we discovered he has osteoarthritis in his hands, but I know he WILL use that workshop after all the gifts—no matter what! I was in Sunnyvale for more literacy workshops but did call Piet on his birthday, October 8th!!

Nov: Home for the month but working on next workshops.

Dec: Worcester and Reading MA, were the two districts I spent time at during the first two weeks of December. One weekend during that time, I drove up to Vermont and visited wonderful, long-time friends, Russ and Betty Tidd. Even managed to get some bread baking and had a great time sharing the past and present of our lives. Am now home ready to enjoy the true meaning of Christmas with my family. Life is GOOD and I am loving every minute of it. Happy 2003!

BRET

Dear Friends and Family,

I'm hoping this will be the last year I write to you from Ohio, the power-plant-polluting heartland of America. Althea and I are planning our last hurrah here by celebrating our marriage in the scenic southeast region of the state next year on May 31. I'm now applying for assistant professor and post-doctoral positions and Althea is sounding out architecture grad schools around the continent. We're hoping our "two-body" problem will work itself out without too much trouble.

The newest member of our household is a black-furred bundle of chaotic kitty energy named Nyxo. She and Sylvie, our other cat, are finally coming to terms, and even curl up together now and again. Thanks to their cuddling powers and Althea's endless support, I passed my doctoral candidacy exam, and my research is on track for finishing a dissertation by spring quarter. This year Althea has been working at the American Classical Music Hall of Fame, so stop by next time you're in downtown Cincinnati.

This summer Althea and I used a conference as an excuse to visit Sydney, Australia. I presented the central chapters of my dissertation, and we toured the city, enjoying the food and sights. We're not currently looking for schools in that part of the world, but we certainly left feeling that would be a wonderful option to explore someday. It would take us even further from friends and family, however, whom we already see far too infrequently. Speaking of which, the commuting lifestyle leaves us with almost no visitors to our home, so do stop by if you find yourself driving through Dayton on Interstate 70 or 75. Best wishes for the coming year, Bret

PYRA

Happy Holiday Greetings to you all!

Many things have come to a resolution this year. Medical school is finished. I will take my licensing exams and graduate in May. Nothing like the gratification of adding some initials to your name.(Right!) That leaves me, however, with only five months of not being directly responsible for anyone's death. My car, however, has been declared dead. There has been no replacement. We are still in the grieving process. I have permanently and happily left the "heartland" state of Nebraska. I am still dating and have no children (that I am aware of). At least a dozen oocytes have been again wasted this year. My cats are in good health and always are available for creating that instant-Angora look, if so desired.

As an ever-present part of my life's adventures, my traveling this year included Chicago, New York City, Sarasota, Belize, South Africa, Swaziland, and Lesotho. They are all part of my master plan to entwine education and traveling pleasure. A HUGE thanks to my friends who housed me for a month each and to each of those who made my trips so wonderful!

Belize, a Tropical & Wilderness Medicine rotation, assisted in my selection of Emergency Medicine for a career. Living in the middle of the jungle allowed opportunities you just couldn't predict, which I loved. (Like watching tarantulas catch their prey right above your head in your classroom...or inner-tubing through seven miles of caves, and someone getting dragged under a log pile by the current...or figuring out how to make a stretcher out of banana leaves and branches.)

The last three countries started as a rotation for school in Capetown's Victoria Hospital where a classmate and I worked a little and played a lot. We partook in Capetown's beaches, mountains, theatre, markets, city life, clubs, restaurants, museums, wineries, historical monuments and sites, and wonderful local friendships. We were so lucky to have a host family take such good care of us. I then left for Johannesburg to start my vacation safari. It was an Environmental Ranger's Guide Course (basically a guide-training course), where we hiked/camped in the Drakensberg Mountains for three days, set up camps, created and cooked our own meals, learned the history of the country, the spoor and droppings of many animals, and slept in the middle of the bush. (An amazingly weird feeling to be awakened by rhinos fifty feet away at night, and by lion's baying in the morning).

We, ten travelers, were unofficially sponsored by Castle beer (the local brand) and learned all about AFNI trees and fauna while having a fan-TAB-u-lous time. I'd love to show off my photo album if anyone ever wants to see it.

So to close—it has been an amazing year with plenty of great memories and accomplishments to add to my growing treasure chest. Here's a shout out to my close friends and to the distant ones—I love you all and send the best holiday wishes for a year of love, laughter, peace, and adventure. I miss you and am waiting for our next reunion. Please make note of the address and phone number changes and write, or call sometime just to say, "Hi!" Be forewarned another address change will happen around May/June. Merry Christmas and have a Wonderful New Year!

Pyra Aarden, 3720 Buena Vista Way S. Ellenton, FL

Little did we know what the next year was to bring. Our lives would be forever changed.

Enjoying Portugal!

Celebrating their dad in Holland.

CHAPTER SIXTEEN
The Year That Totally Changed Us Forever: 2003

2003 started out with exciting plans for the entire family.

Pyra chose Emergency Medicine as her field of study and applied at Syracuse, New York, for her three-year residency. She temporarily lived with us as she finished up odds and ends before her May graduation. During her famous safari in South Africa, she just happened to meet Luis, a young man from Mexico, and a budding romance began. In February, Luis was scheduled to visit us at our Florida home, so we could meet this "knight in shining armor."

I could hardly wait to meet this man who had captured our daughter's heart. I was in Sunnyvale, CA, teaching a Six Traits workshop, but planned on being home the day before Luis arrived. Due to a plane malfunction, my flight was canceled, so I would not be home when Luis arrived. There were some mixed communications. Luis arrived at our house while Pyra was picking me up at the airport.

Luis describes that meeting as unusually difficult. He was nervous with his first introduction to the Aarden family. Pyra had assured Luis that her mom would make a joke of things and all would go smoothly. Instead, he had time on his hands with her quiet dad, and he didn't quite know what to say or do. Luis remembered there were long pauses in the conversation, but things flowed easier when Piet offered him a beer. After all, they had some things in common to talk about. Both were men from another country who had fallen for women from the U.S.A. Piet certainly could give him some tips from his own experiences! The ice definitely was shattered when the raucous Mom and daughter burst upon the scene.

We ended up having Minnesota friends, Jan and Tony Ferraro, pop in for a visit just as we were starting to visit with Luis. Oh, well, the more the merrier! Luis might as well get baptized by fire and get acquainted not only with his future in-laws, but also their zany friends. Piet and I thought everyone might enjoy watching the manatees that came in droves in the winter to enjoy the warm waters near the electric plant at Apollo Beach. For the twenty-mile ride, we all hopped into our old, spacious Cadillac that Pyra referred to as a Winnebago. At times like this, the spaciousness that our Cadillac offered was greatly appreciated.

After learning about manatees in the local information center, several of us took silly photos stretched out on the floor beside paintings of these huge mammals. We wanted to see the contrasts of us short "Lilliputians" compared to the "Giants" among us. By the time we returned home, everyone was ready for libations and learning more about each other's lives. Of course, Jan and Tony begged Luis and Pyra to share how they met, as well as their myriad adventures during the safari. It was a good visit. Piet and I liked Luis, and thought Pyra had chosen well.

Laura, Pyra's close friend from medical school, arrived soon after Luis left for Mexico. She and Pyra decided to take a chance that they would both pass their boards, and not have a huge fee to pay for re-takes. Why not go to Argentina on a cheap vacation with that money? Off they flew in the middle of February to have another opportunity to practice their Spanish, while enjoying beaches and bumming around the area.

The funniest story that sticks in my memory is their decision to go into a lingerie shop and try on the scanty bikinis and tops. Since Laura was small of stature, she quickly found her treasures. It was a different story for Pyra, with her tall, muscular build. The Argentinian women were of slightly different builds. Pyra was having no luck, even after the women clerks had tried to stretch every known piece to fit her body. She decided it was futile to try to squeeze into those scant pieces of material, no matter how much stretch they claimed to have.

Pyra walked out of the store and started walking down the street, only to be surrounded by people wanting to take her photo. They also begged to have their photos taken with this giant woman who flaunted flowing, long blond hair. Laura stayed on the sidelines, enjoying the spectacle. Someone came up to her to ask who this model was that everyone wanted a photo of. Laura turned to the person, and with a very straight face, said, "Como se dice, pornstar?" With that, she clawed her way through the crowd and acted as Pyra's agent, as they took off running and laughing back to their hotel.

When I picked them up at the airport, Pyra insisted that we go directly to Home Depot, even before they had dropped off their suitcases. She wanted me to buy paint to replace the "god-awful" striped wallpaper in our dining area. "Mom, it is SO outdated and ugly. How could you have put up with it all these years?" She threatened to take over the steering wheel if I did not do as she wished. Piet was "pleasantly" surprised when we returned home with not only their luggage, but paint cans, brushes, and all the equipment needed for the paint job.

Ignoring any jetlag they might have had, Laura and Pyra had Piet helping us put blue masking tape strips around the window frames and wallboards. It took three coats of paint to cover the ugly stripes, and we had to wait for each coat to dry. That meant indulging in a few beers and laughs while Laura and Pyra shared their fun, crazy adventures with us.

Pyra and Laura had to return to Nebraska before the paint job was done, but they assured me it would be easy to do the last of the sand painting. Piet informed me this had been a girls' decision and he wanted no part of it. Even though the end result wasn't exactly what it should have looked like, I agreed it was far better than the former striped wallpaper. Pyra did have great ideas for interior decorating. I wondered what her next suggestion would be.

In March, Pyra received her letter of acceptance for Syracuse and, magically, Luis appeared on the scene to help us celebrate. This time, it was a much easier and smoother visit. We celebrated by making raised doughnuts. This had become a traditional practice whenever Pyra celebrated milestones in her life. Luis and Piet helped with sugaring and glazing of doughnuts, while sampling a few during the process.

At the end of April, I flew to Massachusetts to teach more workshops. In May, Piet and I drove to Nebraska for Pyra's graduation ceremonies and party. Pyra's friend, Cathy Hallstrom, and our friends, the Ferraro's, as well as Bret and Althea, joined us for this gala ceremony. Pyra and her two close friends, Laura and Anise, had decided to have one celebration party for the three of them.

After the graduation party, Piet and I decided to drive to Minnesota and Wisconsin to do some memory lane visits. We wanted to visit some of the places he had been as a priest, check in on the cabin he had built on Midge Lake, stop in Naytahwaush to visit my relatives, and then head for the Twin Cities to see Flo and her family, as well as a stop at Mary and Dan's home in Amiret. We managed to spend time visiting Connie and Bill Fisk, as well as Nick and Eileen Rosandick, old friends from Hudson, Wisconsin. Both Bill and Nick were suffering from cancer.

Bill, Connie, Piet, and I started to reminisce way back to when we first met in 1970. Bill and Piet both worked for the state, and Connie and I taught together in St. Paul. As couples, we had invested in coupon booklets, sold as a fundraiser for our school. Bill did not like to use coupons and was embarrassed by them. The rest of us were definitely thrilled to be able to have the discounts. Who could ever forget how Bill hated to show his coupons whenever we went out for supper? Bill would practically crawl under the table when Piet boldly showed the waiter that we wanted the special discount. This was always followed by the remark, "OK, Bill, you can come out from under the table now. The waiter knows you also have a coupon!"

Then there were the hilarious stories of times I would accidentally run into Bill at the local drugstore. I would see Bill and loudly greet him across the aisles with salutations such as, "Hi, Bill. We need to stop meeting here like this or Connie will find out. Which condoms should I get?" or "Hey, Bill. Did you have a coupon for those suppositories you said you needed?" Bill would turn redder than a beet and try to ignore me. It was such fun to tease him. I'm sure he prayed every time he went to the drugstore that I would not be there.

Eileen taught our kids piano when I realized that the "Mom as teacher" just wasn't working. Nick and Piet had interests in building and repairing anything and everything. We would go out for suppers together, or meet in one another's home. Eileen and I would go on for hours about our sewing and music. Piet and Nick were totally taken up with their building projects and the latest tools they had purchased. Eileen's basement sewing center rivaled Joanne Fabric's, while Nick's woodworking shop was like visiting the local Fleet Farm with all its organization and number of tools. We four never lacked for conversation, and enjoyed every chance we had to arrange a get-together.

Piet commented on the way back to the Twin Cities that he did not think we would ever see Nick and Bill again in this lifetime. Both men had good days when we visited them, so we had time to share lots of great stories of our past years together.

This Minnesota trip was also a time to get reacquainted with the couples from our Guardian Angels group. It seemed like only yesterday we had been together planning retreats and sharing our lives on so many different levels. Judy and Carl Scheider, once again, were our special hosts and made sure everyone had a good time. Going down the road called Memory Lane always brought laughter and tears. This amazing group had been our lifeline those many years earlier, when we had been shut out of our parish in Hudson.

We even squeezed in a visit with two of my close friends, Jan Phillips and Nancy Morrow, who had worked on their Master's degree with me in River Falls, WI. A supper and drinks at a local restaurant made that a special evening laced with fun memories of our adventures together in the old days. Piet listened on the sidelines as Jan, Nancy, and I talked shop, but joined in when they asked him about his life of retirement. We ended our Minnesota trip by visiting Dan and Mary before we headed to Ohio for Bret's wedding.

Bret and Althea had decided to get married in the hills of southeastern Ohio on May 30th. They had asked Piet early on if he would officiate at their wedding. Piet told them he was no longer a priest and could not do that. They were disappointed and later came up with another plan. What if they got married by a Justice of the Peace for the legal aspect, and then he could be the Master of Ceremonies at their outdoor wedding? Piet was still hesitant.

I urged him to do it. What an honor that they had asked him to perform the ceremony! They were writing their personal wedding vows and procedures, and really wanted Piet to perform the ceremony. I told Piet that if they asked me, I certainly would jump at the chance. We laughed and then talked more about Bret and Althea's request. Finally, he reluctantly accepted, and everyone was happy.

We arrived the day before the legal wedding to help with any last minute preparations. Piet and I, Althea's parents, plus Pyra and Luis attended the justice-of-the-peace wedding on May 29th. After the wedding, we had a luncheon at an Amish restaurant where Pyra had Althea wear a humorous net veil, complete with red devil horns in the front! That afternoon the couple did a dry run of the next day's ceremony with Piet. It was to be performed on a wooded knoll near the resort—weather permitting. That night it rained.

The next day arrived with more rain in the forecast, so plans changed for the location. It would be held on the deck beside the wedding hall. The men donned their tuxedos in one building and the women prepared themselves in another. When the flowers for the men arrived at our building, I offered to take them to the guys. As I opened the door, the first person I saw was Piet dressed in his rented black tuxedo.

Piet had said he would never again wear a black suit after leaving the priesthood, and he had followed through on this promise until this moment. Althea had insisted that he wear black to contrast with Bret's gray suit. My mouth fell open. I stopped dead in my tracks. Dejavu! Standing right before me was my husband, looking like that dashing young priest I met that first night in Kelliher when he had asked me why nuns were ironing on Sunday. I almost dropped the flowers as I rushed up to him, hugged him uncontrollably, kissed him passionately, and told him how handsome he looked. As I turned to leave, I winked at him and said that I just might want to marry him again!

It was a beautiful ceremony, and Piet did an amazing job. Althea's friends performed a quartet of music and song to add to the richness of the occasion. Afterwards, we had champagne and an elegant evening meal at which the wine glasses were never empty. Many toasts

Piet and I toast.

were in order. Bret asked all of us to limit our toasts to a minute or two. He must have sensed that I had prepared a somewhat longer diatribe. I had worked TOO long and TOO hard on my fairytale version of their togetherness. My dramatic solo performance on the dance floor lasted many extended minutes, despite my son's directives.

Dancing and lots of sharing of stories followed the meal, as well as many wine and beer refills. Somehow, Mary's black and tan straw hat managed to find itself worn by many of the people attending the wedding, including the bride and groom. Photos don't lie!

Later that evening, when only the younger set was still celebrating, Bret told my sister Mary and me that maybe it was time for us to join our hubbies at our cabin. The younger participants left to party elsewhere. Mary and I were alone to continue our celebrating. Bret and entourage had disappeared with all the leftover bottles of wine, but the head table still contained unfinished wine glasses. We managed to remedy that situation before we attempted to crawl back to our cabin. One does not want to remember the headaches we suffered the next morning!

While Bret and Althea went on a short honeymoon, Piet and I drove back to Dayton to pack their belongings for their move to Cincinnati, Ohio. This was one of our gifts to the new bride and groom. Finding boxes, buying rolls and rolls of tape, and escaping from stores with their advertising newspapers, we managed to get most of the packing done before the newlyweds arrived.

Family photo at Bret's wedding.

On June 6, the hired moving van arrived. We drove in separate cars—packed with more of their belongings—to their new home: A rented loft apartment in Cincinnati that had once been a warehouse. When the movers arrived, they had no idea that the apartment was on the third floor, and that there was no elevator. The other surprise was that much of the heavy furniture needed to be carted up a unique, narrow, spiral staircase. Those men earned every penny of their day's labor! Piet and I stayed on for a few days to help the newlyweds unpack. We also tried to avoid the two cats that appeared at strange times for attention. Not a cat lover, I definitely chose to ignore their wants.

Our car then headed back to Nebraska for our next job: Help Pyra relocate to Syracuse, New York. She had found an old Victorian home to rent in which she would have the entire second floor. This move meant we needed to rent a huge U-haul truck and drive that, plus our big, old Cadillac. Since Pyra did not want to abandon her two cats, Lucy and Linus, they had to be accommodated in the car. Not something I was looking forward to!

We worked out an arrangement for driving the long distance to Syracuse. One person would drive the truck, one person would drive the car, and the other person would take a rest, reclining in the passenger seat of the car. We had mapped out a route and made copies for each vehicle. The car would follow the truck along the way, since it would be easier to locate the truck in traffic. Pyra started out driving the truck, while I drove the car, and Piet was to rest.

Since cell phones were not as common at that time, Pyra said we should buy two walky-talkies so we could communicate, as needed. Soon after we started, Pyra decided to try out our new system. Pretending to be a seasoned truck driver, she began "10-4. We need code names like truckers have. I'll be 'Big Bitch.' What are you going to be, Mom?"

My answer was, "If you're Big Bitch, then I'll have to be Little Bitch."

We guffawed, and then she asked her dad what his code name was going to be.

Not finding this funny, he told us he would be "Piet." And so it was.

We managed to arrive in Syracuse without any harrowing close calls, except when Piet was driving the truck and took the wrong turn. He was headed west back to Nebraska and we were going east to New York. Because he was beyond the range of our walky-talky, we decided the best plan was to pull over on the highway, and hope that he would soon realize his mistake. An hour later we spotted our U-Haul truck coming up behind us. We radioed to get off at the next exit and regroup. That delay, and not finding motels that would allow pets, were the only glitches in our search for Syracuse.

Since Pyra's old car had died, we tried to find her a reasonably priced, reliable replacement. After several visits to dealers, Piet found a good deal with a newer car than expected. Piet said she needed a good car for the upcoming Syracuse winter. He wanted his girl to be safe.

The Victorian, multi-roomed, second floor needed lots of work and cleaning, so we stayed to help. Pyra decided to make the third, full-sized bedroom into a walk-in closet. She had never had a closet that could accommodate the length of her clothing, and she decided this was the time for that. Piet began the renovation after Pyra had spent hours acting like an architect to plan every detail. Hours spent at Home Depot getting the shelving she wanted, was nothing compared to the hours Piet spent trying to construct her masterpiece plan. It was an OLD house with the plaster behind the studs and nothing was in sync or level. Piet earned a Purple Heart just building this amazing walk-in closet for his baby. It was nothing but a true work of LOVE.

Luis came to visit over the 4th of July and had fun helping us change the house into a beautiful living space. Every wall was newly-painted with different types of paint designs, pictures hung, closets completed, and floors waxed and polished. Even plants adorned the rooms. Pyra's dream came true: She was living in New York, in an older home, and ready to set up her Emergency Medicine residency. Piet and I left to return to Florida to collapse.

In August was the annual LaVoy family reunion, but Piet said he had had enough travel for a while. Besides, we had already made plans to travel to Ohio for Bret's graduation on August 28th. From there we were to fly to Holland for the fiftieth wedding anniversary of his brother, Gerard, and wife, Riek. Planning a month-long vacation in Europe with family and touring other areas was on our calendar. For now, Piet felt he could use a few weeks to recuperate from our whirlwind summer.

I decided to go to the reunion alone, for a fun time with friends and family from August 4 – 16th. First off, I spent four days with Nancy Morrow and Jan Phillips at Jan and Kent's beautiful cabin in northern Wisconsin. We three gals had a gala time reliving our university life, when we had worked so hard to get our Master's degree. Kent, Jan's husband, was our chief cook. He just shook his head as we three giggled our way through the days and late nights. We were so grateful that we had such fun times together and were still connected. Pontoon rides, visiting the nearby pubs and shops, and simply lazing in the peaceful lake setting were enough activities for us. Being together was the most important. We vowed we would meet once a year at one of our homes, to keep our ties of friendship woven tightly.

While I was there visiting, Pyra called to share her great news. Luis had proposed marriage and she had accepted! No date had been set, but she just wanted us to know! I then called Piet, and we couldn't believe that so many wonderful things were happening within such a short time: graduation, wedding, and engagement. We were two proud parents!

The next stop on my agenda was Pinehurst Lodge, our cousin's resort, in Naytahwaush. Mary and I decided to rent a cabin together for the week of the family reunion. Our sister Flo and her family had made it a tradition to have an annual vacation at the lodge, since their early years of marriage. That meant they had been coming to Pinehurst for forty-three summers! Now their married kids and extended families joined them, as well. Some of the cousins we had grown up with also came with their families, so it was a huge family reunion. We ate, drank, danced, watched videos from former reunion years, and enjoyed the non-ending conversations among the relatives. This always reminded me of Cynthia Rylant's book called, *When the Relatives Came*.

On Monday of the reunion week, the La Voy family group always had a golf tournament, which involved fun golf prizes of all sorts, and then we took over the lodge with a potluck supper. Several evenings, we joined together at one another's cabins with everyone bringing food and drinks. Bar bingo was a big highlight, as was building a fire near one of the cabins so we could enjoy the traditional s'mores with chocolate, graham crackers, and roasted marshmallows. I can't ever forget the Texas Hold 'Em card games, or the constant chatter as we walked from cabin to cabin with our coffee cups every morning to visit with the relatives. Childhood stories abounded and the "kids" were wide-eyed as they listened and learned about the antics of their parents.

I returned home on August 17 and had several days to prepare for our Ohio and Holland trips. Piet was happy to have some quiet time together before we started our next trek.

The morning of August 28th dawned, and our neighbors, Ed and Jeannie, drove over to help us load our suitcases. We then set off for the Tampa airport. On the way, I noticed sweat trickling down Piet's neck. I asked him if he was all right. He said it had been difficult getting the suitcases in the trunk and that he was just perspiring from that effort. After saying goodbye to our friends and thanking them for the ride, we headed for our check-in at the airport.

On the way up the escalator, Piet said he wanted to find a place to sit down. I looked at him and asked what was wrong. "I just need to lie down for a little while and rest."

Alarmed, I said, "Piet, if something is wrong, I need to call a medic. I know they have them in airports."

"NO," he said sharply and with a twinge of anger. "We are going for Bret's graduation, and Pyra will be there tonight. She's a doctor and can do whatever needs to be done, if anything. Don't ask me again."

He lay down in an uncrowded area of the airport. I went to buy some water and aspirins. I didn't know what else to do. After a while, he said he felt better and that we should go through security to our gate. "I will be all right, don't worry or ask me more questions!" he said, as he looked at me with those determined eyes.

When we got to the gate area, he chose to lie down again until our flight was called for boarding. On the plane, he had a soda and peanuts, but was very quiet and now complained of being cold. How strange! This man never complained, was always hot, and perspired at the drop of a hat.

In Atlanta, we had to change airplanes. Piet said he needed to find a restroom. I kept his backpack, but had the strangest feeling that something might have happened while he was in the bathroom because it was taking him so long. Much to my relief, he came out from the bathroom, and we boarded the plane for Columbus, Ohio. We had talked with Bret that morning. He was planning to be at the airport to pick us up and would be waiting outside of the baggage area.

When we debarked from the airplane and were walking to the baggage area, I thought Piet was definitely walking so much more slowly, but I did not want to aggravate him by asking more questions. We would soon be at the hotel, and he could lie down and relax there. Pyra would fly in from Syracuse that evening. She would know what to do if he needed medical help.

The luggage carousel started, but I told Piet to sit down in one of the more comfortable chairs. I would get our luggage. After retrieving the first two pieces of luggage, I glanced over to see Piet looking around at other passengers in the airport. One more piece of luggage and we would be on our way. Playing the waiting game, I wondered when it would arrive. Not seeing it yet, I looked over to check on Piet.

"NO!!!!" I screamed loudly! I couldn't believe it. Piet was sprawled on the airport floor. Medics were hovering over him with paddles on his chest. I screamed again, "NO!!!!" I pushed people aside and yelled, crying, "That's my husband! That's my husband! What is wrong? Oh, my, God, what is wrong?"

I remember one of the black, female security officers rushed over to me and pulled me back from the medics. "Honey, stay back. We pray, honey, we pray," she pleaded with me. "They're doing everything they can, but they need space."

People started crowding around to see what had happened. Security attempted to keep them away. I was screaming and crying as I watched them giving CPR and using the paddles on Piet's chest. An officer appeared at my side to say an ambulance had arrived to take him to the nearest hospital. With that, the medics placed Piet on a gurney and told me to follow.

"What do I do?" I wailed in my confusion. "Our son was supposed to be outside waiting for us. His name is Bret Aarden, in a blue car. We don't have all our luggage! Help me, I don't know what to do. Oh, my God, Piet, what has happened to you? Please, please, help me. Where do I go? What do we do?" I sobbed.

A woman, who was a nurse, came rushing up and said that they had better find me a place to sit or I would be their next patient. The officer took me by the arm and told me that I was to go with the ambulance. Medics were loading Piet in the back of the ambulance. They said I could not sit back there, but could sit in the front. Just as I was about to get in the ambulance, I turned and saw Bret getting out of his car nearby.

A policeman had approached him at the curb. Bret thought at first that they were going to tell him to move his car. He saw the ambulance race up to the airport door right beyond where he was parked. The officer asked him if he were Bret Aarden. He was to follow the security person and park on the side of the ambulance. Bret realized, then, that something had happened to one of his parents.

I screamed, "Bret, it's your dad. I don't know what's wrong, but I have to go with him, to the hospital. They said they would take care of you and our luggage."

They quickly closed all the ambulance doors, and with sirens going full blast, we left the airport. Sobbing, I kept turning back to see what was happening to Piet. The ambulance driver said, "Just look straight ahead. I'm going to get us to the hospital as fast as I can. He's in good hands."

That surreal ride never seemed to end. Why wouldn't cars pull over for us? Piet needed help immediately. Didn't drivers know what those sirens meant?

Arriving at the hospital, they rushed Piet into the nearest ER room and took me to the receiving desk. My hands were shaking so hard and I was sobbing uncontrollably. How on earth did I know his social security number? Why were they asking me all these silly questions? I needed to be with my husband and not answering such absurd questions. PLEASE —let me go. I wanted to only be where Piet was!

A nurse took me to the ER area where they had pulled the curtains around the bed. Piet had a plastic tube and bag coming out of his mouth and the medics were still applying the paddles. I could not see any up and down movements in Piet's chest, and his eyes were shut. No movement anywhere. What was wrong? What had happened??

A doctor came over, put his arm around me, and asked if they should continue the paddles. "OF COURSE!" I shouted, "He needs them, right? Please, please, help him, doctor. He wouldn't let me get any help at the airport. Please?"

After a few more minutes, the doctor once again put his arm around me and said, "My dear lady, there has been no response or heartbeat since they started trying to revive your husband in the airport."

I couldn't believe my ears. Piet was dead??? Oh, no, it couldn't be true. I looked at the doctor to ask if this was really real. Was my husband really dead? How could this be?

The doctor nodded and quietly assured me that it was real. "So this means the paddles aren't doing any good?" I asked.

"No. The medics did all they could and won't stop until you say so."

"If he's dead, then, yes they can stop." As they removed the paddles from his chest and tube from his mouth, I let out an anguished wail of despair and disbelief.

At this point, Bret appeared in the room and rushed to me. I desperately clung to him, crying, saying that his dad was dead. How could this be, Bret? He was alive just a bit ago, in the airport.

The doctor and nurses quietly and calmly stood by, and then said that some decisions needed to be made. What were our plans for his body? We needed to make some final arrangements. Sobbing, I shared that Piet wanted his body donated to a medical school and that we had done all of the paperwork for this. Piet had the permission card in his billfold. Was there a medical school at the university?

I will never forget the professional and caring ER personnel as they called the medical school for me. I answered all the questions they asked about Piet. They said they would be honored to have Piet donate his body to their Ohio State University medical school. There were some restrictions regarding the length of time before his body had to be refrigerated. The pathologist at the hospital told us that the length of time was ten hours. Piet had died at 2:20 p.m. We had until midnight.

While I was talking with the medical school personnel, Bret called Pyra to tell her what had happened. She was unable to get an earlier flight. She would arrive at 9:30 p.m. Bret called Althea, who was at the shopping mall. She ended up, ironically, arriving in an ambulance a short time later. An ambulance had appeared at the mall entrance just as she was trying to get a taxi. In desperation, she asked if she could get a ride to the hospital, and in this emergency, the driver said he would take her.

My thoughts suddenly turned to our Catholic ritual, the Last Rights. I should ask for them, for Piet. I told the doctor and nurses that Piet had been a priest, and wondered if there was any Catholic priest in the hospital to perform this ceremony. In a few minutes, we had a nun appear in the ER, who happened to be visiting the sick. She said she had called the Monsignor, who would come shortly. Next thing I knew, we had two other ministers appear in the room as well. Clergy from many denominations surrounded Piet, all saying prayers. How fitting! I then shared that I had been a nun. The doctor just shook his head and said he didn't know if he could handle any more surprises. The nun rushed over to hug me and held my hand in support.

Monsignor arrived at about the same time as Althea. We witnessed the anointing of oils that Piet, himself, had done so often for others during his priestly life. We shared how selfless and giving Piet had been during his life, and thanked all those surrounding us for their kind deeds of mercy. As they all respectfully left us, the doctor said he would find a small private room, so that we could be alone with Piet until the time came for them to take his body.

The staff could not have been gentler or kinder. They were there for whatever we needed as we spent our final hours saying our goodbyes to Piet. When Bret and Althea drove to the airport to pick up Pyra, I had my time to be alone with this amazing man who had graced my life thirty-four years earlier when he caught me ironing in his parish laundry room.

Our life, like everyone else's, had had its ups and downs. But, oh, I had learned so much from him, and experienced the deepest meaning of what it was to truly love a man of such strength and depth. I had never dreamed it would end so soon, or like this. As I stood looking at Piet, I prayed, "God, give me the strength to bear this. Help me be strong for my kids as they suffer the loss of their father at this time of their young lives."

When Pyra, Bret, and Althea arrived, we hugged, wept and viewed the now silent, motionless body of a man who rarely took time to rest during his life. I shared the events of the day, from the time I noticed sweat trickling down their father's neck that morning, to the last efforts to restore his life. I told Pyra her dad was sure she could take care of him when she arrived. We left the room at different intervals so each person could say their own tearful goodbyes to Piet. At midnight, we had to give that final hug and last kiss, and thank him for all he had done for us.

When we walked outside to the car, we could not believe our eyes. In their shock and hurry, no one had noticed the car motor was left running as they rushed into the hospital. The car had been running all that time. No one had stolen it, nor had it run out of gas! I told the kids that their dad was definitely still protecting us.

We drove to the hotel, checked in, and gathered together in the room that Piet and I had reserved for ourselves. The other room was to be for the kids. Bret said he was not going to attend graduation the next day. I immediately responded, "Oh, yes, you are! Your dad would not even let me get a medic because he so wanted to be here for your graduation. You will attend, as we all will. Your dad would have wanted that."

After much discussion, Bret acquiesced, but said he did not want the party that was planned for afterward. We agreed on that, but I thought we should have a quiet lunch in Bret's honor and invite his advisor, Dr. Huron, as well as his best friend, Sean. I said that the luncheon was not to be about Piet, but about Bret. This was to be Bret's celebratory day for accomplishing the completion of his Doctorate in Music Cognition. His dad would have been so proud of him!

Pyra came into my room that night to comfort me and sleep with me in my bed. We desperately clung to each other as we hugged and sobbed, trying to come to grips with the reality of Piet's death.

In the midst of all this, I realized that I needed to let Piet's family in Holland know of his death, and explain why we would not be coming to celebrate the 50th wedding anniversary with them. With a six-hour time difference, that call needed to be made early in the morning, before we left for the graduation ceremonies. It was a call I never thought I would be making on the day of Bret's graduation.

With Bret at his graduation.

Somehow, we made it through Bret's graduation, trying to concentrate on his great achievement, but we were dazed with disbelief that his dad was not here to help him celebrate. It was just the day before that Piet was so excited to be a part of this celebration. How could this be? How could we carry on without him?

The luncheon was difficult, as we tried to keep the conversation on Bret's happy event and not talk about his dad's sudden death. We managed to get through it with stories about the winding and twisting paths of schooling that led to Bret's Ph.D.

After lunch, reality set in. There were lots of decisions to be made and plans for what needed to be done next. Payment for the transportation of Piet's body to the medical school needed to be completed before we left Columbus. Pyra received a call: Luis was at the Columbus airport. How wonderful that he came to comfort to Pyra and the rest of us.

We picked Luis up first, then drove to the funeral home. The director of the funeral home was very kind, explained about the death certificates that he would create for us, and shared other details that needed to be done after the death of a loved one. We listened, asked questions, and then paid for the transportation cost, as well as the death certificates. It was the beginning of all the legal work that lay ahead.

The kids did not want me to return home alone. We decided that we would spend the upcoming Labor Day weekend together at Bret and Althea's apartment in Cincinnati. I rented a van so we all could ride together. Bret left his car with friends in Columbus, and would pick it up when he returned the rental van. It was decided that after the weekend, Bret, Althea, Pyra, and I would drive to Syracuse for two weeks together. Since Bret had just graduated and had more freedom, it was logical to go to Pyra's. She wasn't sure how much time they would allow her to be absent from her ER Residency. Luis could only stay for the long weekend, before returning to Mexico.

Since Piet had a small life insurance policy, I told the kids that we would use that money for all expenses while we were grieving together.

When I phoned my sisters to tell them of Piet's sudden death, they both wanted to know what they could do for me. I told them about our New York plans and said it was not necessary for them to come right then. I shared with them that Piet had declared that he did not want a funeral, and that his body was given as a gift to the medical school. Maybe later, they could come to Florida to spend time with me.

The following afternoon, as we were driving to Cincinnati, I got a call from Mary that she was at the Cincinnati airport. She had rented a car and needed to know how to get to Bret's apartment. I couldn't believe my ears—Mary was there for me! She and Flo had talked and decided that Mary would come right away. Flo would wait and fly to Florida to be with me when I got home. This way, I would have the support and love of both my sisters at crucial times, when I most needed them.

Mary had also booked a hotel room for the two of us, not knowing how much living space Bret and Althea had. She thought it would be good for the kids to have time alone, as well as the two of us to have time together. How right she was! It was such a wise choice in this time of unexpected loss and difficulty.

On Sunday, the kids asked if I wanted to attend Mass in honor of their dad. They had done their research and learned there was a Catholic church just down the street. It had an early Mass with Gregorian chant—chant that their dad had loved so much and chant that I had learned in my convent years.

As I stood between my two children in that church, the priest came out in his vestments and started the liturgy in Latin! I sobbed as I remembered all those years Piet had done the same. Listening to the rich, melodic voices of Bret and Pyra as we sang the Gregorian chants, I was overwhelmed with grief and memories. I felt Piet's spirit and closeness, and knew he was with us at every moment.

After Mass, we found a unique coffee shop that had a back room, just as if it had been made for us. It was filled with books and the ambiance was comforting and so personal. We shared memories as we ate breakfast and enjoyed the rich coffee, memories and each other…a perfect memorial place.

That afternoon back in the apartment, Mary had all of us sit in a circle. She wanted us each to take some time and silently think about our greatest memories of Piet. After several minutes, she told us that while she was on the plane, she had written notes to share with us about her Piet memories:

Quality man

Appreciative

Generous

Self-giving

Respectful

Appreciation of what Vonnie, Bret, and Pyra did

Love of family

Soft quiet manner

Skills – a man similar to Dad

Love of good food

Never complained

Beautiful voice: Dutch songs and lullabies

Creativity: Hudson home, retaining wall, wood, memorial to his Dad

Genuine caring and thoughtfulness

Love for classical music

Stamina – work ethic, physical ability

Frugal – no frills needed

Enjoyed quality

Love of nature

Stimulated: painting, tutoring

Stood firm for what he believed

NEVER boastful, yet proud

Disciplined, liked routine

Productive – never wasted time on trivial matters

His orange truck

Winemaking

Squirrel and deer feeding

Trails
Firewood – cutting finger on wood splitter
Skinny legs; long curved nose
Mom and Dad's 50th-anniversary prayer for Peace
Memories of the Hudson house fireplace
Washing dishes, cleaning the table, clean, clean, clean
Laundry detail
Love for a beer

As she shared each memory, Mary asked if anyone had a memory that linked or had a connection with the one she had shared. That person then shared their related memory before Mary shared another of hers. When she was finished, none of us had a dry eye. We sat there hugging each other and allowed our tears to flow until it seemed there could be no more. Then each of us, amidst tears, clearing of throats, chuckles and more tears, shared other ways that Piet had made an impact in our lives and how much he had meant to each of us.

On Tuesday, Luis and Mary left. How grateful we were for their comfort and support during this unexpected loss of Piet. After they left, the four of us packed the van and set off for Syracuse. We needed time to process how we were going to survive without a husband and father to help us.

One of the things we all felt strongly was a desire to create some unique and personal way to recognize and remember Piet. A generic card telling of his death was not suitable or honorable enough. After brainstorming different ideas, we decided that with Bret's computer expertise, we could create and print a fitting pamphlet, sharing what Piet had meant to everyone. We decided it would be great if we had a photo from the time Piet and I had met, as well as a current photo of him for the booklet we would create. Pyra happened to have a framed, favorite photo of her dad displayed in her living room. It was from 1970, a professional photo taken when he started work at the state prison. We had more-recent photos of Piet taken two months earlier at Bret's wedding. So we had the photos we wanted. Now came the difficult task of summarizing, on paper, Piet's remarkable seventy-five years of life.

Since many of the Holland family still spoke Dutch, we decided it would be great if we could have someone in Holland translate our English version into Dutch. Our booklet could then be in both languages, to honor Piet, his family, and ancestry. Thanks to the age of technology, we had our Dutch translation a few days later.

We chose his 1970 photo for the cover and even found a copy of one of Piet's signatures to add to the originality of our booklet. The last page was his photo taken May 31st in his tuxedo: The man in black, once again, minus the Roman collar! The following was our tribute:

PIET F. AARDEN

8 Oct 1927 – 28 Aug 2003

Piet was born in Uden, Nord Brabant, the Netherlands, of Jan Aarden and Elizabeth van den Berg on October 8, 1927. He was the second youngest and had six siblings: Johanna, Cor, Martien, Hein, Karel, and Gerard. After attending a seminary boarding school during the Nazi occupation, he emigrated to the United States in 1948 to become a missionary priest.

His seminary training began in Onamia, MN, with the Crosier priests. He completed his studies at the St. Paul Seminary and was ordained in 1954. Piet served as a priest in the Crookston diocese in Minnesota until 1969, where he was known for his beautiful singing voice, for his inspiring, articulate sermons, and as a pastor whose foremost concern was always with the needs of his parishioners. Over the course of his life, he designed and helped build a church addition in Grygla, a rectory in Kelliher, a cabin at Midge Lake, and a home in Hudson, Wisconsin.

In 1970 he was laicized and married Yvonne Rumreich, a former nun. They had two children, Bret and Pyra. For 23 years he worked as a social worker and Activities Coordinator at the Stillwater State Prison. In addition to his involvement in the church, educational politics, winemaking, woodwork, and his children's activities, he was constantly building, improving, and maintaining an idyllic home in five acres of Wisconsin woods. In his view, travel was an important part of child-rearing, and he made efforts to bring the family on frequent trips to the Netherlands, around the U.S.A. and around the world. After retiring in 1993 and selling the Hudson home, he traveled with Yvonne for several years before settling in Florida.

He will be remembered for his welcoming demeanor, charitable attitude, love of family, generosity of time and effort, and constant attention to people, as well as his meticulous laundry, the superabundance of grapefruit, enthusiastic motorcycling, skill with wood and watercolors, and love of nature.

In recent years he shared his teaching talents by volunteering with Project Light, a non-profit organization that tutors English as a second language. Piet always preferred to give gifts rather than receive them, and in the spirit, he ultimately donated his body for medical student study. He was a doting father, a devoted and supportive husband, a good neighbor, a gentle man of deep convictions and few words who was loved by many.

Please share your memories and pictures of Piet for a memorial book by emailing Yvonne or at his memorial website (www.pietaarden.com). If you would like to give a gift in commemoration of Piet's life, please consider donating to Project Light.

"...that best portion of a good man's life, his little, nameless, unremembered acts of kindness and of love."

William Wordsworth

The day before Piet died, Bret had called to say how excited he was to have us come for his graduation and that he couldn't wait to see us.

That same day, a card and letter had arrived from Pyra with this verse by Linda Lee Elrod:

In our family,
Dad, you've always been
"the strong one."
The one who is there for us,
who always says,
"Don't worry, we'll handle this."
But what happens
When life throws you a curve?
I know you have this thing
About not burdening your family
And that protectiveness
Is part of
What makes you "you"...
But I'm all grown-up now, Dad,
And I really want
to be there for you.
Sometimes just talking
To someone else can really help,
And I'm a good listener.

> Of course, you're still
> Your own boss,
> But I just want you
> To know that
> I love you and I'm here for you,
> Just like the thousand times
> You've been there
> For me.

Pyra had added her thoughts to this poem:

OKAY—

So I guess I missed "Father's Day" (official)...but then again, it is really just a day where we remind you how fantastic you are & how loved you are—so I guess today is it!

Just wanted to remind you of how much I love you & love hearing from you. Please feel free to call me at any time—especially if you are doing the bachelor thing! (tee hee)

I am so glad you have leaped over these past few years of medical turmoil without damage. I have dreams that this will continue for years to come. We have so many things and experiences to share...(including walking me down the aisle!!)

So my dear father—thank you for all the support (physically, emotionally, financially, etc.) and love over the years—for the memories and the dreams for the future—I love you, daddy. Please take care.

Love, Pyra

After reading the card and hearing from Bret that evening, Piet had turned to me. With tears in his eyes, he shared how he had always hoped that he would live to see his children graduate from high school.

"Imagine that," he had said that night. "In May we celebrated Pyra's graduation as an ER doctor, and tomorrow we will be leaving to watch our son receive his doctorate in music."

With that special twinkle in his eye and his flirtatious wink, he had said proudly, "We didn't do too badly, did we?"

My Ode to Piet

Strength, determination, perseverance
    Were your footholds.

Depth, intellect, and listening
    Were your pillars.

Caring, loving, concern
    Were your supports.

Faith, belief, and wisdom
    Were your roof beams.

Architect, builder of dwelling –
    Home and human.

These are your legacies
    Your strongholds.

Amen.

EPILOGUE
Life After Piet: 2003-2017

"In the midst of winter, I found there was within me, an invincible summer." (Camus)

I tried to make sense of Piet's death. Since I believe that poetry is the spontaneous overflow of powerful feelings, I wrote this poem while grieving in Syracuse:

DEATH
Death is a
Summer thunderstorm
A lightning bolt
Zigzagging,
Targeting my husband's heart
Zapping life's energy
Tearing him from me
Within a split-second.

Claps of thunder raging as
Medics rushed
Seizing imitation life supports
Desperately pounding life
Into a body ravaged
By cruel heart attacks.
Heartstrings – broken –
Playing their last tune.

DEATH –
A thunderstorm
Forever striking my heart.

Returning home after Piet's death was something I dreaded, but my sister, Flo, and cousin, Sharon, flew to Florida to be with me. They arrived at the airport an hour or so before I did. When I went to the luggage carousel, I looked up and saw their smiling, yet sympathetic, faces. They came running over with their arms spread wide for comforting hugs—angels in disguise.

Flo and Sharon offered to help me in whatever way they could. I certainly was in no shape or frame of mind to accomplish all the things that needed to be done alone. They sat with me to create a list of things that needed to be taken care: Social Security, banking, legal documents that had to be changed, phone calls that must be made and answered, and the task of deciding what to do with a closet full of Piet's clothing.

As friends came to share my grief, I shed never-ending tears, re-living the still-hard-to-believe story of how Piet had died. If I had been alone, I would have had a breakdown. Flo and Sharon were pillars of strength to shore me up when I thought I could not go on.

At the Social Security office, I learned that I could not make over $14,000 if I wanted to receive Piet's Social Security, otherwise the government would take a huge percentage of the earnings. I knew it would be too difficult to do workshops, anyway. It would not be fair for the teachers and students to have a person shedding tears at the drop of a hat. So I made the decision to not work, and gave myself the gift of time to grieve. I needed to figure out how I was going to live without Piet.

Flo's family sent me a landscaping stone, roughly-hewn, with the following words engraved upon it:

Piet Aarden 1927-2003:

In His Will is Your Peace

Tulips were etched next to the words. I placed this near the entry of my home as a beautiful memorial. I decided to get colorful wooden tulips on my next trip to Holland and place them next to the stone.

On October 8, Piet's birthday, I chose to have a celebration of his life with my neighbors. It would be our Memorial Service for him. On a table, decorated with pictures of Piet, and surrounded by various Dutch artifacts, I placed a can of his favorite beer, Old Milwaukee, and a bottle of white wine to symbolize all his years of wine making.

I told my Florida friends the story of Piet's winemaking saga and his love of cheap beer. I also shared how Piet always reminded me of Paul Bunyan, with his mighty strength, and how he was always doing things for others. To demonstrate these amazing qualities, I read part of a sympathy letter I had just received from Joan Thompson, a friend from Wisconsin. She wrote:

"One day I met Piet at Fleet Farm and asked if I could pay him to split some wood I had in my driveway from a tree that had fallen…for some reason I

thought he would stop over with his "gas powered" splitter and complete the job. When I came home the next day in ninety-degree heat, there was Piet just finishing the last of many logs, by hand! My winter supply of wood, cut, split, and stacked for the long winter ahead, was all neatly completed. Piet would accept no money and I had to force him to stop for iced tea and pie. He was such a kind and generous man. I will always remember Piet's caring and support. To be without him must be a struggle. He truly lived his life to the fullest to the very end—truly a blessing! Now I am sure he prompts you to do the same."

There were no dry eyes in our group as each person shared their memories of Piet. So many of my friends remembered or focused on his utmost respect for women, and how special they felt whenever Piet was in their presence. He truly had been a gentleman to the core.

In November, I flew to Minnesota where our Guardian Angel friends held a Memorial for Piet at Carl and Judy Scheider's home. John Riehle led us in song and prayer, then each person gave testimony to what they held most dear in their encounters with Piet. They all remembered his tasty rhubarb wine, his gentleness, strong baritone singing whether in the church choir or our group's sing-a-longs, as well as his willingness to tackle any task with cheerfulness and determination.

Since my friends knew how talented Piet was in creating anything out of wood, I had to share a story that our Hudson neighbor, Pat Heinzen, had written to me when she heard of Piet's death. Piet had built a small wooden bench for Bret and Pyra when they were little. Pat's daughter wondered if Piet could do the same for her and, of course, he did.

The Bench

(In loving memory of Piet)

At first glance the little bench was small and plain; some might even say homely. But closer inspection showed it to be sturdy, well balanced, and able to make the little girl six inches taller. She learned to brush her teeth because the bench made her tall enough to spit in the sink. She liked to spit. The little girl helped her Mama wash the dishes because the bench made her feel like a big girl. She often carried the bench with her. It was a sit-upon respite in the woods where she reigned as queen. If she flipped it over, she could give her kitty a ride. Standing on tiptoe, she could reach the cookie jar. But, most of all, she was always six inches taller.

The little girl is grown now but she still has the bench. When seeing it, she often reflects on the carpenter who made it for her. He, too, was sturdy and strong, and well balanced. He did not make the bench for show. It was simply to make a child taller. Magically, he made everyone whose lives he entered feel six inches taller. If he didn't know, he'd ask. If he knew, he shared. If you needed help, he was there. He was a neighbor, a friend, a husband, a father, and a child of God.

The gift of a small bench carried the spirit of the man. The little girl would pass this gift on to her children, and they to their children, and the spirit of the builder, Piet Aarden, will live on for many years to come.

As our Memorial tribute to Piet came to a close, we toasted him with a glass of wine, and gave thanks for this man who had graced our lives all those years.

After spending time with friends, I traveled to Dan and Mary's for Thanksgiving. Because Piet and I had been married the day before Thanksgiving, this holiday added to my intense sorrow. It was the first anniversary day without him. Mary took me cross-country skiing through their woods on the day of our anniversary. As we skied, memories of our Hudson woods flooded my mind. I sobbed uncontrollably, wishing Piet were with me. How could I continue without him?

The kids came home for Christmas, and we shared our grief and memories of their dad. Piet always read the Nativity story to us before opening presents. (This was a tradition handed down from my family. Dad always read the story of the Birth of Christ before we were allowed to open gifts.) I felt it was a beautiful tradition that I wanted carried on in our family. Since Piet was not there, I took his place and read.

Pyra stayed on for several days after the holidays, and viewed the thousands of slides that Piet had taken during his lifetime. We discovered boxes of slides we had never seen before. In all his travels before we met, Piet had been all over the U.S.A. as well as many European countries with his friend, Father Reynolds.

 Setting up the projector screen, we loaded carousels of Piet's slides. We spent hours laughing and crying as we re-lived the life of Piet before we knew him, as well as all the slides he took of our family over the years. All of a sudden, we looked at a slide of a young man in jeans and a white t-shirt riding a horse across the plains. Pyra and I stopped, looked at each other in total puzzlement. Was that her dad? We took a closer look to see if it could possibly be him. It was Piet in his younger days—maybe when he was a seminarian. Never once had Piet shared his love of horses or riding. Were those slides showing a one time experience he had in the "Wild West," or had he ridden many times before? We would never know

—an unsolved mystery of Piet Aarden! Pyra reminded me once again that she had always loved horses and wanted one, even though Piet and I wouldn't let her. Now, just maybe, it could be that it was in her genes! Maybe her dad had been a cowboy way back then!

We also viewed slides of Piet building his cabin at Midge Lake during priestly days. Then one slide really caught my eye. It showed Piet pensively looking off into the distance, while riding alone in a gondola on the canals of Venice, Italy. I wondered how many young women, looking at this good looking young man, wanted to jump aboard! As we viewed more and more of his slides, we discovered many unknown parts of Piet's life. If only Piet were with us to share "the skinny" about those unknown adventures he had experienced before he knew us!

The year 2004, after Piet's death, would have been terribly lonely if it had not been filled with travel and time with family and friends. Connie lost Bill in October of 2003, and Eileen lost Nick in December of the same year. We three friends suddenly found ourselves trying to learn the new role of widowhood. In March, Connie and Eileen flew down from Wisconsin to spend time with me. We decided to travel to the Florida Keys. Being together, sharing what we each were experiencing with the loss of our husbands, we decided to plan future travels together. This made our farewell much easier when I dropped them off at the airport.

During the year of 2004, Luis and Pyra did extensive research on expediting the green card process for Luis. Since he was from Mexico, it was necessary to have that piece of paper, if he wished to live in the U.S.A. Luis had proposed to Pyra in August, a few weeks before Piet died. We were happy that Piet had had several occasions to meet his future son-in-law. Pyra and Luis learned that if they got married, it would be a faster process to get the green card. In March they decided that they would have a legal wedding. Why not have a FUN wedding, and do it up right in Vegas, at an Elvis Presley chapel? Since Luis' dad enjoyed the Vegas scene, this would be great for everyone.

There was one small catch. Pyra and Luis decided on a costumed wedding. All those in attendance would wear a costume of their choice. Pyra became Foxxy Cleopatra and Luis was Austin Powers. Pyra's two best doctor friends, Anise and Laura, came as flapper girls of the 20s, while Bret and Althea decided to come as famous literary people. This plan changed, and Bret assumed the role of a wealthy, Southern pork farmer (so fitting, since he was a strict vegan), and Althea became the geisha girl he had acquired on his world travels! So what should I dress as? A group from my neighborhood had just performed the play, *The Sound of Music*. I had been chosen for the role of Maria so, of course, I just knew I had to dress as a NUN!! (So fitting, I thought, in so many ways!) We all wondered what Luis' mom and dad would pick for their costumes.

When the time came for us to take the ride in a sleek, white limo to Elvis' chapel, we descended the stairs of the MGM hotel down to the lobby. All the people at the slot machines stopped as we paraded through the casino area. Catcalls, whistles, and shouts arose from the crowds when they saw Pyra, this tall woman-goddess in gold stilettos and a daring gold lamé gown, complete with Afro wig. She was leading her motley entourage. Pyra's purple-velvet-suited-sidekick (Austin Powers) was wearing his ruffled white shirt, as well as his unique wig and teeth. Naturally, he walked just a few steps behind his lady. The rest of us paled in comparison, but I did manage to get a few catcalls of my own: "Say a prayer for me, Sister!" and "Use those beads for luck, Sister!"

Imagine our surprise when we meet Luis' parents in the lobby, only to discover them in dressy, but ordinary, attire. They did not think Pyra and Luis had been serious when they talked about costumes! One could write a book just about the Vegas wedding, but suffice it to say, we all had an amazing, fantastic evening, never to be forgotten.

November became the time to travel to Mexico for Pyra and Luis' formal wedding. It was in an ancient, beautiful Catholic church bedecked with flowers, pomp, and circumstance. Pyra chose a white, long, flowing sateen gown and simple veil. In her hands, she carried a gorgeous purple iris bouquet. (My mom's favorite flowers that she had always grown around our home.) Since Piet was not there to walk his daughter down the aisle, I felt deeply honored when Pyra asked me to take his place.

The church ceremony was followed by a gala afternoon of appetizers and drinks at Luis' parents' home in Cuernavaca. Tables decorated in white and blue linens and bows were set up while waiters filled our wine and drink glasses. The catered meal was followed by a live band and dancing. The late evening (or should I say early morning) exploded with fireworks lighting the sky. The newlywed couple could boast, in years to come, that it took two marriages to make them the happy couple of today.

Christmas was spent in Syracuse with the newlyweds along with Bret and Althea. It was our second Christmas without Piet, and still difficult to accept that he was gone.

The year of 2007 ended with the earth-shaking news that Pyra and Luis were expecting not one, but TWO, babies the following April. They had moved to San Francisco, in May. Knowing they would need more room than just the apartment they were living in, they purchased a five-bedroom home in Pleasant Hill, about an hour east of the city. Luis began his daily ride on the BART (Bay Area Transit System) each morning at 4:30, so he could be in the office when the markets opened in New York City. Pyra accepted a job as an ER doctor at Martinez County Hospital.

This was also the year that Bret began a new teaching position as an assistant professor of music at the school he had attended for undergrad studies: New College in Sarasota. He had spent the prior three years teaching at U. of Mass, Amherst. I was thrilled to have him close by!

Then came the year 2008. How could 2008 ever be forgotten? It was the year that gave me a new title. I became a Grandmother. For Piet, being a grandfather would have been the crowning glory of his life. He would have won the title of "Opa Piet."

ER work became too strenuous for Pyra, and she began having early contractions. Because of this, she ended up spending a week and a half in the hospital flat on her back. It was the middle of March, and I flew out immediately to stay with her in the hospital. Then I ended up staying until the end of July to help with the newborns.

Pyra had chosen not to know the sexes of the babies. A week before the twins were born, I asked if I could try to predict their gender with her dad's trusty Dutch method. In one hand, I held a piece of thread attached to a gold wedding band which I dangled over an empty water glass. Then I placed my other hand on Pyra's stomach in the two different locations where I felt a kick. If the baby were a boy, the thread on the ring would move back and forth. If a girl, it would turn in circles. I proudly announced that Pyra would be giving birth to a boy AND a girl. I just knew how proud Pet would be that I had carried out his Dutch tradition!

I had thought long and hard during Pyra's pregnancy about what I wanted the grandbabies to call me when they reached the stage of uttering sounds. I decided on the name, "Nikoma." Nikomis was the Ojibwe name for grandmother, and "Oma" was the Dutch name. Since these children would not have the pleasure of having a Dutch grandfather to spoil them, I would combine the two ancestries and be called, Nikoma. I liked it. It was different. Let's face it, I was different, so it made natural sense to veer from the norm. And Nikoma it was, now, and forever.

How does one describe the absolute JOY of seeing your daughter give birth to not only one, but two babies? The twins, Mariano and Javier, were born on April 30. Can you imagine how surprised I was to see TWO boys, not a girl AND a boy? Did I miss some trick in Piet's tried and true methodology? Buying green and yellow baby clothes and accessories ended up being a wise choice, after all.

Mariano made his entrance into this world at 3:26 a.m. weighing in at seven pounds, two ounces and measuring twenty-one inches. Four minutes later, Javier joined him weighing in at five pounds, ten ounces and measuring nineteen inches. After counting all the fingers and toes, and examining them carefully, they were announced to be in perfect health.

BUT when Luis' mother, Chelo, first laid eyes on them, she looked at them in wonder and surprise. Those babies didn't look like Mexican babies; they looked like little Dutch babies, with fair skin and the little hair that was there! We all laughed. Piet's Dutch genes had ruled! We assured Chelo that the babies had Mexican names to prove their heritage.

When Pyra and Luis brought the twins home, everything about their life changed. A new flavor and tone with baby bottles, diapers, binkies, and nights that did not know the meaning of the word "sleep" for the parents, or the rest of us. Having to have two of everything was another learning curve. How happy Pyra was to have TWO people there when both babies needed attention at the same time!

2010 was a year of changes, especially for Bret. He filed for divorce and that became official in October. He continued his teaching at New College, and began a whole new chapter in his life.

Three years later, Pyra and Luis broke the news that they were expecting again—another set of twins! In September, Pyra needed to have bed rest so I flew out and stayed to help until the following January. For this pregnancy, when she had the ultrasounds, she didn't prohibit the doctor from telling her the sexes of her babies. After all, she had two sets of everything for boys, so now she wanted to know if there would be any reason to start collecting girls' clothing. The results came in: This time it was to be a girl AND a boy. (No need for Piet's Dutch method, this time.)

On October 1, 2013, Stefano appeared into this world weighing in at five pounds, fourteen ounces. Two minutes later, his sister, Gabriela, joined him. She outdid him by weighing in at seven pounds and fourteen ounces! Both were healthy babies. Chelo was all smiles when she saw the beautiful dark complexion of Gabriela. She had one Mexican baby, for sure! We rejoiced that all went well. Now the new learning curve for the Lopez Aarden household would be to learn how to survive with two sets of twins needing attention at all times!

As I finish this epilogue in 2017, Bret is currently working as a computer engineer in Boston, Massachusetts. He began working for his firm, Wayfair, an online retail company, three years ago. Bret is able to apply all the management skills and people skills that he learned while being a professor. All those myriad jobs involving computer programming that he had done over the years ended up being a great advantage for him.

Bret and I in Greece!

Pyra is still working as an ER doctor at two hospitals. She and two other ER doctors are beginning a new company. It is called, VIVIFY, a personalized IV Therapy and Supplement Service to help people recover from illness, detox, escape painful conditions, or enhance their fitness regimen. Luis continues to work at Wells Fargo, and he still gets up in the wee hours of the morning to catch the BART into San Francisco.

Mariano and Javier are nine years old and entering fourth grade. They are almost as tall as their Nikoma and proud of it! Gabriela and Stefano will turn four this year in October and are enjoying their Spanish Immersion School every day.

Pyra, Luis, Mariano, Javier, Gabriela, and Stefano.

As for me, in the years since Piet died, I have found the following adage to ring so true:

> "Death leaves a heartache no one can heal,
> love leaves a memory no one can steal."
> (From an Irish headstone)

To heal my heart over these past fourteen years since Piet died, I chose to continue my literacy consulting workshops until 2015, learned how to quilt with the help of friends and classes, acquired many new friends, enjoyed the challenge of many writing classes, visited my children and grandchildren numerous times each year, and spent a majority of my time traveling both in the U.S.A. and internationally. Having traversed over forty-five different countries, I have many more on my "bucket list."

This year of 2017 is the year I am putting finishing touches on this book that my kids and friends have told me that I absolutely must write. Whenever I shared the story of how Piet and I met, everyone always said, "You've got to write your story. It would make a great movie!" Finally in June of last year, I approached a young man named Eric Wyatt, and asked if he would help me edit and revise my story. I had taken several writing classes from Eric over the past four years, and he always encouraged us to take up the challenge and write our life's story.

So, my dear family and friends, this book is my attempt to write that story of a little girl who spent her first thirteen years on the White Earth Reservation, those many moons ago. I, as a young girl, NEVER could have dreamed of where my life might take me. The many twists and turns and amazing travels and adventures were only in books, not real life.

Or so I thought...

In one of my writing classes, we were asked to write about who we really were. Our poem was to start with the words: " I am…" I wrote the following poem and feel that these words still ring true as I now live my live as a widow, loving life and whatever adventures it may yet bring:

I am a liberated, nomadic woman seeking life's adventures-
I wonder why it is so difficult for me to learn languages
I want walls of prejudice to become embracing arms of peace
I hope to be vibrant and outspoken to my dying breath
I believe education is the key that opens doors for all.

I am a liberated woman seeking life's adventures –
I feel that I need to live life to its fullest at every moment
I cry when I talk about my deceased husband, Piet
I try to bring a smile and laughter into people's lives
I believe that everyone comes culture-rich, filled with potential.

I am a liberated woman seeking life's adventures –
I understand that life throws us multiple curves
I think the adventures of travel are life's best education
I hope to foster a love of reading/writing in all the lives I touch
I believe that there is a reason for everything.

I am a liberated woman seeking life's adventures –
My name is Yvonne Marie Rumreich Aarden
1940 - ?

If I had never had the unforeseen privilege and honor of falling in love with a handsome, dashing, Dutch priest, this book would never have come to life in every meaning of the word. Piet was my forever-lover who believed that nothing was impossible. He believed in me like no other person in my life had, and he sacrificed so much so that his "Indian maiden" could follow her heart and dreams.

Thanks, Piet! You live on forever in my heart and memories...

Playing Nikoma is one of my all-time favorite roles!

Acknowledgements

No book about one's life is ever written without the encouragement and support from others. Mine is no different. If there had never been a Piet Aarden in my life, this book would never had a chance for a beginning, middle or end. So my first thanks is to him for always loving and believing in me.

Of course, Bret and Pyra have said over and over, throughout the years, "Mom, you NEED to write a book about your and Dad's unique life. After all, we wouldn't be here if you two had not met!" So, thanks, Bret and Pyra, for never giving up on your insistence for this book to be written.

My mom and dad were certainly the first encouragers in my life, no matter what paths I chose to take. I owe them everything for showing me what boundless love and acceptance really look like. Thank you, Mom and Dad, for never giving up on me.

My two sisters, Mary and Flo, also need to be thanked for their support and generosity over all the years. Thanks, and know I truly appreciate each of you for also never giving up on me and helping me through thick and thin.

Thanks to all those multitudes of friends and extended family who showed interest in the lives of Piet and myself. You, too, told me that I needed to write and share the story of Piet and myself. So many of you became our strong foundation of support in both the good and difficult times. I am eternally grateful for having each of you in my life then and now.

Lastly, how can a book like this become a reality without an amazing mentor and editor? I often count my blessings when I think how fortunate I have been to take classes from Eric Wyatt (www.WordsMatterESW.com). Eric taught the first Legacy Writing class I took, and he ignited the spark to put pen to paper and make this book a reality. He is a gifted writer himself, as well as an amazing teacher and encourager. Thanks, Eric!

APPENDIX 1

My play, written in New Hampshire - 1989

1989: Case of Product vs. Process #10087

EXTRA! EXTRA! READ ALL ABOUT IT! 49 YEAR OLD GREY-HAIRED TEACHER OF 28 YEARS WINS US WEST AWARD! READ ALL ABOUT IT!

Scene One: Inside Mr. Over-Used Basal's Office

Narrator: Who was this gal? Why did she win it? What did she do? When did it happen? How come? These were the questions Mr. Over-used Basal wanted to be answered and fast. He'd have to get his brother's detective agency on the line immediately and have them investigate this lady. His basal multi-million dollar a day business could be in big trouble if this article in the local newspaper WE'VE ALWAYS DONE IT THIS WAY was really true.

Mr. Over –used Basal:
Hello, can I speak to my brother, Sergeant Boring Basal? This is urgent. Yeah, Boring? Can you get on a case real fast? I think Lieutenant Fill-in-the-Blank Workbook and Captain Drill Skillsheet are the men to work with you on this case. Get over here on the double. We've gotta get our isolated skills developed to crack this case! Comprehend?

Scene Two: Detectives at Basal's Office

Mr. Over-used Basal: "…so you see we need to quickly post these wanted posters all around the United States before she's aware of what we're doing…"

<u>BE ON THE ALERT FOR LATEST THREAT TO ALL BASAL ENTHUSIASTS:</u>

-YVONNE AARDEN –
MOST WANTED TEACHER BY BASAL READING COMPANIES IN U.S.A - LAST SEEN CARRYING BOOK BAG LABELED: "READING TEACHERS ARE NOVEL LOVERS" AND CONTAINING LATEST HEINEMANN PUBLICATIONS AND PERSONAL WRITING JOURNAL.

DESCRIPTION:
5'4", 135# (GIVE OR TAKE A FEW) ONE BROWN AND ONE BLUE EYE, SCAR ON LEFT CHEEK NEAR BOTTOM LIP, WEARS GLASSES AT ALL TIMES, WEDDING BAND, TURQUOISE RING, PETOSKEY STONE RING ALL ON LEFT HAND WITH MULTI-COLORED STONE RING ON RIGHT RING FINGER. REPORTED TO HAVE WEIRD SENSE OF HUMOR AND WILL TALK TO ANYONE WHO WILL LEND A LISTENING EAR – ESPECIALLY IF ASKED KEY QUESTION: "WHAT DO YOU MEAN BY WHOLE LANGUAGE?" $10,000 REWARD: READ OR ALIVE!

"Get these posters printed and out in all our warehouses, catalogs, and in the hands of all our in-service reps throughout the land and especially in our city of "We've Always Done It This Way.""

<u>Captain Skillsheet:</u>
Using our Palmer-Method handwriting, we copiously copied all the significant details in our detective logs. We need all the info we can get about her May 5, 1989, U.S. West Award and all the accomplishments that led up to the award. If we could capture her in the process of doing this anti-basal activity red-handed, the reward would be profitably placed in our very own hands.

Scene Three: Inside Detective Agency Office:

Captain Skillsheet: "Hey Lieutenant Workbook, listen to this. The newspaper article says there are no fill-in-the-blanks in her classroom. And Sergeant Basal, can you believe this? No reading series either. Howz kids gonna know if they 're in 3-1 or 3-2 after bein' in her room for a year?"

Lieutenant Workbook: "Yeah, Captain Skillsheet, they won't even know how to spell correctly cuz' it says here that she don't give 'em weekly spelling tests like we grew up with. Says here she don't even have a formalized spelling class."

Sarge Basal: "Get this, Lieutenant Workbook, it goes on to say she used only library books and kids did all their own writing. Says somethin' about HANDS AROUND THE WORLD theme following Will Steger's Antarctica expedition this coming August. Kids studied the country of each explorer goin' with this Steger guy. They did it with fiction and non-fiction books of the country, used resource people, videos, and filmstrips."

Captain Skillsheet: " Sarge Basal, what's this stuff about fiction and non-fiction? Any clues? Says some kids read over 250 library books in one year. Must a been a messy room with so many books lyin' all around. Why not be clean and efficient with just the 3-1 and 3-2 basal readers?"

Lieutenant Workbook: "Hey, Capn' Skillsheet, can you believe the school cook helped in this gal Aarden's room? Took the kids OUT of the classroom every Wednesday to bake the bread of the country they was studyin'. Whatever happened to the good ole days of REadin', Writin' and Rithmetic?"

Sargeant Basal: "Lookin' pretty serious, guys! Let's see if we can capture some real live evidence on this chick. Oh, no, look at this! Kids publish own books, write own poetry and have their choice of books and writing! Could run my brother's basal company out of business! We gotta move fast. Let's check back with my brother, Boring Basal, and his assistant, Mrs. Contrived Curriculum, and see if they have any new clues. We've gotta find this woman creating change in her basalized school. Grab them cameras. No rest 'til we find her."

Scene Four: Two days later.
(Detective using remote video cameras to spy inside Aarden's 3rd-grade classroom. Time is 8:30 a.m. Total silence except for a few whispers here or there. Children seated on cushions in the reading center, lying anywhere on the floor, or sitting in chairs.)

Lieutenant Workbook: "Hey, Sarge Basal, can you believe every kid getting to CHOOSE their own book to read? They're REAL books – can't find the teacher. Where is this gal? Where's the teacher's desk? Where are the kids' desks? Is this teaching?"

Captain Skillsheet: "Look, Lieutenant Workbook, there's a grey-haired lady on the floor leanin' against the wall reading "Loudmouth George". Real strange! Let's come back when there's some learning or teachin' goin' on. Mr. Boring Basal would NOT like this scene of smilin' happy kids reading all those different books! But this does give us some real LIVE evidence that the basal is nowhere to be seen in this room. Why'd she get that award anyway??"

Scene Five: One month later inside Mr. Basal's Office

Mr. Over-Used Basal: "Well, boys, what's up? What did you find for real live evidence on this gal? Enough to pull the plug? Let's hear your report first, Lieutenant-Fill-in-the-blanks Workbook."

Lieutenant Workbook: "To fill you in on the latest blanks and summaries, Mr. Boring Basal, I'd like to report on two major offenses against basals I saw in this weird classroom:
#1: Students write daily on any topic they choose and receive no red mark corrections from the teacher. Have this thing called peer-editing and peer-help. Teacher seldom gives answers but instead returns a question with a question. No need for your basal workbooks or worksheets! They use tons of paper and can write with anything and then save it in folders. Bad for your production line of ready-made fill-in-the-blank books!"

#2: Four resource people seen comin' into the classroom to tell about Japan, the country they were studying for this whole past month. Students were learnin' to read and write in Japanese and even doin' some math problems with Japanese writing. One lady left video letters for students to see real Japanese kids of today and how they lived. Caught teacher readin' to kids from Japanese authors. The kids' families had to help research country and make 1,000 origami cranes to send to Hiroshima to the Sadako Shrine. School cook made rice crackers with students every Wednesday of that month. All got to eat and enjoy them during school time. What a waste of good fill-in-the-blank workbook time! This stuff called Haiku, Tanka, and Japanese writing covered the walls along with the real Japanese art of both these 3rd graders and their Japan penpals.

What happened to those tidy commercial posters and neat wall hangings from Trend Publishing Company? I'm sorry to report, Mr. Boring Basal, there was NO evidence of fill-in-the-blank workbooks, basals or skill sheets anywhere. Even when she opened the cupboard doors, they was bare of your manuals and materials. Only evidence for positive clues for signs of your popular basal method teaching was next door in the super quiet, tidy, organized second grade where everyone still gets to do the same thing and all are neatly packaged into three ability groups using your wonderful pre-packaged materials,

<u>Mr. Over-Used Basal:</u> "Well done, Lieutenant Workbook. You are to be commended on your filling me in on the latest blanks and skillfully filling in the isolated facts which will hopefully lead to the whole message. What do you have to report, Captain Drill Skillsheet?"

<u>Captain Drill Skillsheet:</u> "Mr. Basal, I noticed two big glaring offenses against all your years of trying to keep teachers as technicians. Hope these will show how your hundred page ditto skill sheet packets are being totally ignored."

#1: Everything was hooked or tied together. We couldn't tell what class was what. Japan was everywhere and the kids seemed to know what to do. The teacher sat on the floor most of the time. They had this thing called "Author's Chair." Kids were teaching kids. (Wow, to be a teacher like this and still get paid, much less receive an award!) No time in her day for skill sheets. What's gonna happen to these kids? Hope the parents get good and upset havin' to read to their kids every day outside of the school time and report it in Reading Passport Booklets. Can you imagine askin' parents to turn off the tube to read and then spend time talking to the kid about what they read? Then to make matters worse, she expects the parents to get library cards for every kid and go to the library with the kid to do research on whatever country they was studyin'. Too much parent involvement if you ask me – almost like she's tryin' to connect home and school learnin'. Ain't she getting' paid to teach? Why involve the poor parents?

#2: Chief Rote Memory would hit the roof if he saw the things she does in Math. No workbooks or no skill sheets – just junk the kids constantly use for countin' and makin' up their own problems. She's all over the place again like usual instead of standin' upfront teachin'. She uses this book called, "Math, A Way of Thinking". How can they think without your drill and skill worksheets, Mr. Basal?"
Saw things called geoboards, Cuisenaire rods, unifix cubes, tiles, tangrams, blocks, bathroom tiles and all kinds of other noisy stuff that they called math. No timed tests!
Then there was three computers going all the time with kids totally unaware of all the other noise in that room. I kept askin' myself: 'Where are the workbooks? The memorizing of the multiplication tables and facts? The REAL math?" Sorry to say, Mr. Boring Basal, I was totally depressed to see what that gal has turned that room into – sure glad my severely labeled John ain't in that room. We've gotta stop this gal before she spreads this stuff to other teachers!"

<u>Mr. Over-Used Basal:</u> "Serious offenses you've cited, Captain Drill Skillsheet. Just when I've got 300 new skill and drill black master sheet books runnin' on the presses due to come out this July. A migraine headache comin' on. Let's get your report over and done with Sergeant Overused Basal. Hopefully, you'll have some news to cheer your brother."

<u>Sergeant Over-Used Basal:</u> " Would that I did, brother. Sergeant Basics of your THROW OUT WHAT IS NOT BASIC department would have a stroke if she saw the time spent on poetry and art. This gal Aarden even takes every Friday afternoon to have Parent's Poetry 'n Punch. Can you believe the waste of parent's time to come in the week their child has been Star of the Week and share experiences of their child

and their favorite poems? Every student memorizes a different poem every week for this poetry hour. As we listened, several students recited poems they had created themselves and one kid even memorized a two-page poem from this guy called Silverstein or somethin' like that. Was about this Sara Stout who wouldn't take the garbage out. My thoughts of what she's doin – garbage!! Waste of time, don't you think, Mr. Boring Basal?

Last day of the month we couldn't believe it – in walk several Moms and Dads with video cameras and the place looks like grand central station. Kids running here and there. Costumes appearing, props being set up, kids laughing, talking and acting as if learnin' was fun. This gal Aarden gets in front of the camera and welcomes all to Japan and then each student does his Japan research report in such unique ways. Nobody read from a paper sounding like an encyclopedia we used to do. The one girl was dressed in a real Japanese kimono and demonstrated a Japanese tea party. Another kid sets up a canoe and comes in a fishing costume and catches fish that have Japanese facts on them. (Sound fishy to you, brother?)

Lieutenant Workbook: "Yeah, and remember the kid who had colored charts and diagrams on how to build a Japanese rock garden and even brought in a rock garden he made to show the rest how to do it? No kid did the same thing. Is this that creativity stuff you hear about? And then to top it all off, I heard the kids all rushing up to the gal Aarden and begging to be the first one to take the video home to show their parents. What's this world coming to anyway?" Give up MASH television time for a school video? Where are the Basics, Boss? Where are the Basics?"

Mr. Over-Used Basal: "Detectives, I can't believe how much evidence you got in such a short time. We'll have to…"

Captain, Drill Skillsheet: "Wait, Mr. Boring Basal, we've got more. If you think all the things we've reported are bad, you should see how she even asks parents to come and help her in the classroom every day. If they couldn't come in during the day, could they help by doing things in their home for her? Pushing her luck, I even heard her ask grandparents to come and help. What's her problem" Can't she handle 29 kids in that small room with no sink?"

"Seems to me that if she'd hand out lots of skill sheets and got back to ability groups, the kids would sit quietly in their seats and she wouldn't need all that extra help. Someone should give her the simple message to cure her radical needs. GET BACK TO THE BASALS."

<u>Lieutenant Workbook:</u> "We ran out of videotape and time but felt we had enough evidence to turn this woman's subversive anti-basal activities over to you. She's leavin' for a sabbatical that she won from this U.S. West outfit. Can't figure out why they didn't choose someone from Tradition City for that award. Sure would have helped your market, Mr. Boring Basal."

<u>Mr. Over-Used Basal:</u> "Great work, men, you captured enough evidence of the who, what, when, where, why, and how of this gal to fill volumes. We can move in for the real take-over and return of the basals while she's on leave. We'll keep close tabs on her in case she tries to continue this de-basalization stuff. Afraid she's too far gone for us. I'd go so far as to say she's BEYOND THE BASAL.

Footnote:
BEWARE: The teacher pursued above may turn up at your school at any time. Any information as to her whereabouts will be richly rewarded with commercial basal materials if she is found to continue her campaign to wipe out the basals.

Footnote #2:
The detective agency has been put out of business by Heinneman Press, which was able to put Mr. Over-Used Basal behind bars and locked out of classrooms. Twist of fate has granted his reward money to the gal Aarden whom they pursued for reading-writing process destroying the basalization products.

Those seeking more info on her "GIVE POWER BACK TO THE KIDS AND TEACHERS: campaign may write to:

Yvonne Aarden, 594 White Oak Drive, Hudson, WI 54016

APPENDIX 2

U S WEST REGIONAL FINALIST AND MINNESOTA AWARD RECIPIENT

Yvonne Aarden

OUTSTANDING TEACHER OF THE YEAR

Yvonne is acclaimed not only as a talented and creative teacher, but for her abounding love for each child in her third grade class at Bayport Elementary School. Her dedication to Process Learning for her students and to Children's Literature by having authors and illustrators come to her class have shown that she clearly deserves to be this year's winner of the U S WEST "Reaching Beyond Classroom Walls" Outstanding Teacher Award.

Yvonne has great enthusiasm for teaching and tries to provide special opportunities for her children to expand their learning horizons. She also focuses on one student each week of the school year when they are the "star", and his or her parents are invited to take part in special activities in the class.

She has implemented the Whole Language theory (child-centered, experience-based learning) with her students the past two years and has found it to be the most exciting and challenging of her past 28 years of teaching. The students are empowered to become independent learners capable of making choices within a no-ability grouping and non-threatening environment.

Children's literature is another of her favorite teaching areas, and Yvonne is dedicated and persistent in acquiring fine authors and illustrators to come to her small school so her children have access to these outside sources in the language arts.

She was instrumental in forming a RAISING READERS committee formed to encourage parents and students to read at home.

Yvonne says that she has always tried new ways to motivate students to love the learning process whether they were her students she taught in Mexican migrant villages in Texas, native American Indians on her home reservation in northern Minnesota, disabled prison inmates, special education students or the middle class white of the Midwest. She has never stopped being a student herself and constantly updates her personal life and library with the latest of research in education.

Yvonne belongs to a number of Piano Associations, Reading Associations and Whole Language groups and has held offices in these groups as well as others.

Update Interview: Yvonne Aarden

Yvonne Aarden was recently chosen as a winner of U.S. West's Outstanding Teacher Award. As part of the award she will receive a year's sabbatical to continue her study of reading instruction. Yvonne is a third grade teacher in Bayport, Minnesota, in the Stillwater School District. Yvonne, who lives in Hudson, WI, is a past president of the St. Croix Valley Reading Council.

Update: *Please tell us about the award and how you began this process.*

Aarden: The Outstanding Teacher Award is sponsored by U.S. West, a telecommunications business that services fourteen states. Last year, U.S. West decided to appropriate 20 million dollars for education. One of the programs they developed is the Outstanding Teacher Award program. In this program they award five thousand dollars to state winners from each of the fourteen states. Each state winner is then sent to Denver to compete for a year's paid sabbatical, plus expenses. They offer three sabbaticals per year.

Three of my parents nominated me for the U.S. West Award which meant they had to fill out a nomination form and I had to fill out several forms. The program is called "Reaching Beyond Classroom Walls," so I had to state how I felt that I in my classroom reached beyond classroom walls. I also had to write about what would I do during the year if I were granted a sabbatical.

After submitting my application, I was informed that I was one of the six state finalists. I then went to Minneapolis for an interview and later was informed that I was the winner.

Update: *So as a state winner you won the five thousand dollars?*

Aarden: I won five thousand dollars to be used for professional development. I also had the chance then to go to the new Scanticon Conference Center, just south of Denver. They paid for my husband's way and my way and housed and treated us royally.

Update: *Can you tell us about the competition.*

Aarden: They did two things. Each of us was interviewed by a researcher from Fort Lewis College in Durango, Colorado. They wanted to know both our philosophy of education and our life history as to what creates teachers who are chosen for such an honor. We had an hour and fifteen minute interview with these people. The results will be in a publication that is a part of a grant program between the college and U.S. West. Then we had a half hour interview with five individuals, educators, public officials, and representatives of U.S. West. The half hour interview plus the papers we had filed were used to help decide the winners. Three people were chosen for sabbaticals.

Update: *Who else was chosen?*

Aarden: They chose Patience Fisher from Lincoln, Nebraska, who is a secondary math teacher. Her sabbatical proposal was to work for a year at the university level to help especially elementary teachers who she felt were really math-anxious. And to also develop programs to help girls in the math program.

They also chose Allen Marks from Albuquerque, New Mexico, who is a math/English/problem solving teacher who works in a high school that is 80% minority. His proposal was to develop a handbook that would enable minority student to learn how to apply and be accepted into prestigious colleges. He felt that a lot of the minorities had certainly all of the academic and intellectual potential but did not know how to get into these better colleges.

Update: *Can you tell us more about your application? What do you do beyond the classroom walls?*

Aarden: What I have done is use the whole language philosophy; I really prefer Canada's description, child-centered, experience-based learning. I did away with all textbook and basal systems and used nothing but library books. I use a theme centered curriculum. Since I work in a self-contained third grade classroom, I can correlate absolutely every subject across the curriculum with the themes I'm doing.

I had attended last summer the Antarctica Institute at Hamblin University, which gave us so much background on Antarctica. Will Steger from Minnesota is going to be leading that expedition starting this August; it will be the first non-motorized crossing of Antarctica. So I chose "Hands Around the World" as a theme. Each month we took a country of one of the explorers who will be on this expedition. Starting out with Will Steger's Minnesota, we did a general study of the U.S.A. and zeroed in. In my reading program I had nothing but Minnesota authors and we studied Minnesota in a very unique way. I happen to have a wonderful cook in our school and so I worked out with her so that every Wednesday she would take five of my pupils and would bake the bread of whatever country we were studying.

That has worked out beautifully. We did a bread of each one of the countries. As we studied the culture, I was able to bring in resource people from absolutely every country. The kids learned at least some of the basic words of every language. At lunch they would say please and thank you in the language of the country we were studying. We studied the U.S.A., England, France, China, Japan, the Antarctica and the Arctic together, and then Australia because that's where the explorers will be landing.

As we did our month's study about each country, I also developed what we call our Passport to Reading program to involve parents. I met with parents at the beginning of the year and explained my program. I expect and I asked them to pledge fifteen minutes of reading with their child and to record it in the Passport to Reading. Also the children are to record what they read for their fifteen minutes alone. So I require a half hour of reading. Then I asked that they research the country with their children. I put in extra copies or extra sheets in their Passport to Reading. As a family they research facts and kids can put in drawings and whatever each month.

Interview...continued

At the end of each month we culminate with different things. Sometimes it's videotaped reports. I send these videotapes home. Because a lot of parents can't make it to school to see the reports, though the videotapes they can see not only what their child is doing but also what the other kids in the room are doing. That's part of how I felt I had gone beyond classroom walls.

When I would study Japan, we would I would fill it with library books that had settings in Japan, that were by Japanese writers or illustrators, and then I always tied in non-fiction books and all the current magazines. I also have them interested in looking at newspapers. They would bring in articles and they would say " I don't understand, Mrs Aarden, every country that we study, that's what's in the newspaper." It made them aware that what we're learning in the classroom is right out there in the world. I firmly believe that reading has to be not a schooltime activity but a life long activity. I felt by involving parents, by bringing in all of these people, by showing how reading was an important part in their life, and by studying what happens in different cultures, the kids could do a lot of comparisons and understanding.

We did a really exciting thing when we were studying the USSR. The kids wrote their own personal letters to Gorbachev and to Bush explaining how they felt peace could be obtained. The kids made little banks; they saved their pennies and nickels. We ended up sending thirty dollars with the L.D. coordinator who was on the Ski for Peace program. He took and changed their money into rubles, and was able to hand the money and our letters to Gorbachev to a high official in Russia. He also went into classrooms in Russia. My kids had written individual pen pal letters and I had taken photos of the school and the kids, which we used to make up a beautiful booklet. When Bill returned he showed slides of the actual school where our pen pal letters were sent. The kids that got our letters sent gifts back to my kids. This type of activity shows the interrelatedness of reading and real life.

Update: *The enthusiasm seems contagious.*

Aarden: It is. The kids get so excited and energized by it. I have no ability groupings in my classroom. My kids become responsible for their own learning in that they model and help each other; they are teacher-learners all the time .

Update: *What will you do with your year's sabbatical?*

Aarden: In my proposal I said I'd like to spend about a month in each of four areas that I saw as being very strong in germinating and spreading the whole language philosophy, namely working with Donald Graves, Jane Hansen in New Hampshire, Lucy McCormick Calkins in New York; going up into Canada, into Nova Scotia where whole language is very strong; working in Arizona with the Goodmans; and then going into Missouri with Dorothy Watson. Those would be the four main areas.

Then my idea was to go there and learn and assimilate much, try to be a teacher-researcher and come home then and write about what I had experienced. I said I would try to do a book on it. I has also said that I would look into the idea of working on a doctorate.

I've begun talking about the possibility of writing a book about experiencing whole language across the United States. My year would be the perfect setting for it. What I would want is to be able to go into all the areas to find out where it's really happening. Then I'd like to go in and observe and see whether it is really whole language, how is it working, who is it working with, what makes it successful, or what doesn't work . That's what I hope I can work it into for next year.

Appendix 3

KELLY CARMODY DAY, BAYPORT SCHOOL 1988

We have gone through many trials
In the past few years
Lots of fun and adventure
Mixed with sadness and tears.

We have been to many exotic places
And experienced miracles first hand
We have been to Mexico and Hawaii
To Disneyworld and Disneyland.

We went trout fishing in North Carolina
Mountain climbing into the Colorado snow
Rode E.T.'s bike in California
We were always on the go.

We have traversed this great country
By boats, trains, and planes
We swam in all our oceans
And walked in tropical rains.

We experienced so many things
With our God leading the way
Now knowing what was in store for us
We lived to the fullest every day.

Most of you have known Kelly
From first grade and before
Riding bike and playing ball
Or walking to the store.

You knew him as any other kid
With his good points and his bad
You might have liked him an awful lot
Or he made you very mad.

I know he got in trouble
More than once or twice
Using nasty swear words
And sometimes not being so very nice.

But that was the Kelly
That we all grew to love
And I think that he is with us today
From his heavenly home above.

I am sure he is overwhelmed
By this outpouring of your hearts
But at the same time probably laughing
As he is letting little angel farts.

Kelly had to go through many changes
Many he didn't like
Like eating brown rice and seaweed
and unable to ride his bike.

We had a long stay in the hospital
Where he almost died twice
In a coma for a week
He paid a heavy price.

He recovered from the surgery
But found he couldn't walk
Could no longer print with his right hand
And found it difficult to talk.

He overcame these obstacles
And was soon riding his bike every day
Now writing with his left hand
And having a lot to say.

He said he saw Jesus
While they operated on his head
"Kelly you will be well"
is all that he said.

He had many months of radiation
And a year of painful shots in his hand
Pills that made him puke at night
A thing he couldn't stand.

After that long terrible year
His therapy finally came to a close
His hair was starting to grow back
No new tumors had arisen.

Things were looking bright
Kelly was feeling good
Working hard at playing t-ball
Doing the best he could

Then something happened last year
At this time in May
Kelly had a seizure at school
And the ambulance took him away.

They said he was very sick again
A new tumor had appeared
They gave him only months to live
The worst that we had feared.

They said there was nothing that they could do
To save him from his fate
A little radiation... maybe
Might postpone the fatal date.

With love from all of you
And every dollar you could afford
You sent us on our way
To catch a rainbow and it's reward.

In Mexico Kelly was very happy
We lived in tropical splendor
The summer spent in the ocean
Our life was warm and tender.

We were very happy for a while
It seemed Kelly had been cured
We sold our house in Bayport
A hardship we endure.

We lived in California
In hopes, Kelly would stay healed
We started life all over
Kelly's death sentence …repealed.

It seemed that we had beat the devil
We overcame his fate
Until fall of last October
Kelly was feeling great.

It was then that his pain returned
And back to the hospital we went
Kelly's cancer was back again
to Minnesota, we were sent.

Kelly was getting very tired
His death was very near
We had done everything we could do
We held every moment very dear.

Then on the first day of December
Kelly passed away at our home
Free from all his misery
And the pain he had known.

We shall all miss him very much
Now that he is dead
But his memory will live on
In these books that will be read.

So I thank God for all of you
And the love you have shared
You were an important part of his life
Showing always, that you cared.

We thank you from the bottom of our heart
For this special day
In honor our Kelly James
As we gather here today.

God Bless You All!
Mitch and Barb Carmody

Made in the USA
Columbia, SC
03 February 2019